P9-CLE-966

Family Values

FRANK MILLER
story and art

LYNN VARLEY
cover colors

STEVE MILLER
logo design

MARK COX
book design

DIANA SCHUTZ
editor

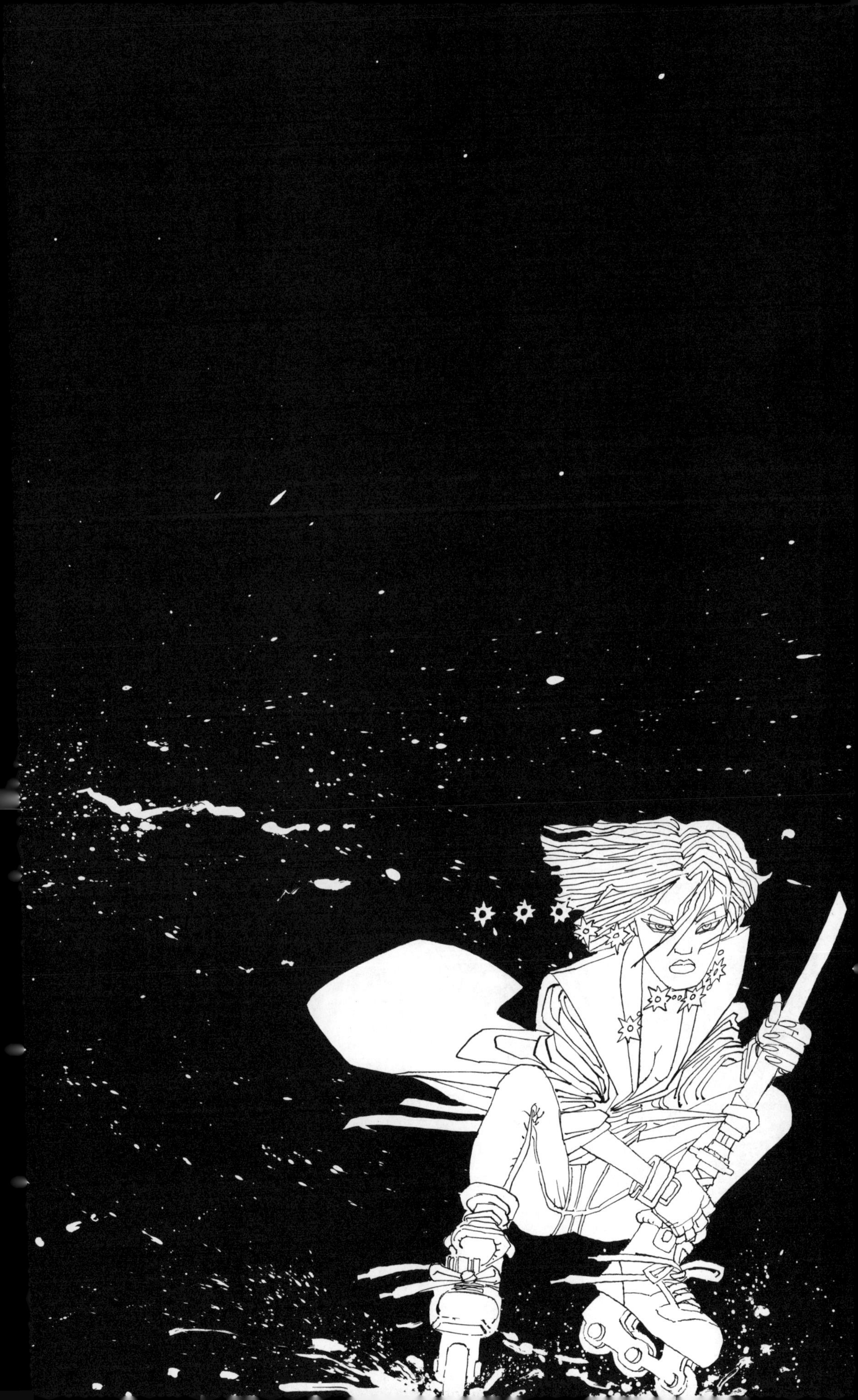

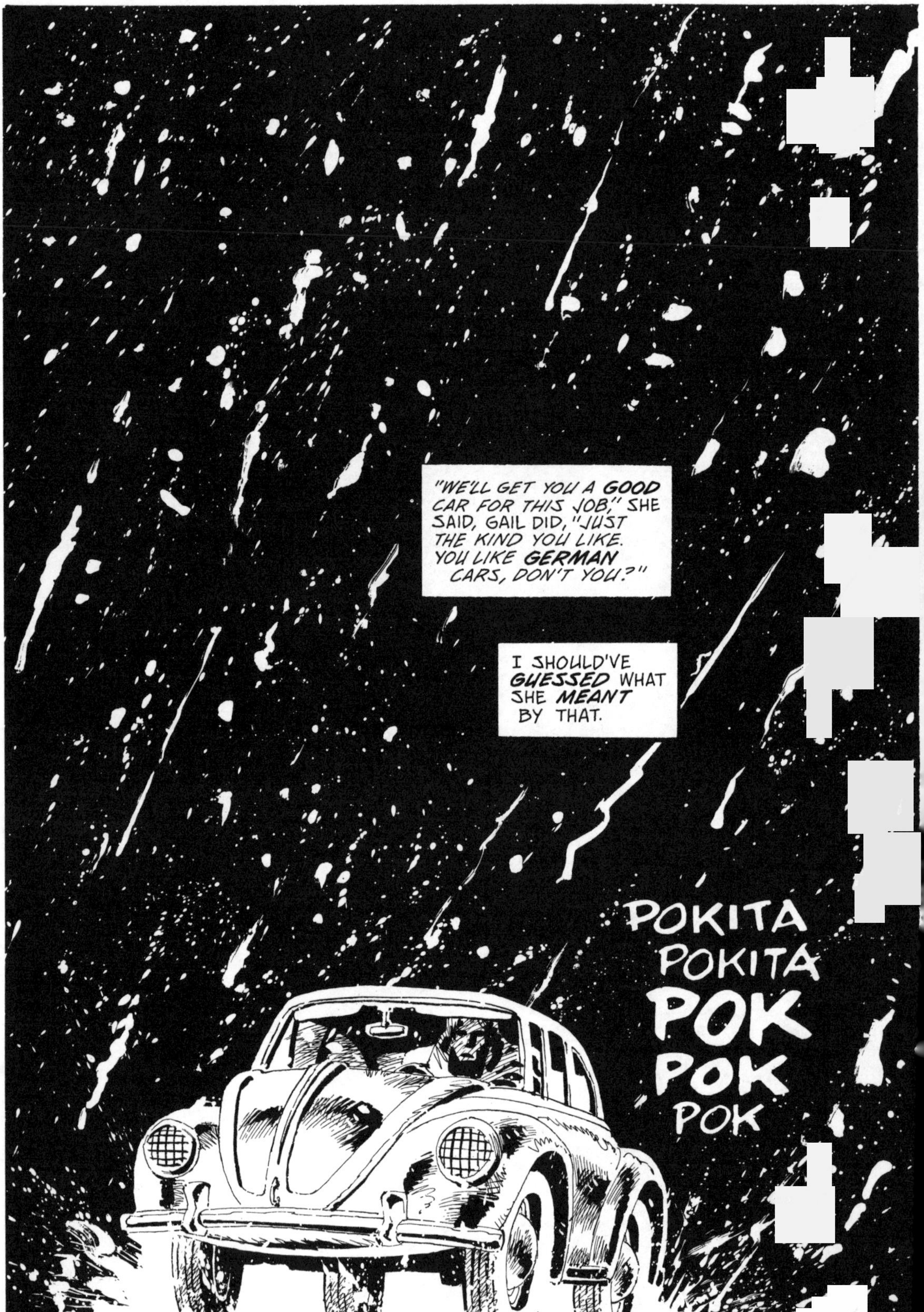
"WE'LL GET YOU A GOOD CAR FOR THIS JOB," SHE SAID, GAIL DID, "JUST THE KIND YOU LIKE. YOU LIKE GERMAN CARS, DON'T YOU?"
I SHOULD'VE GUESSED WHAT SHE MEANT BY THAT.
POKITA POKITA POK POK POK

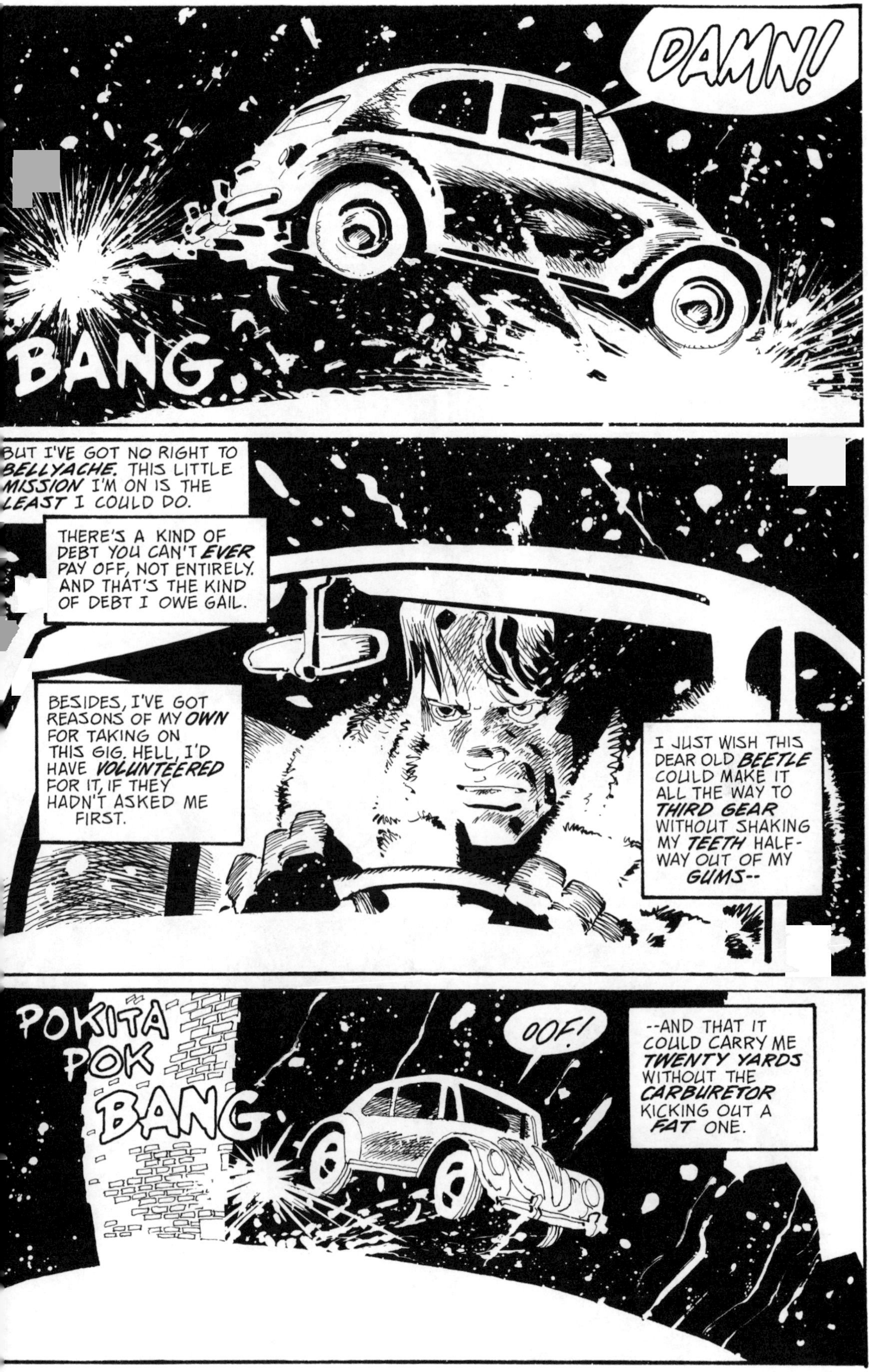
DAMN!
BANG
BUT I'VE GOT NO RIGHT TO BELLYACHE. THIS LITTLE MISSION I'M ON IS THE LEAST I COULD DO.
THERE'S A KIND OF DEBT YOU CAN'T EVER PAY OFF, NOT ENTIRELY. AND THAT'S THE KIND OF DEBT I OWE GAIL.
BESIDES, I'VE GOT REASONS OF MY OWN FOR TAKING ON THIS GIG. HELL, I'D HAVE VOLUNTEERED FOR IT, IF THEY HADN'T ASKED ME FIRST.
I JUST WISH THIS DEAR OLD BEETLE COULD MAKE IT ALL THE WAY TO THIRD GEAR WITHOUT SHAKING MY TEETH HALF-WAY OUT OF MY GUMS--
POKITA POK BANG
OOF!
--AND THAT IT COULD CARRY ME TWENTY YARDS WITHOUT THE CARBURETOR KICKING OUT A FAT ONE.

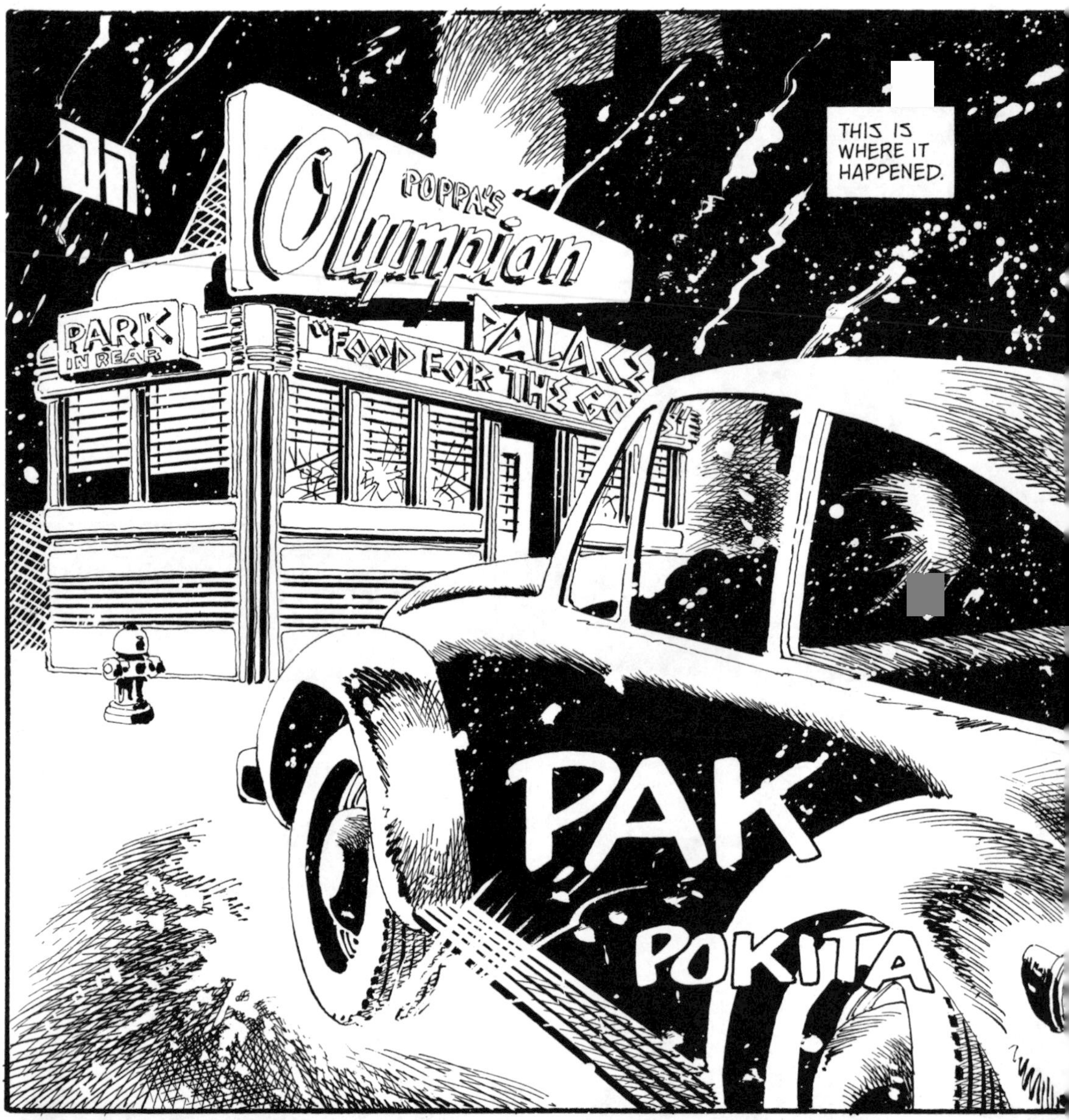
THIS IS WHERE IT HAPPENED.
POPPA'S
Olympian
PARK
IN REAR
PAK
POKITA

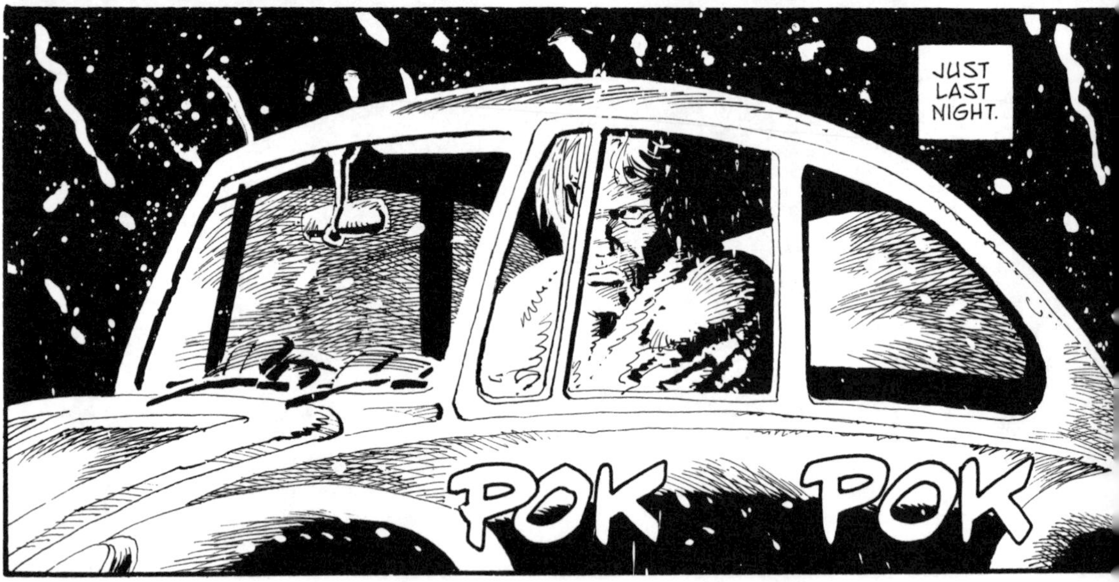
JUST LAST NIGHT.
POK POK

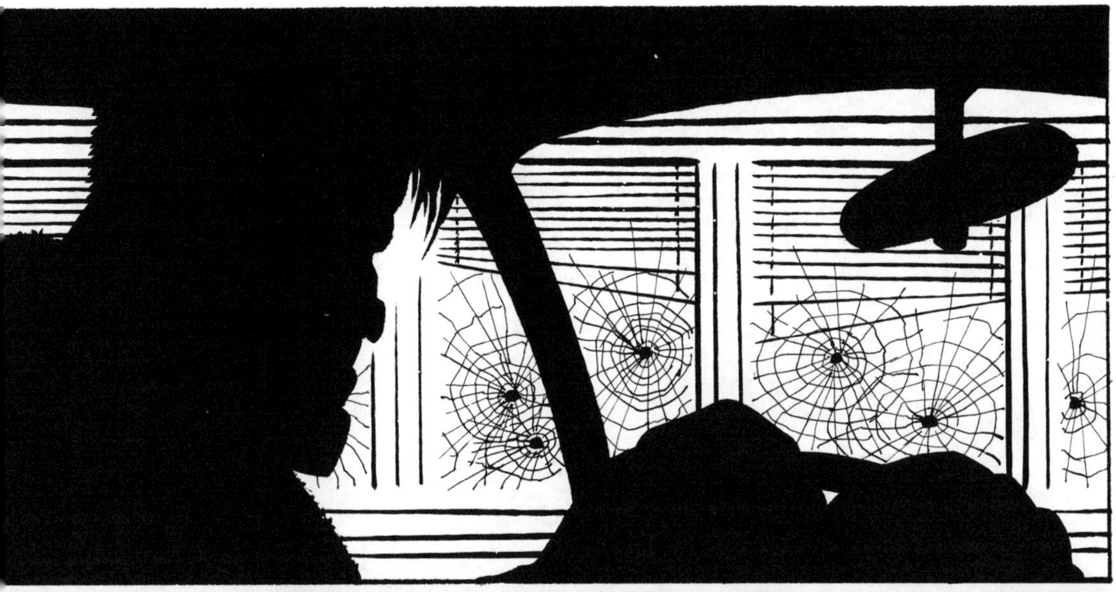

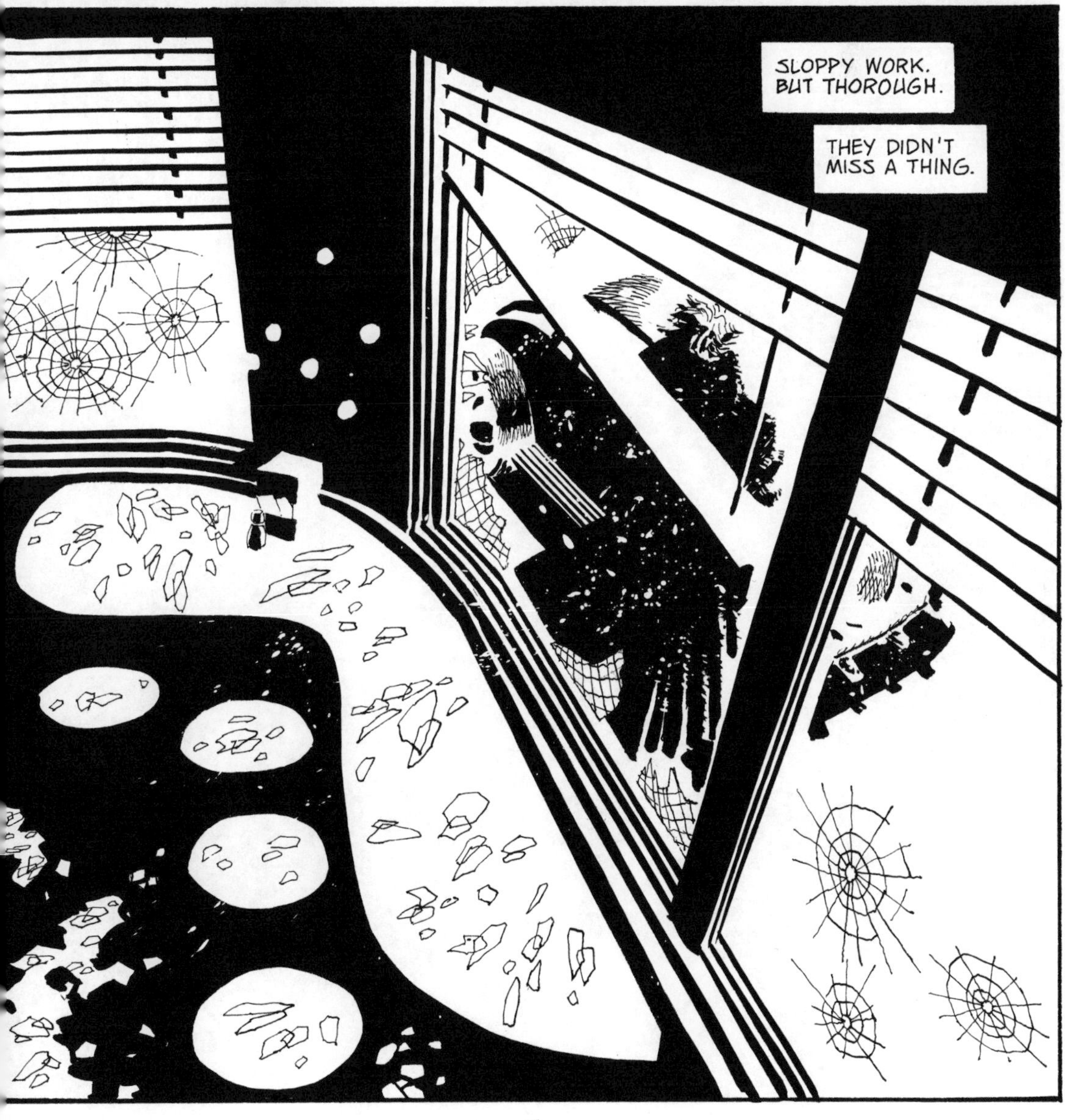
SLOPPY WORK. BUT THOROUGH.
THEY DIDN'T MISS A THING.

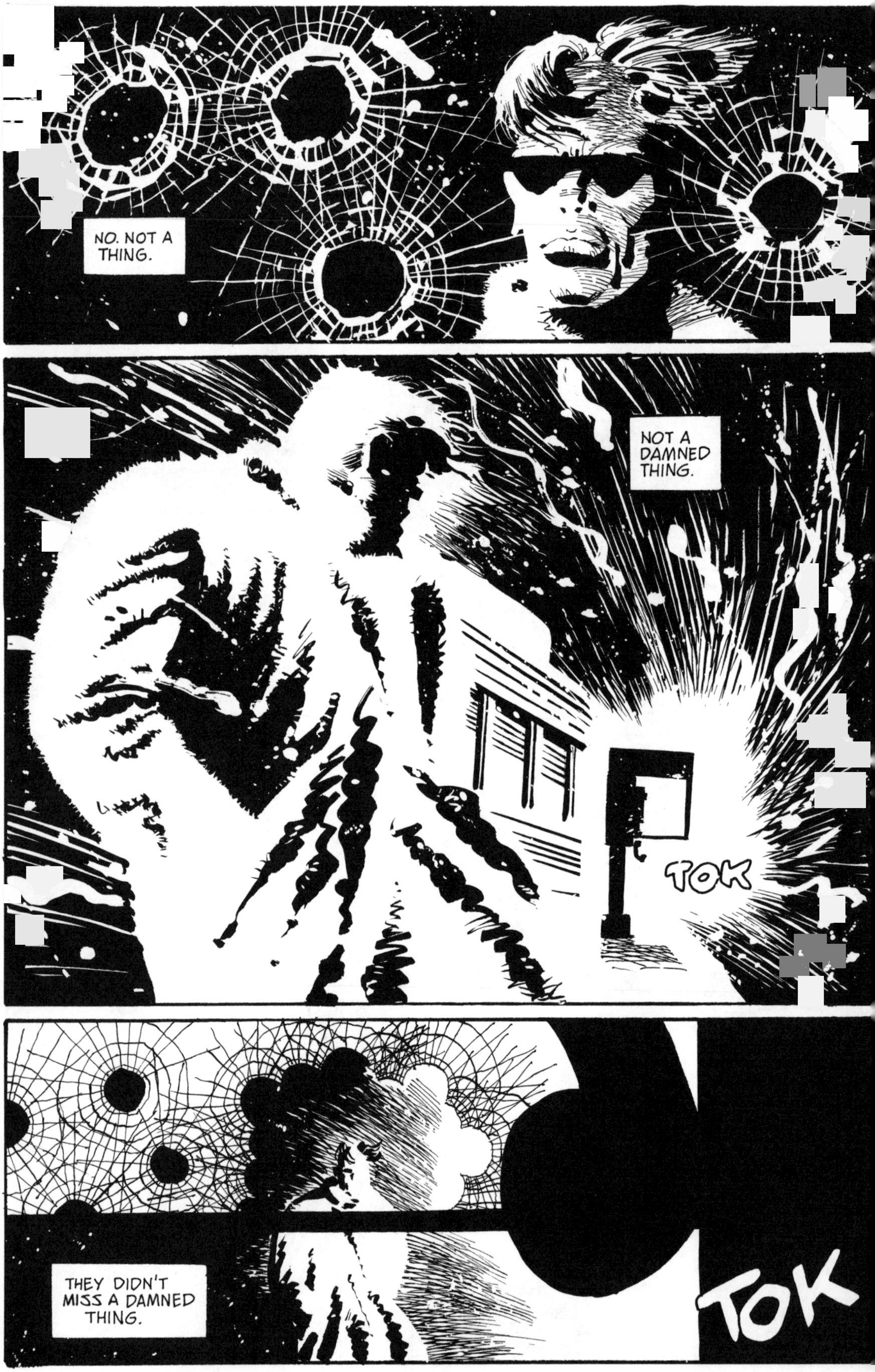

NO. NOT A THING.
NOT A DAMNED THING.
TOK
THEY DIDN'T MISS A DAMNED THING.
TOK

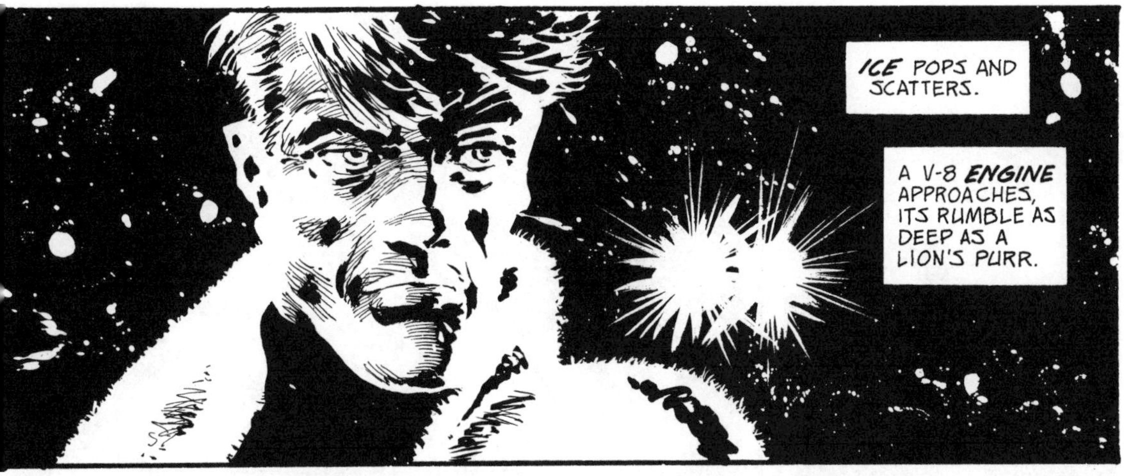
ICE POPS AND SCATTERS.
A V-8 ENGINE APPROACHES, ITS RUMBLE AS DEEP AS A LION'S PURR.

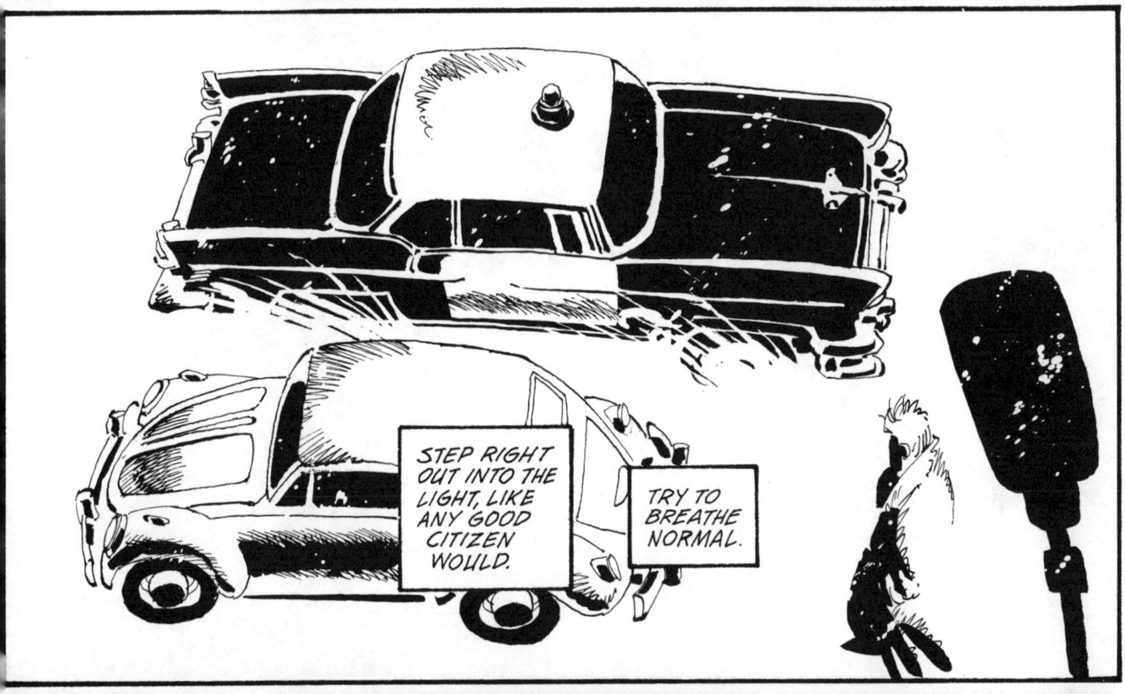
STEP RIGHT OUT INTO THE LIGHT, LIKE ANY GOOD CITIZEN WOULD.
TRY TO BREATHE NORMAL.

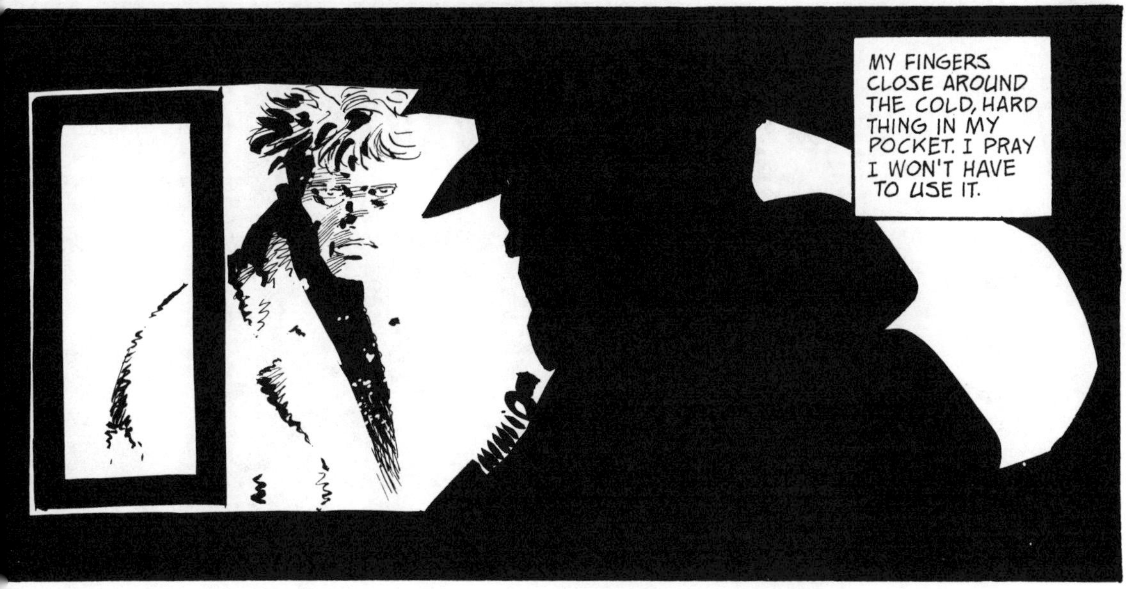
MY FINGERS CLOSE AROUND THE COLD, HARD THING IN MY POCKET. I PRAY I WON'T HAVE TO USE IT.

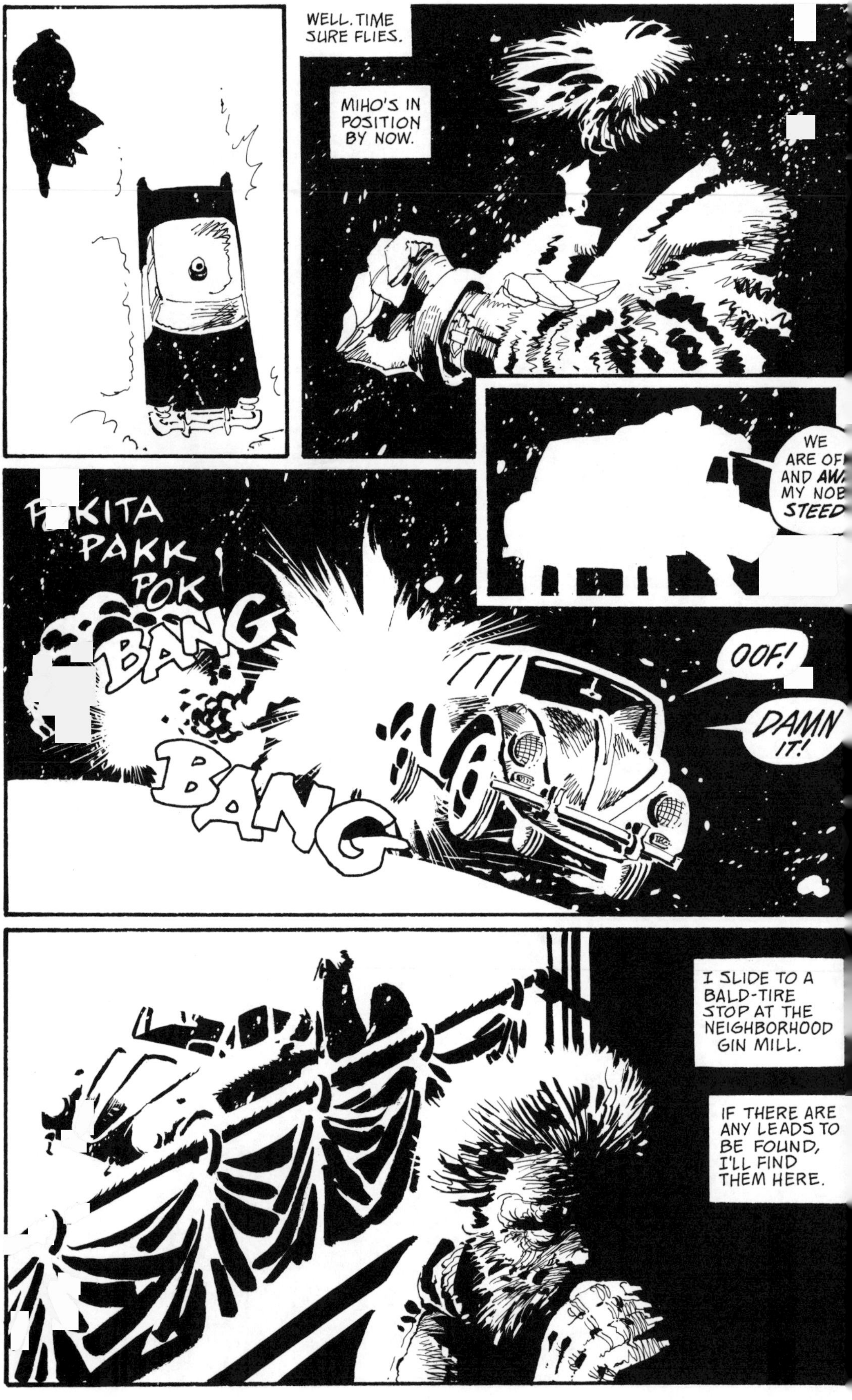

WELL. TIME SURE FLIES.
MIHO'S IN POSITION BY NOW.
WE ARE OF AND AW MY NOB STEED
KITA PAKK POK
BANG
BANG
OOF!
DAMN IT!
I SLIDE TO A BALD-TIRE STOP AT THE NEIGHBORHOOD GIN MILL.
IF THERE ARE ANY LEADS TO BE FOUND, I'LL FIND THEM HERE.

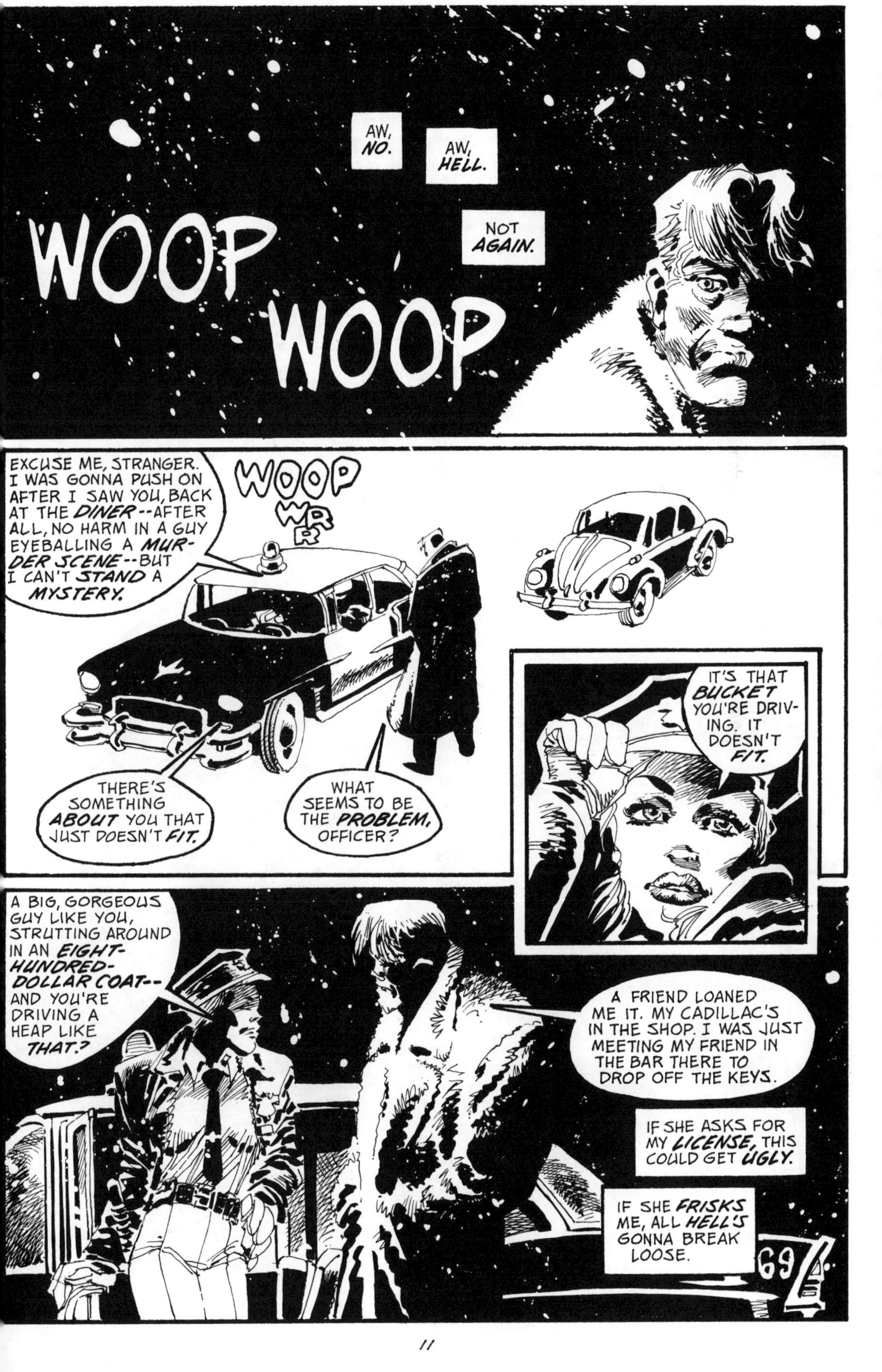

AW, NO.
AW, HELL.
NOT AGAIN.
WOOP WOOP
EXCUSE ME, STRANGER. I WAS GONNA PUSH ON AFTER I SAW YOU, BACK AT THE DINER--AFTER ALL, NO HARM IN A GUY EYEBALLING A MURDER SCENE--BUT I CAN'T STAND A MYSTERY.
WOOP
WR R
THERE'S SOMETHING ABOUT YOU THAT JUST DOESN'T FIT.
WHAT SEEMS TO BE THE PROBLEM, OFFICER?
IT'S THAT BUCKET YOU'RE DRIVING. IT DOESN'T FIT.
A BIG, GORGEOUS GUY LIKE YOU, STRUTTING AROUND IN AN EIGHT-HUNDRED-DOLLAR COAT--AND YOU'RE DRIVING A HEAP LIKE THAT?
A FRIEND LOANED ME IT. MY CADILLAC'S IN THE SHOP. I WAS JUST MEETING MY FRIEND IN THE BAR THERE TO DROP OFF THE KEYS.
IF SHE ASKS FOR MY LICENSE, THIS COULD GET UGLY.
IF SHE FRISKS ME, ALL HELL'S GONNA BREAK LOOSE.
69

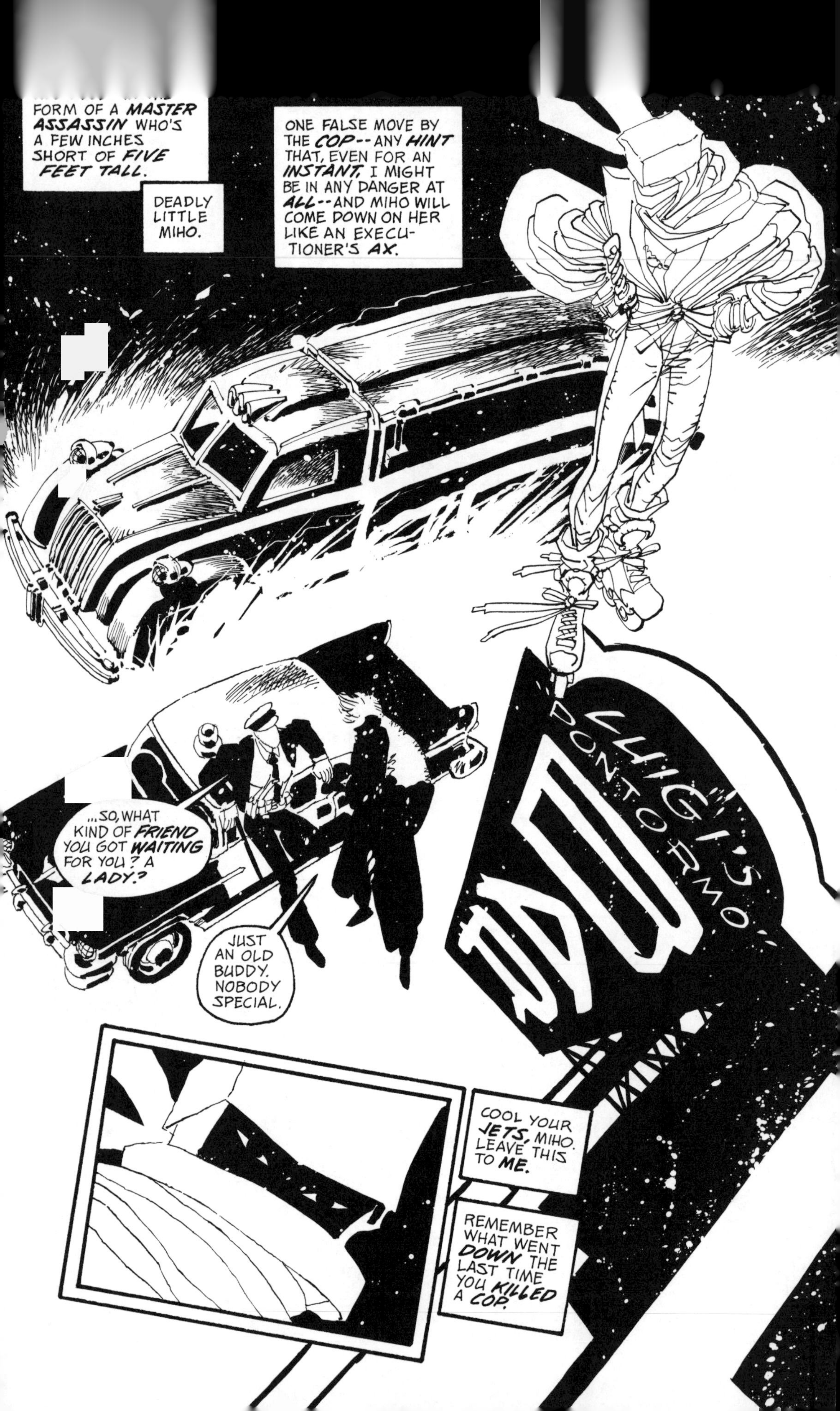

FORM OF A MASTER ASSASSIN WHO'S A FEW INCHES SHORT OF FIVE FEET TALL.
DEADLY LITTLE MIHO.
ONE FALSE MOVE BY THE COP-- ANY HINT THAT, EVEN FOR AN INSTANT, I MIGHT BE IN ANY DANGER AT ALL-- AND MIHO WILL COME DOWN ON HER LIKE AN EXECUTIONER'S AX.
...SO, WHAT KIND OF FRIEND YOU GOT WAITING FOR YOU? A LADY?
JUST AN OLD BUDDY. NOBODY SPECIAL.
LUIGI'S
PONTORMO
COOL YOUR JETS, MIHO. LEAVE THIS TO ME.
REMEMBER WHAT WENT DOWN THE LAST TIME YOU KILLED A COP.

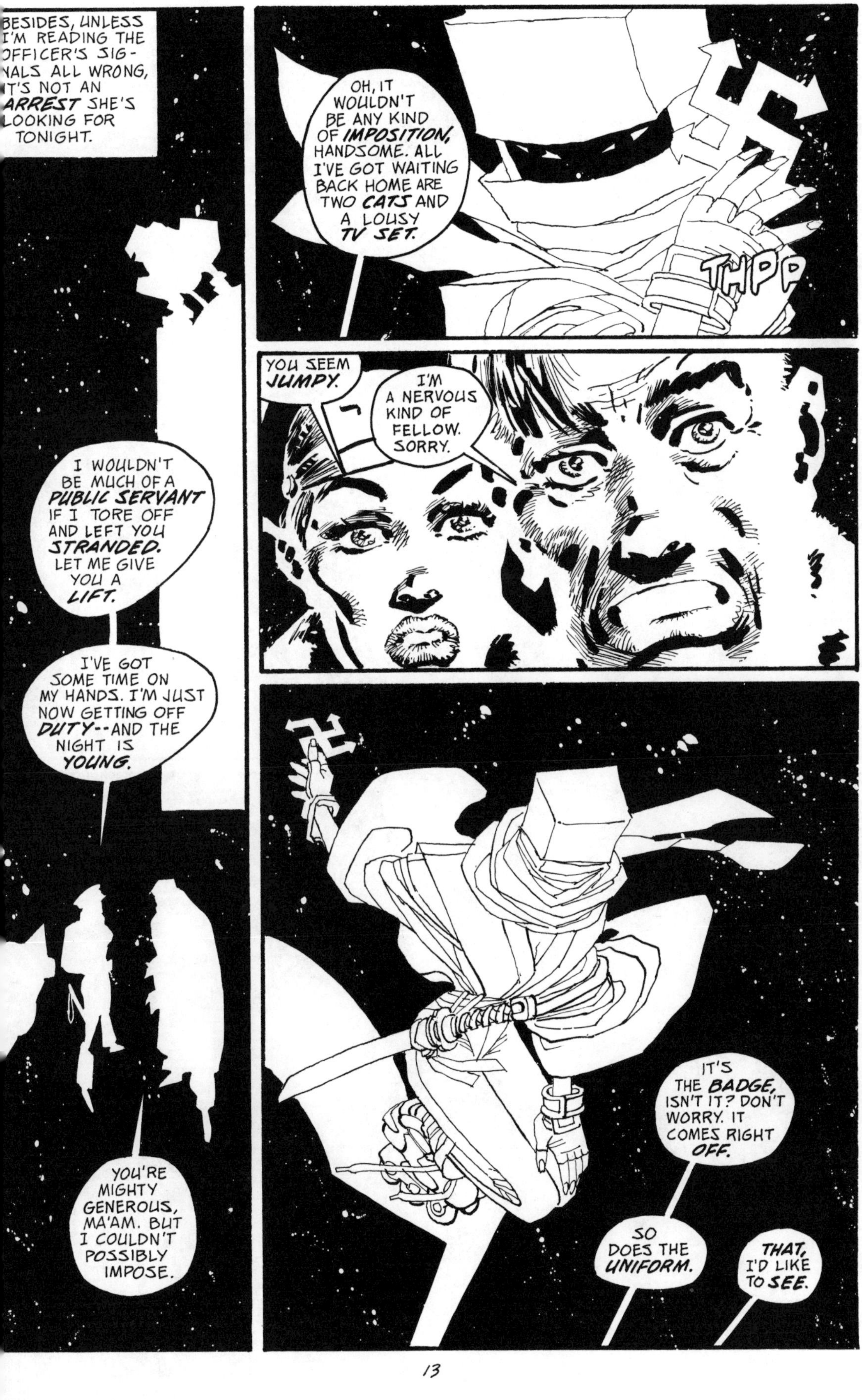
BESIDES, UNLESS I'M READING THE OFFICER'S SIGNALS ALL WRONG, IT'S NOT AN ARREST SHE'S LOOKING FOR TONIGHT.
OH, IT WOULDN'T BE ANY KIND OF IMPOSITION, HANDSOME. ALL I'VE GOT WAITING BACK HOME ARE TWO CATS AND A LOUSY TV SET.
THPP
YOU SEEM JUMPY.
I'M A NERVOUS KIND OF FELLOW. SORRY.
I WOULDN'T BE MUCH OF A PUBLIC SERVANT IF I TORE OFF AND LEFT YOU STRANDED. LET ME GIVE YOU A LIFT.
I'VE GOT SOME TIME ON MY HANDS. I'M JUST NOW GETTING OFF DUTY--AND THE NIGHT IS YOUNG.
YOU'RE MIGHTY GENEROUS, MA'AM. BUT I COULDN'T POSSIBLY IMPOSE.
IT'S THE BADGE, ISN'T IT? DON'T WORRY. IT COMES RIGHT OFF.
SO DOES THE UNIFORM.
THAT, I'D LIKE TO SEE.

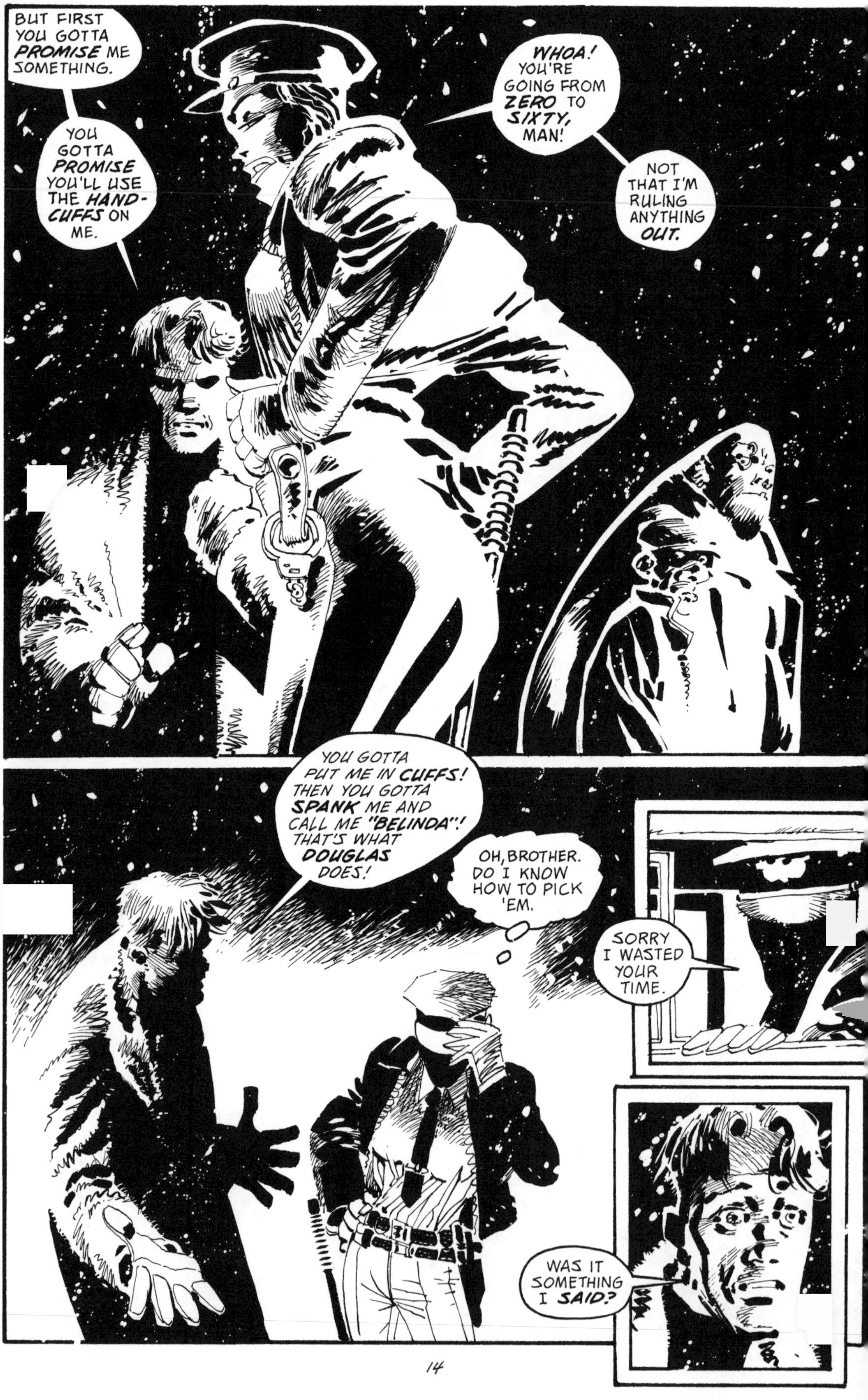
BUT FIRST YOU GOTTA PROMISE ME SOMETHING.
YOU GOTTA PROMISE YOU'LL USE THE HAND-CUFFS ON ME.
WHOA! YOU'RE GOING FROM ZERO TO SIXTY, MAN!
NOT THAT I'M RULING ANYTHING OUT.
YOU GOTTA PUT ME IN CUFFS! THEN YOU GOTTA SPANK ME AND CALL ME "BELINDA"! THAT'S WHAT DOUGLAS DOES!
OH, BROTHER. DO I KNOW HOW TO PICK 'EM.
SORRY I WASTED YOUR TIME.
WAS IT SOMETHING I SAID?

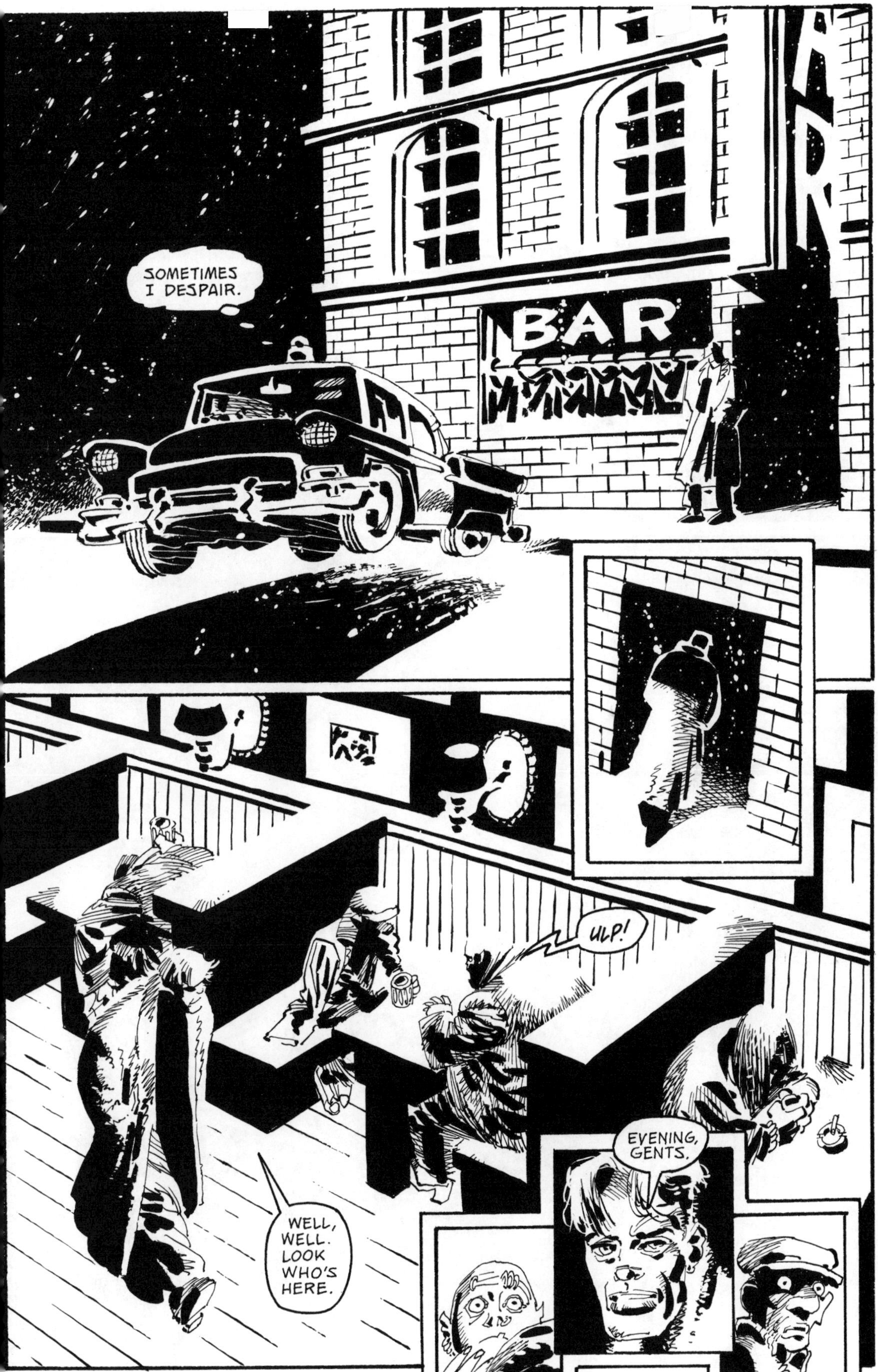
SOMETIMES I DESPAIR.
BAR
ULP!
WELL, WELL. LOOK WHO'S HERE.
EVENING, GENTS.

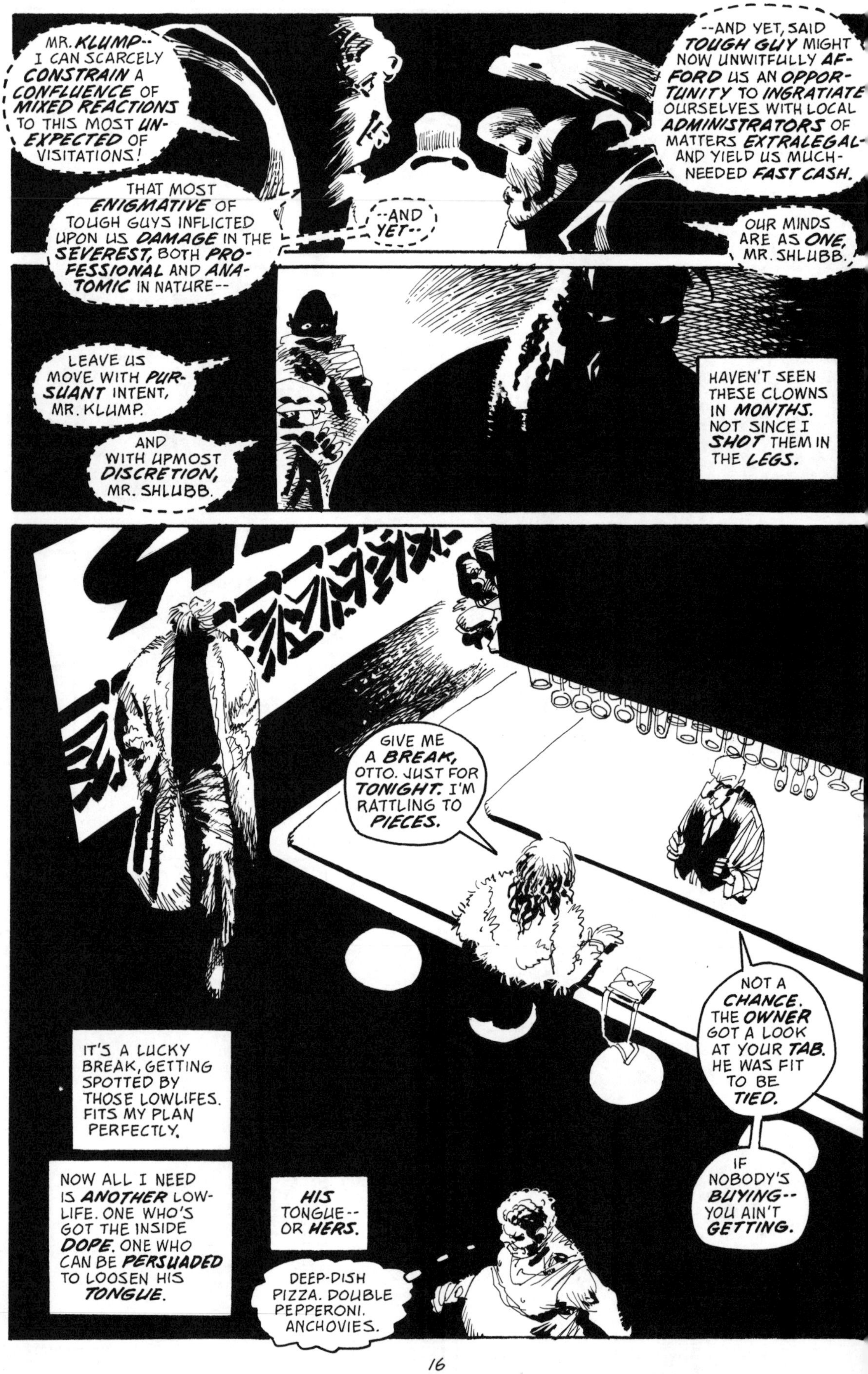

MR. KLUMP-- I CAN SCARCELY CONSTRAIN A CONFLUENCE OF MIXED REACTIONS TO THIS MOST UN-EXPECTED OF VISITATIONS!
THAT MOST ENIGMATIVE OF TOUGH GUYS INFLICTED UPON US DAMAGE IN THE SEVEREST, BOTH PRO-FESSIONAL AND ANA-TOMIC IN NATURE--
--AND YET--
--AND YET, SAID TOUGH GUY MIGHT NOW UNWITFULLY AF-FORD US AN OPPOR-TUNITY TO INGRATIATE OURSELVES WITH LOCAL ADMINISTRATORS OF MATTERS EXTRALEGAL-AND YIELD US MUCH-NEEDED FAST CASH.
OUR MINDS ARE AS ONE, MR. SHLUBB.
LEAVE US MOVE WITH PUR-SUANT INTENT, MR. KLUMP.
AND WITH UPMOST DISCRETION, MR. SHLUBB.
HAVEN'T SEEN THESE CLOWNS IN MONTHS. NOT SINCE I SHOT THEM IN THE LEGS.
GIVE ME A BREAK, OTTO. JUST FOR TONIGHT. I'M RATTLING TO PIECES.
NOT A CHANCE. THE OWNER GOT A LOOK AT YOUR TAB. HE WAS FIT TO BE TIED.
IF NOBODY'S BUYING-- YOU AIN'T GETTING.
IT'S A LUCKY BREAK, GETTING SPOTTED BY THOSE LOWLIFES. FITS MY PLAN PERFECTLY.
NOW ALL I NEED IS ANOTHER LOW-LIFE. ONE WHO'S GOT THE INSIDE DOPE. ONE WHO CAN BE PERSUADED TO LOOSEN HIS TONGUE.
HIS TONGUE-- OR HERS.
DEEP-DISH PIZZA. DOUBLE PEPPERONI. ANCHOVIES.

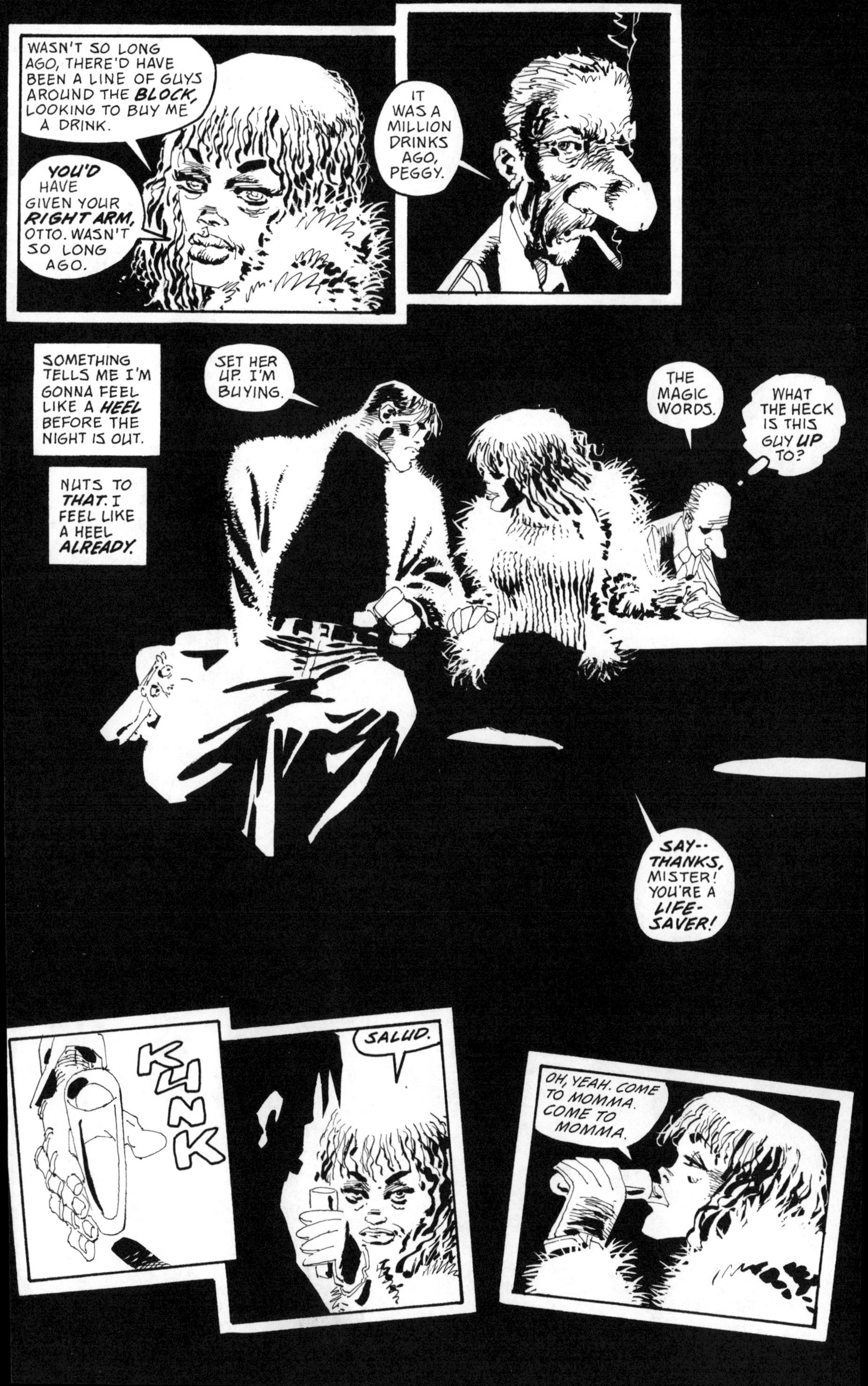

WASN'T SO LONG AGO, THERE'D HAVE BEEN A LINE OF GUYS AROUND THE BLOCK, LOOKING TO BUY ME A DRINK.
YOU'D HAVE GIVEN YOUR RIGHT ARM, OTTO. WASN'T SO LONG AGO.
IT WAS A MILLION DRINKS AGO, PEGGY.
SOMETHING TELLS ME I'M GONNA FEEL LIKE A HEEL BEFORE THE NIGHT IS OUT.
NUTS TO THAT. I FEEL LIKE A HEEL ALREADY.
SET HER UP. I'M BUYING.
THE MAGIC WORDS.
WHAT THE HECK IS THIS GUY UP TO?
SAY-- THANKS, MISTER! YOU'RE A LIFE-SAVER!
KLUNK
SALUD.
OH, YEAH. COME TO MOMMA. COME TO MOMMA.

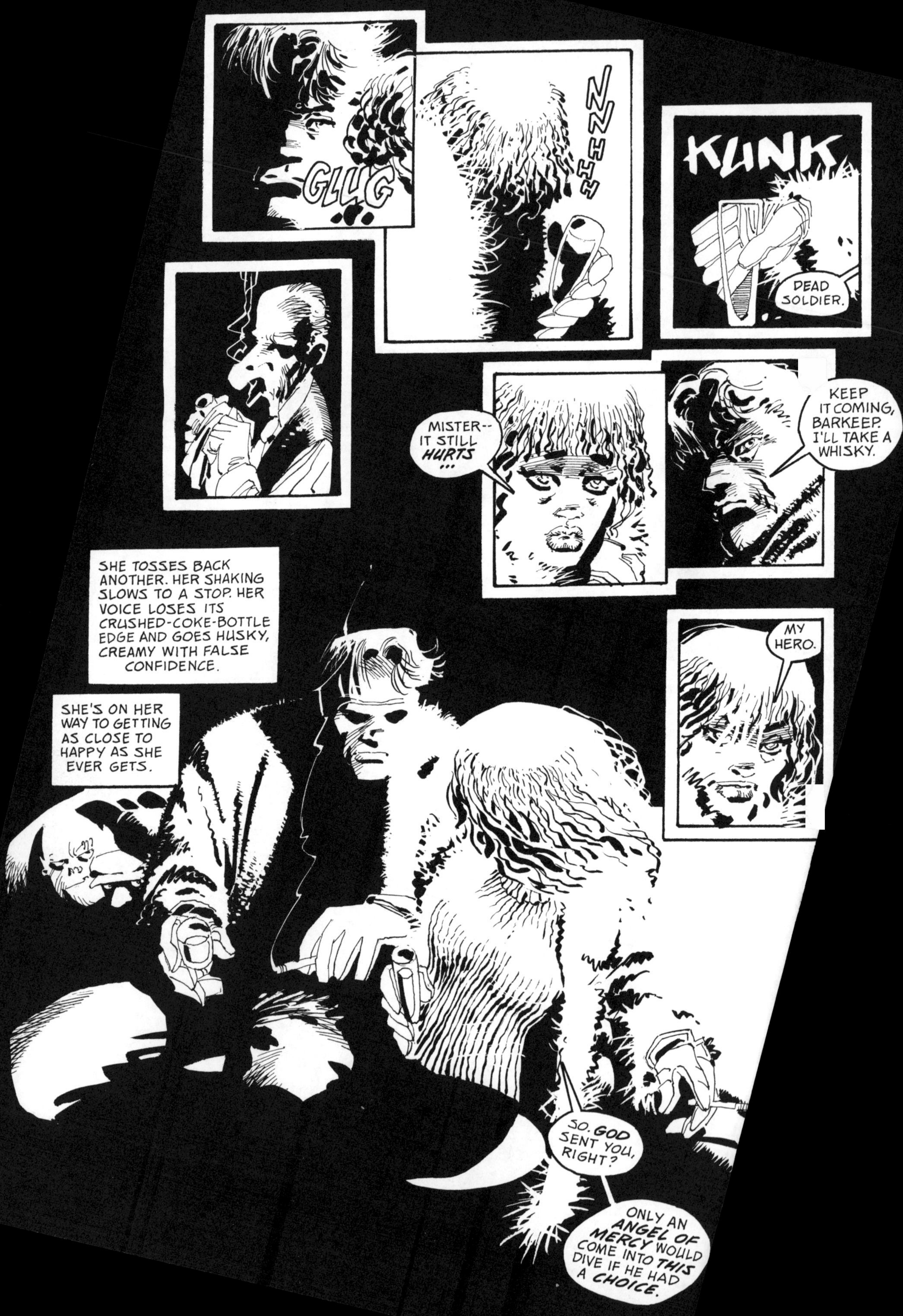
GLUG
NNNHHHH
KUNK
DEAD SOLDIER.
MISTER-- IT STILL HURTS ...
KEEP IT COMING, BARKEEP. I'LL TAKE A WHISKY.
SHE TOSSES BACK ANOTHER. HER SHAKING SLOWS TO A STOP. HER VOICE LOSES ITS CRUSHED-COKE-BOTTLE EDGE AND GOES HUSKY, CREAMY WITH FALSE CONFIDENCE.
MY HERO.
SHE'S ON HER WAY TO GETTING AS CLOSE TO HAPPY AS SHE EVER GETS.
SO. GOD SENT YOU, RIGHT?
ONLY AN ANGEL OF MERCY WOULD COME INTO THIS DIVE IF HE HAD A CHOICE.

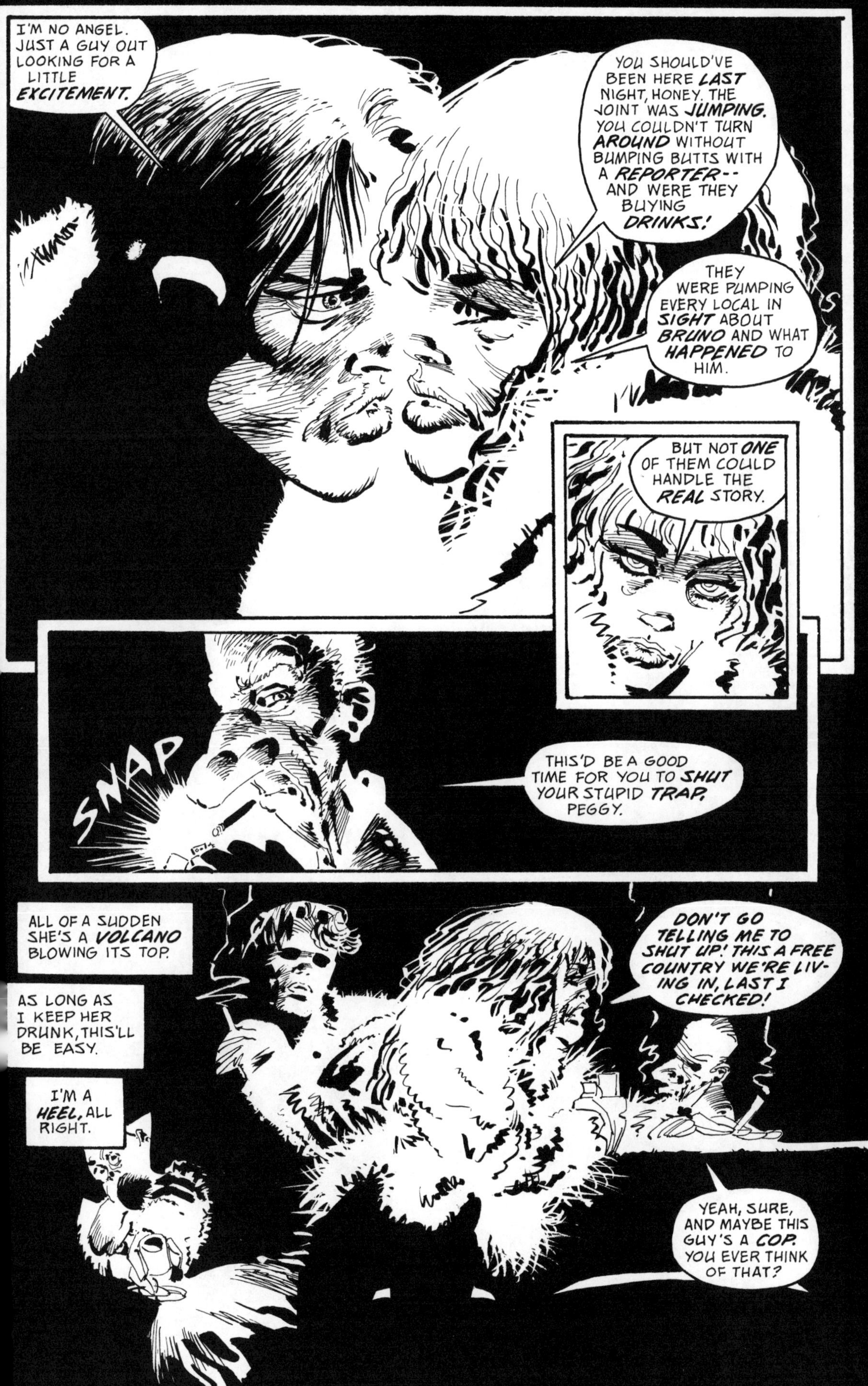
I'M NO ANGEL. JUST A GUY OUT LOOKING FOR A LITTLE EXCITEMENT.
YOU SHOULD'VE BEEN HERE LAST NIGHT, HONEY. THE JOINT WAS JUMPING. YOU COULDN'T TURN AROUND WITHOUT BUMPING BUTTS WITH A REPORTER-- AND WERE THEY BUYING DRINKS!
THEY WERE PUMPING EVERY LOCAL IN SIGHT ABOUT BRUNO AND WHAT HAPPENED TO HIM.
BUT NOT ONE OF THEM COULD HANDLE THE REAL STORY.
SNAP
THIS'D BE A GOOD TIME FOR YOU TO SHUT YOUR STUPID TRAP, PEGGY.
ALL OF A SUDDEN SHE'S A VOLCANO BLOWING ITS TOP.
DON'T GO TELLING ME TO SHUT UP! THIS A FREE COUNTRY WE'RE LIV-ING IN, LAST I CHECKED!
AS LONG AS I KEEP HER DRUNK, THIS'LL BE EASY.
I'M A HEEL, ALL RIGHT.
YEAH, SURE, AND MAYBE THIS GUY'S A COP. YOU EVER THINK OF THAT?

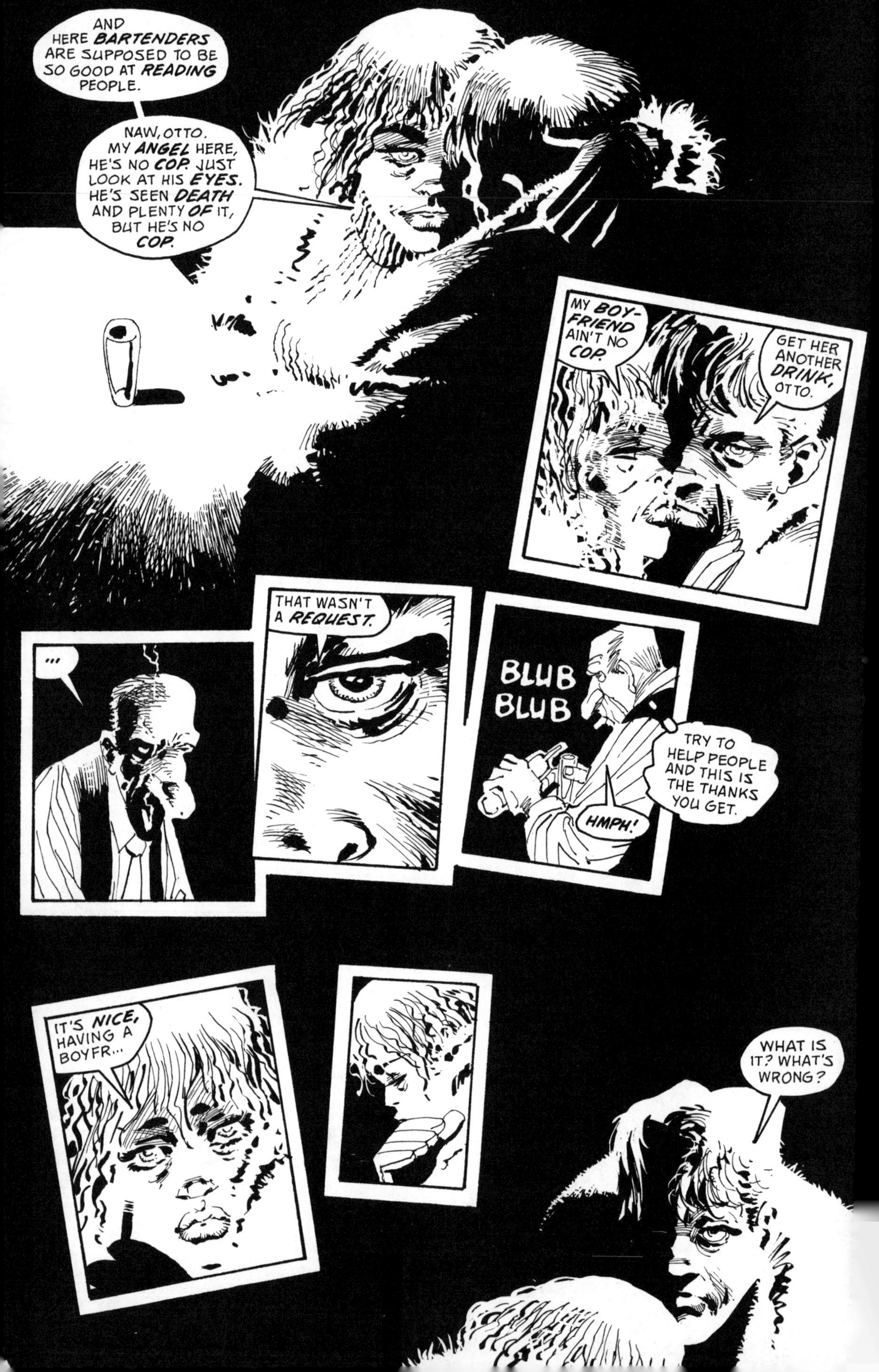
AND HERE BARTENDERS ARE SUPPOSED TO BE SO GOOD AT READING PEOPLE.
NAW, OTTO. MY ANGEL HERE, HE'S NO COP. JUST LOOK AT HIS EYES. HE'S SEEN DEATH AND PLENTY OF IT, BUT HE'S NO COP.
MY BOY-FRIEND AIN'T NO COP.
GET HER ANOTHER DRINK, OTTO.
...
THAT WASN'T A REQUEST.
BLUB BLUB
TRY TO HELP PEOPLE AND THIS IS THE THANKS YOU GET.
HMPH!
IT'S NICE, HAVING A BOYFR...
WHAT IS IT? WHAT'S WRONG?

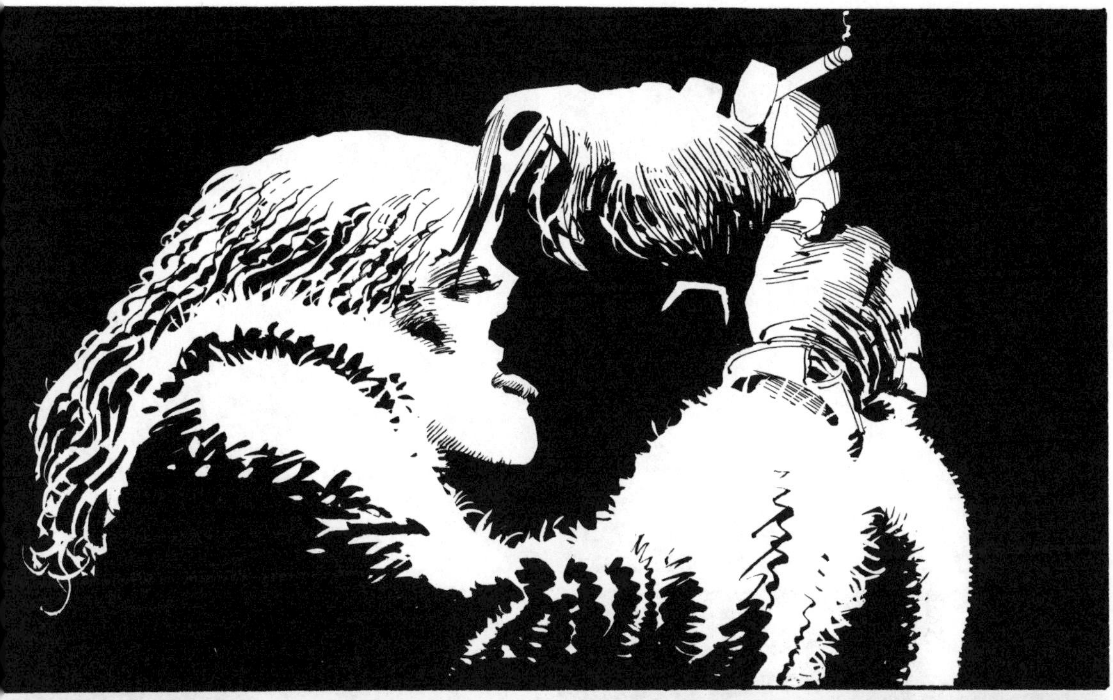

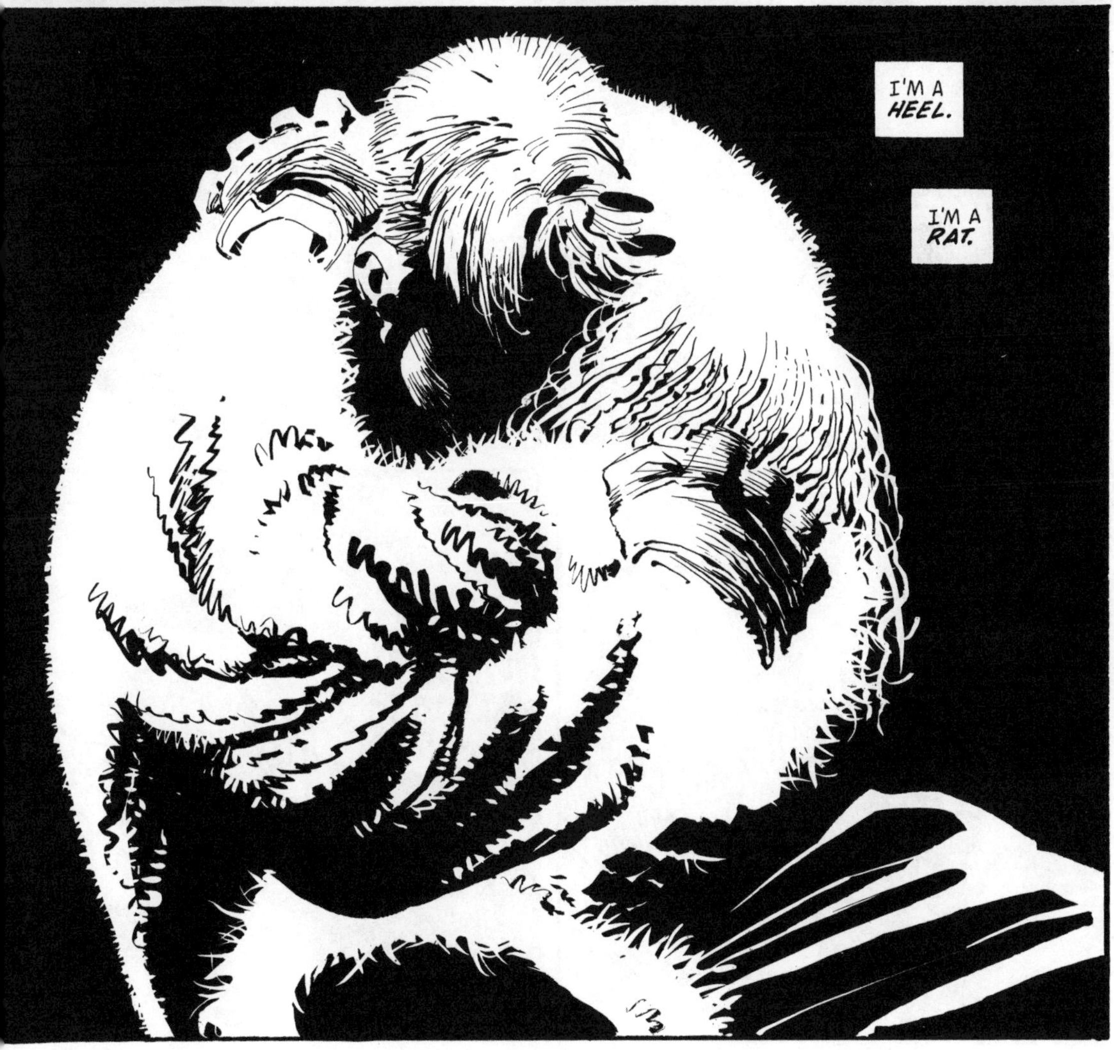

I'M A HEEL.
I'M A RAT.

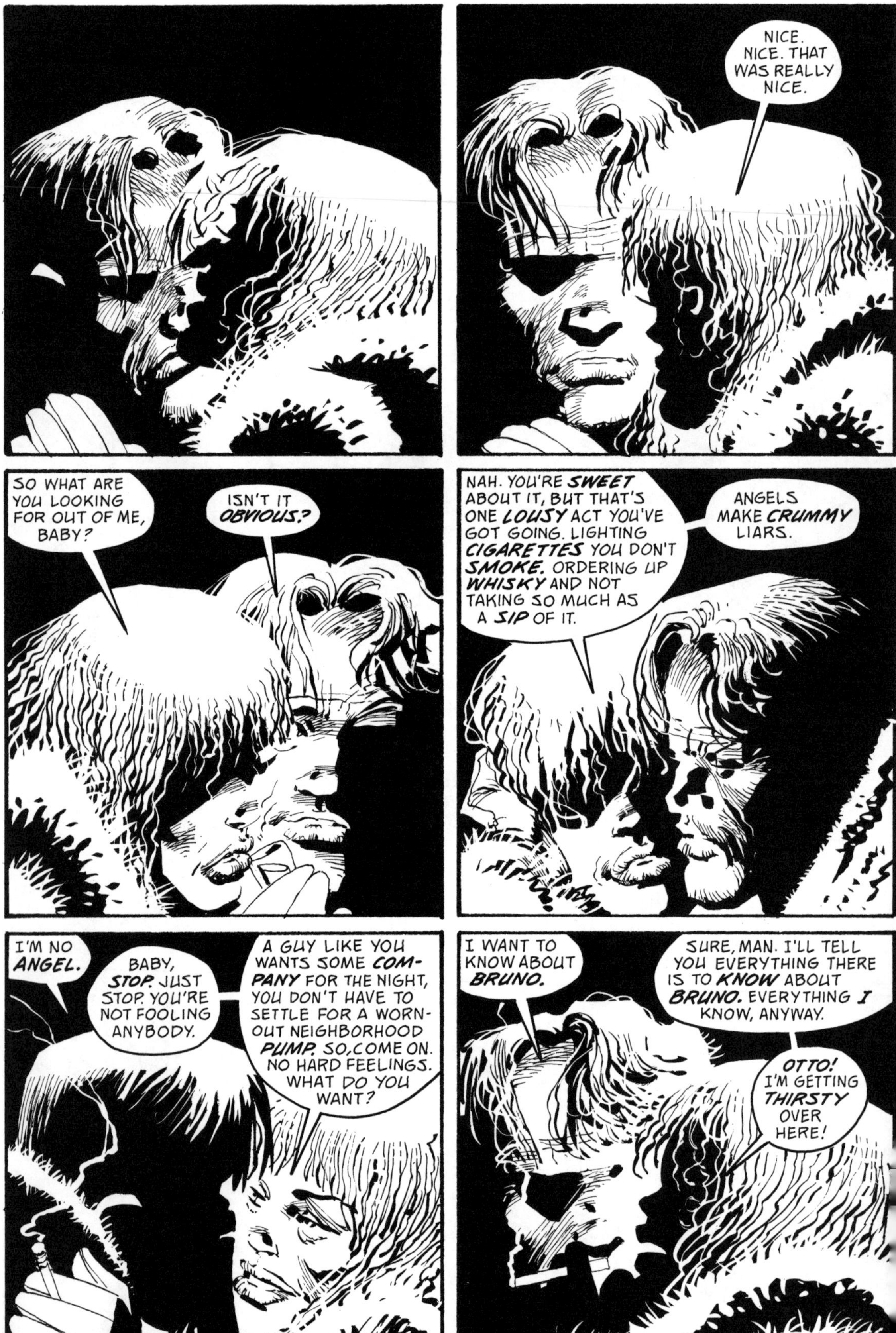
NICE. NICE. THAT WAS REALLY NICE.
SO WHAT ARE YOU LOOKING FOR OUT OF ME, BABY?
ISN'T IT *OBVIOUS?*
NAH. YOU'RE *SWEET* ABOUT IT, BUT THAT'S ONE *LOUSY* ACT YOU'VE GOT GOING. LIGHTING *CIGARETTES* YOU DON'T *SMOKE.* ORDERING UP *WHISKY* AND NOT TAKING SO MUCH AS A *SIP* OF IT.
ANGELS MAKE *CRUMMY* LIARS.
I'M NO *ANGEL.*
BABY, *STOP.* JUST STOP. YOU'RE NOT FOOLING ANYBODY.
A GUY LIKE YOU WANTS SOME *COMPANY* FOR THE NIGHT, YOU DON'T HAVE TO SETTLE FOR A WORN-OUT NEIGHBORHOOD *PUMP.* SO, COME ON. NO HARD FEELINGS. WHAT DO YOU WANT?
I WANT TO KNOW ABOUT *BRUNO.*
SURE, MAN. I'LL TELL YOU EVERYTHING THERE IS TO *KNOW* ABOUT *BRUNO.* EVERYTHING *I* KNOW, ANYWAY.
OTTO! I'M GETTING *THIRSTY* OVER HERE!

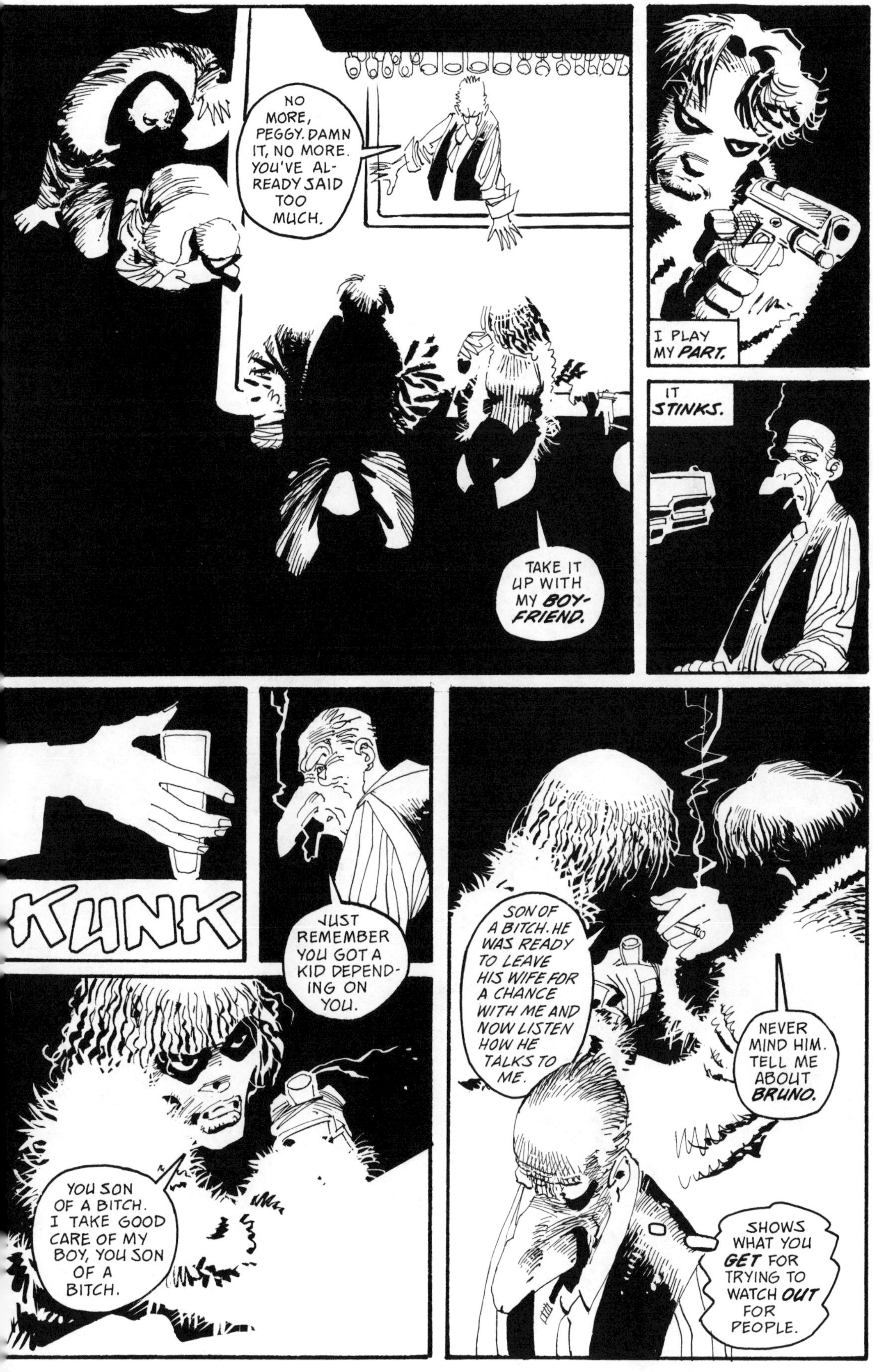
NO MORE, PEGGY. DAMN IT, NO MORE. YOU'VE AL- READY SAID TOO MUCH.
TAKE IT UP WITH MY BOY- FRIEND.
I PLAY MY PART.
IT STINKS.
KLUNK
JUST REMEMBER YOU GOT A KID DEPEND- ING ON YOU.
YOU SON OF A BITCH. I TAKE GOOD CARE OF MY BOY, YOU SON OF A BITCH.
SON OF A BITCH. HE WAS READY TO LEAVE HIS WIFE FOR A CHANCE WITH ME AND NOW LISTEN HOW HE TALKS TO ME.
NEVER MIND HIM. TELL ME ABOUT BRUNO.
SHOWS WHAT YOU GET FOR TRYING TO WATCH OUT FOR PEOPLE.

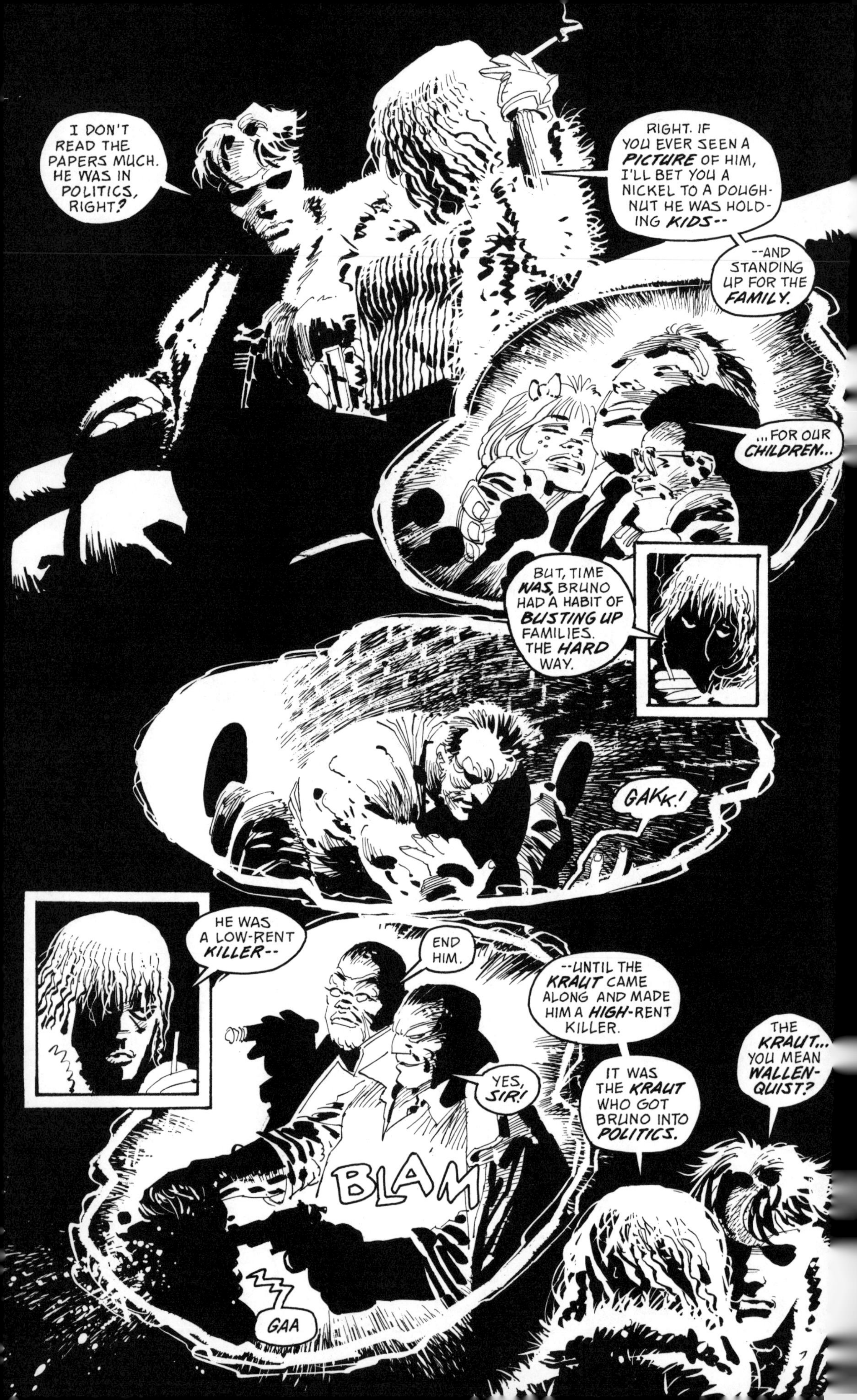
I DON'T READ THE PAPERS MUCH. HE WAS IN POLITICS, RIGHT?
RIGHT. IF YOU EVER SEEN A PICTURE OF HIM, I'LL BET YOU A NICKEL TO A DOUGHNUT HE WAS HOLDING KIDS--
--AND STANDING UP FOR THE FAMILY.
...FOR OUR CHILDREN...
BUT, TIME WAS, BRUNO HAD A HABIT OF BUSTING UP FAMILIES. THE HARD WAY.
GAKK!
HE WAS A LOW-RENT KILLER--
END HIM.
--UNTIL THE KRAUT CAME ALONG AND MADE HIM A HIGH-RENT KILLER.
YES, SIR!
BLAM
IT WAS THE KRAUT WHO GOT BRUNO INTO POLITICS.
THE KRAUT... YOU MEAN WALLENQUIST?
GAA

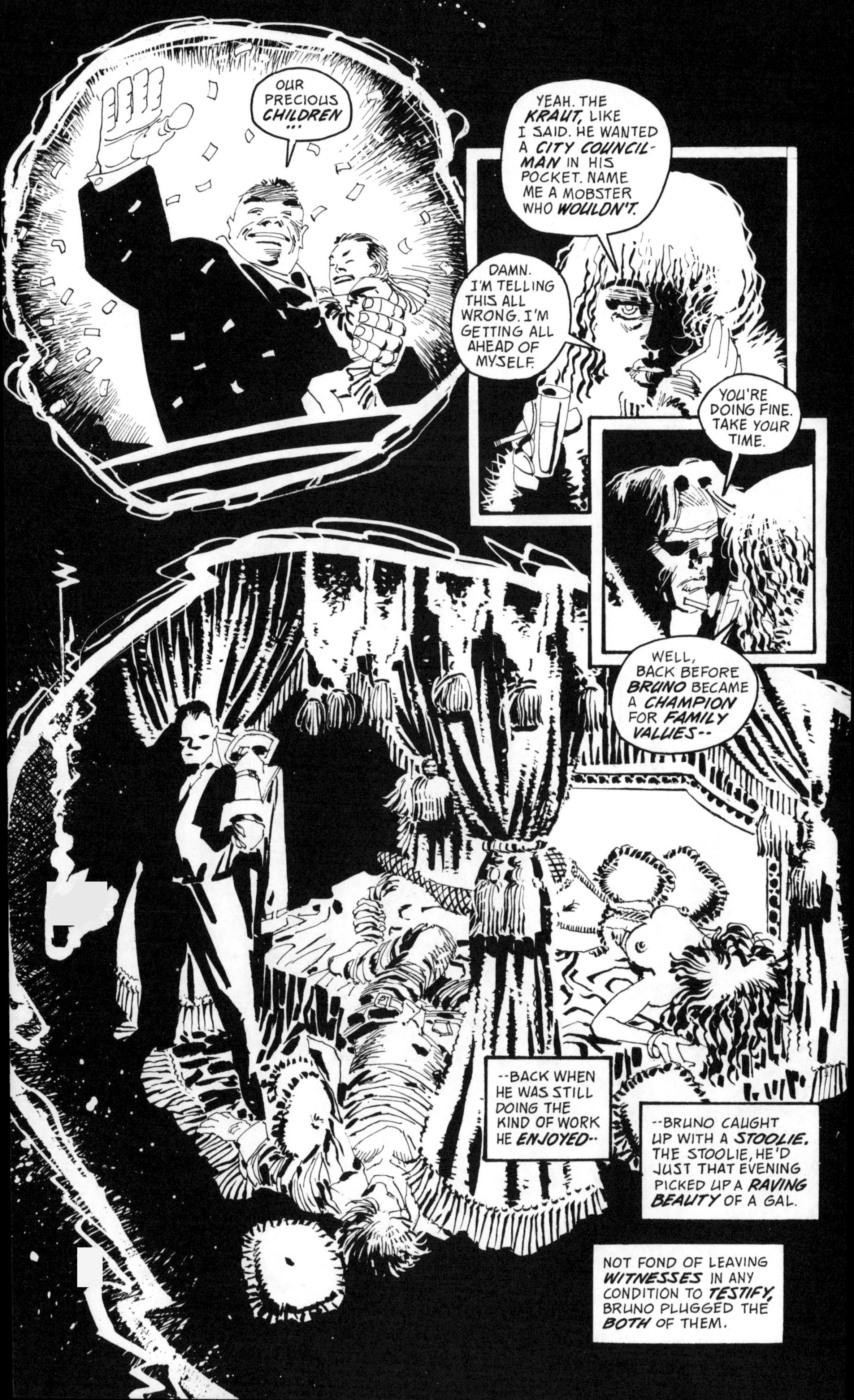
OUR PRECIOUS CHILDREN ...
YEAH. THE KRAUT, LIKE I SAID. HE WANTED A CITY COUNCILMAN IN HIS POCKET. NAME ME A MOBSTER WHO WOULDN'T.
DAMN. I'M TELLING THIS ALL WRONG. I'M GETTING ALL AHEAD OF MYSELF.
YOU'RE DOING FINE. TAKE YOUR TIME.
WELL, BACK BEFORE BRUNO BECAME A CHAMPION FOR FAMILY VALUES--
--BACK WHEN HE WAS STILL DOING THE KIND OF WORK HE ENJOYED--
--BRUNO CAUGHT UP WITH A STOOLIE. THE STOOLIE, HE'D JUST THAT EVENING PICKED UP A RAVING BEAUTY OF A GAL.
NOT FOND OF LEAVING WITNESSES IN ANY CONDITION TO TESTIFY, BRUNO PLUGGED THE BOTH OF THEM.

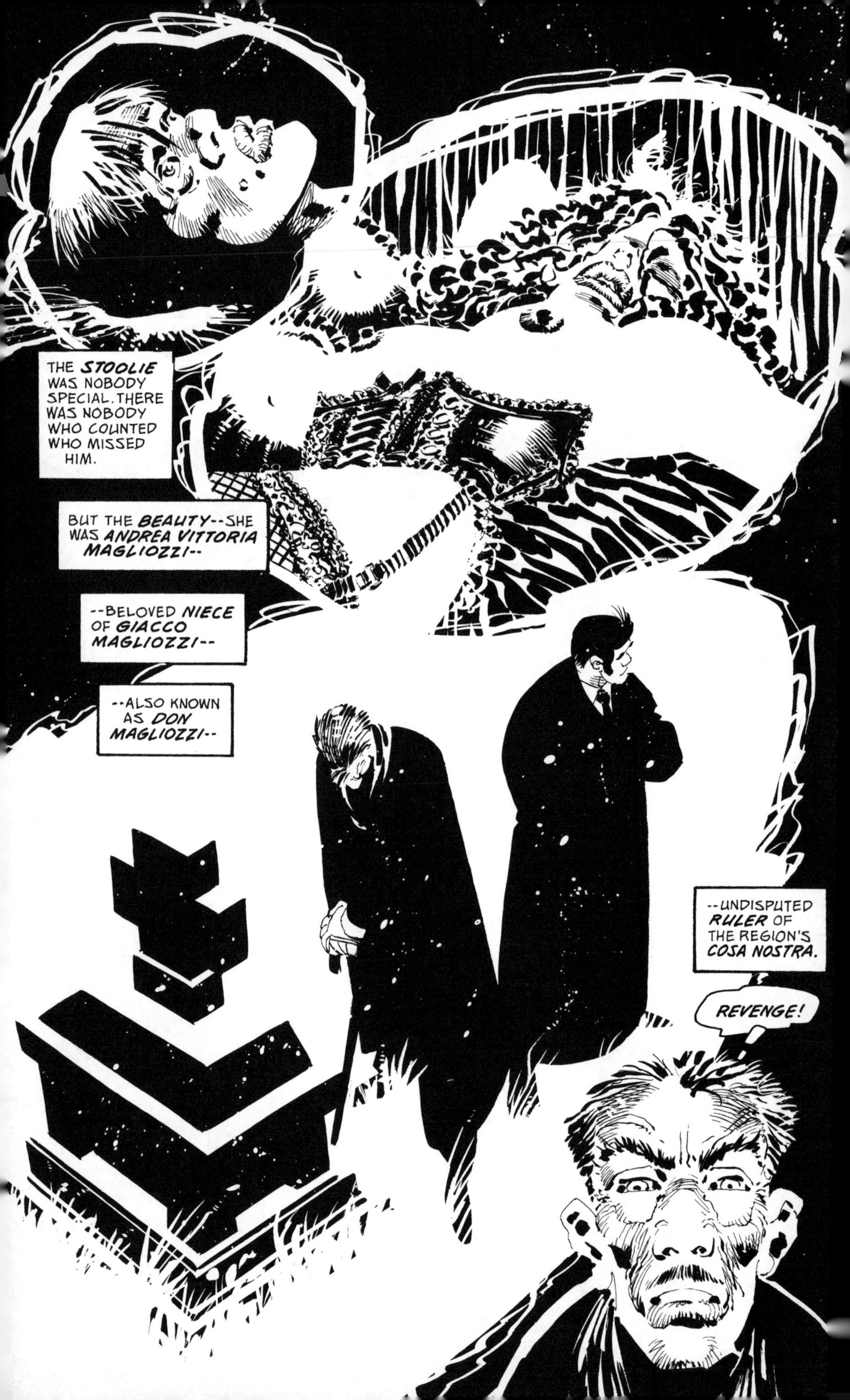
THE STOOLIE WAS NOBODY SPECIAL. THERE WAS NOBODY WHO COUNTED WHO MISSED HIM.
BUT THE BEAUTY--SHE WAS ANDREA VITTORIA MAGLIOZZI--
--BELOVED NIECE OF GIACCO MAGLIOZZI--
--ALSO KNOWN AS DON MAGLIOZZI--
--UNDISPUTED RULER OF THE REGION'S COSA NOSTRA.
REVENGE!

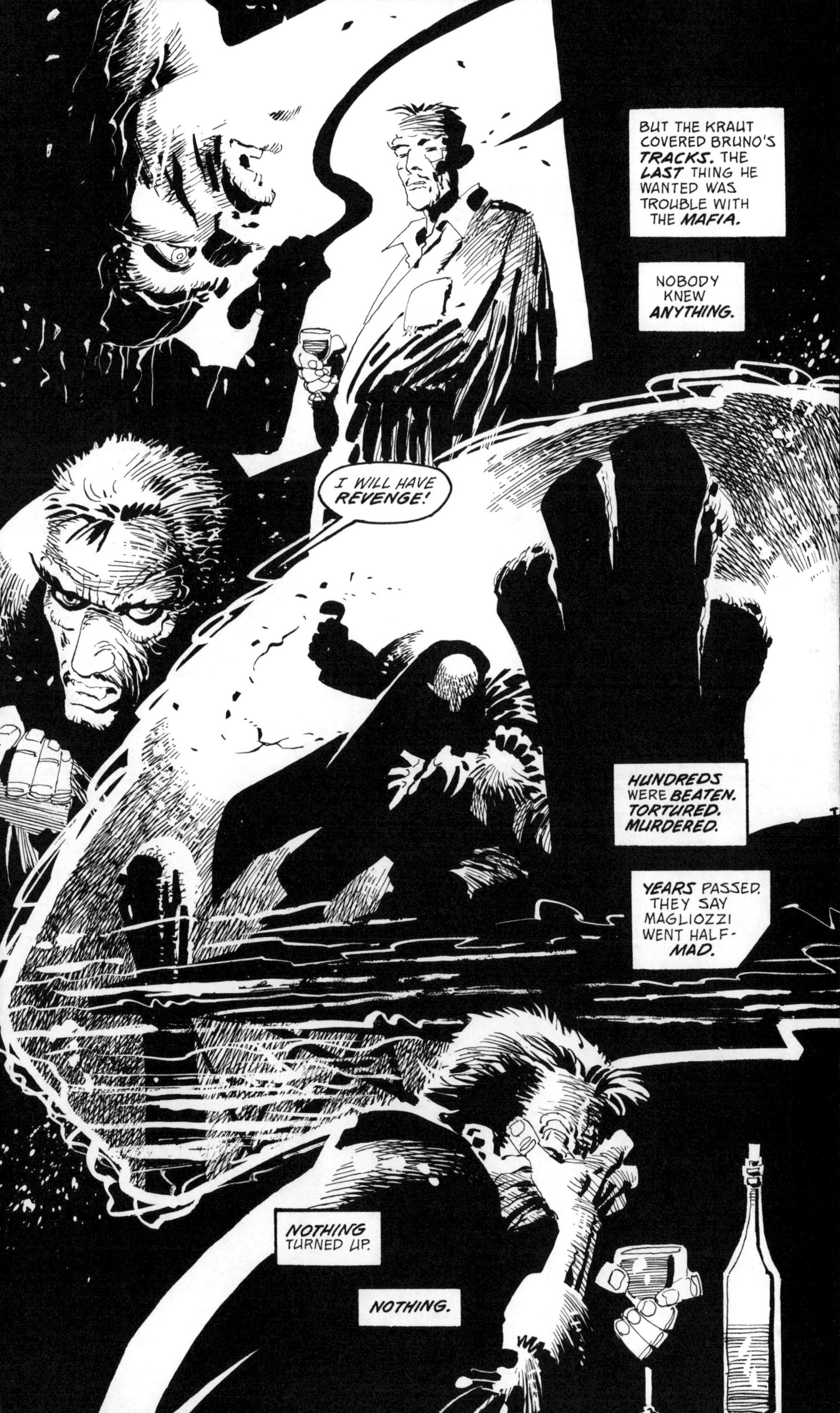
BUT THE KRAUT COVERED BRUNO'S TRACKS. THE LAST THING HE WANTED WAS TROUBLE WITH THE MAFIA.
NOBODY KNEW ANYTHING.
I WILL HAVE REVENGE!
HUNDREDS WERE BEATEN. TORTURED. MURDERED.
YEARS PASSED. THEY SAY MAGLIOZZI WENT HALF-MAD.
NOTHING TURNED UP.
NOTHING.

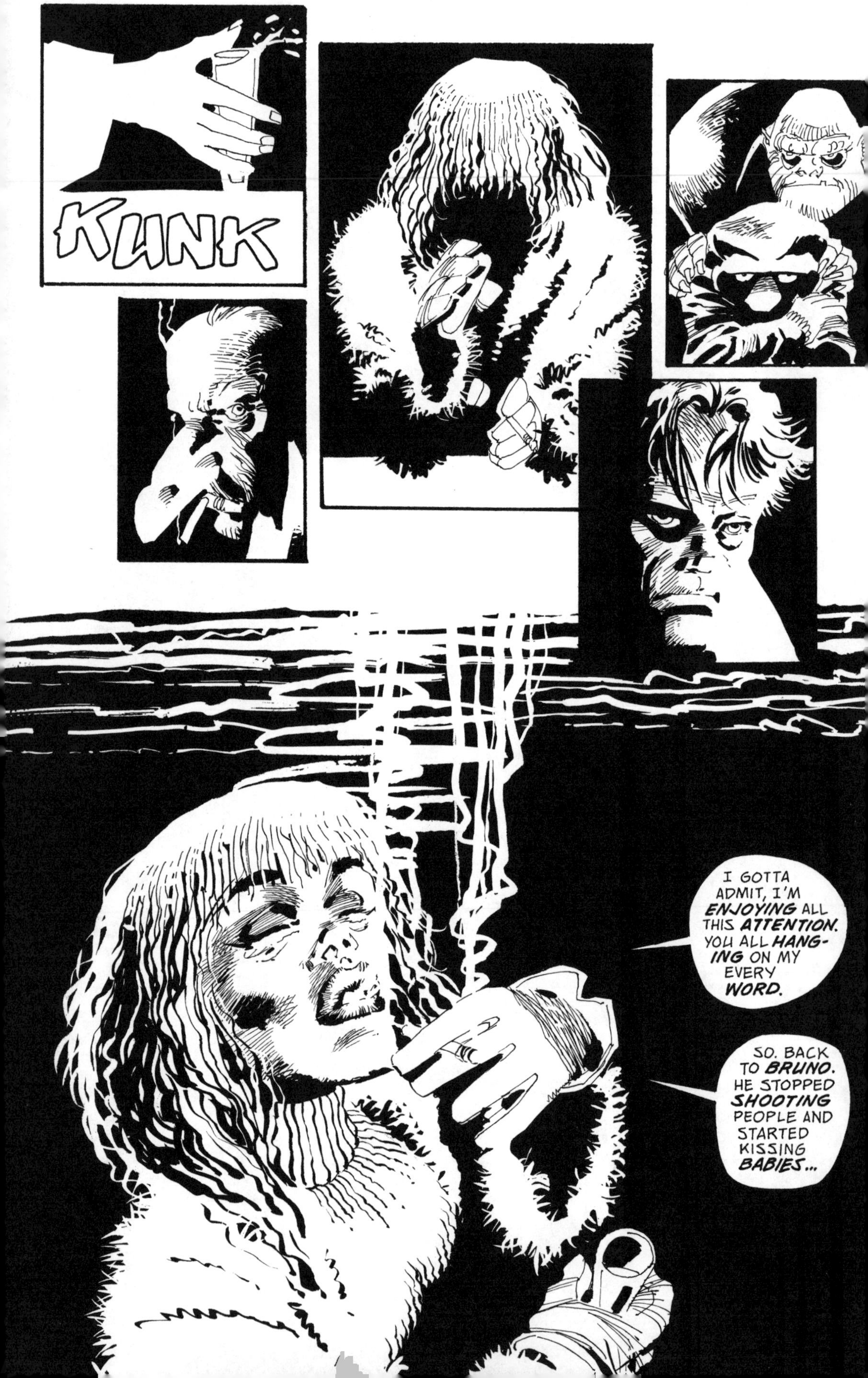
KUNK
I GOTTA ADMIT, I'M ENJOYING ALL THIS ATTENTION. YOU ALL HANG-ING ON MY EVERY WORD.
SO. BACK TO BRUNO. HE STOPPED SHOOTING PEOPLE AND STARTED KISSING BABIES...

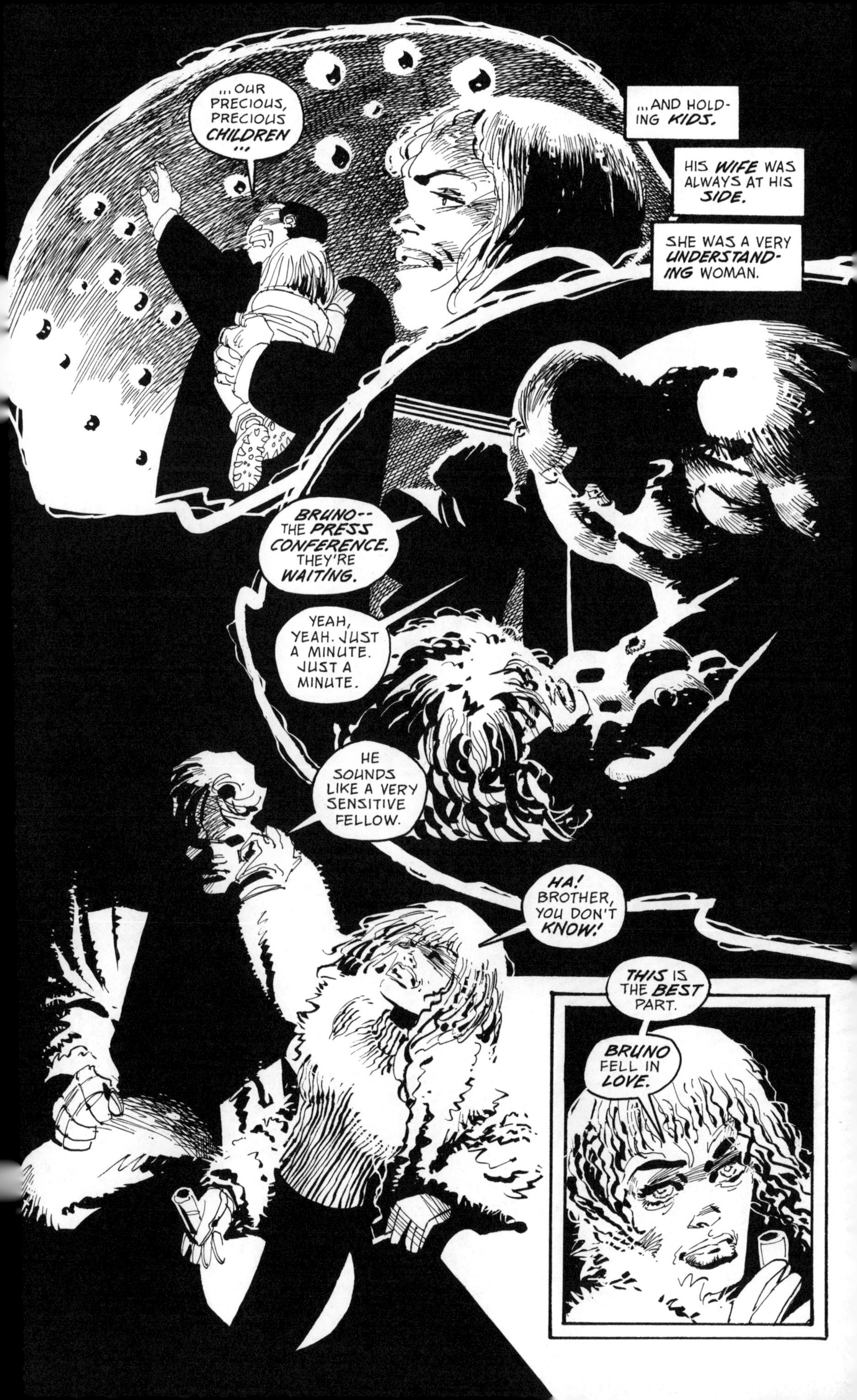
...OUR PRECIOUS, PRECIOUS CHILDREN ...
...AND HOLDING KIDS.
HIS WIFE WAS ALWAYS AT HIS SIDE.
SHE WAS A VERY UNDERSTANDING WOMAN.
BRUNO-- THE PRESS CONFERENCE. THEY'RE WAITING.
YEAH, YEAH. JUST A MINUTE. JUST A MINUTE.
HE SOUNDS LIKE A VERY SENSITIVE FELLOW.
HA! BROTHER, YOU DON'T KNOW!
THIS IS THE BEST PART.
BRUNO FELL IN LOVE.

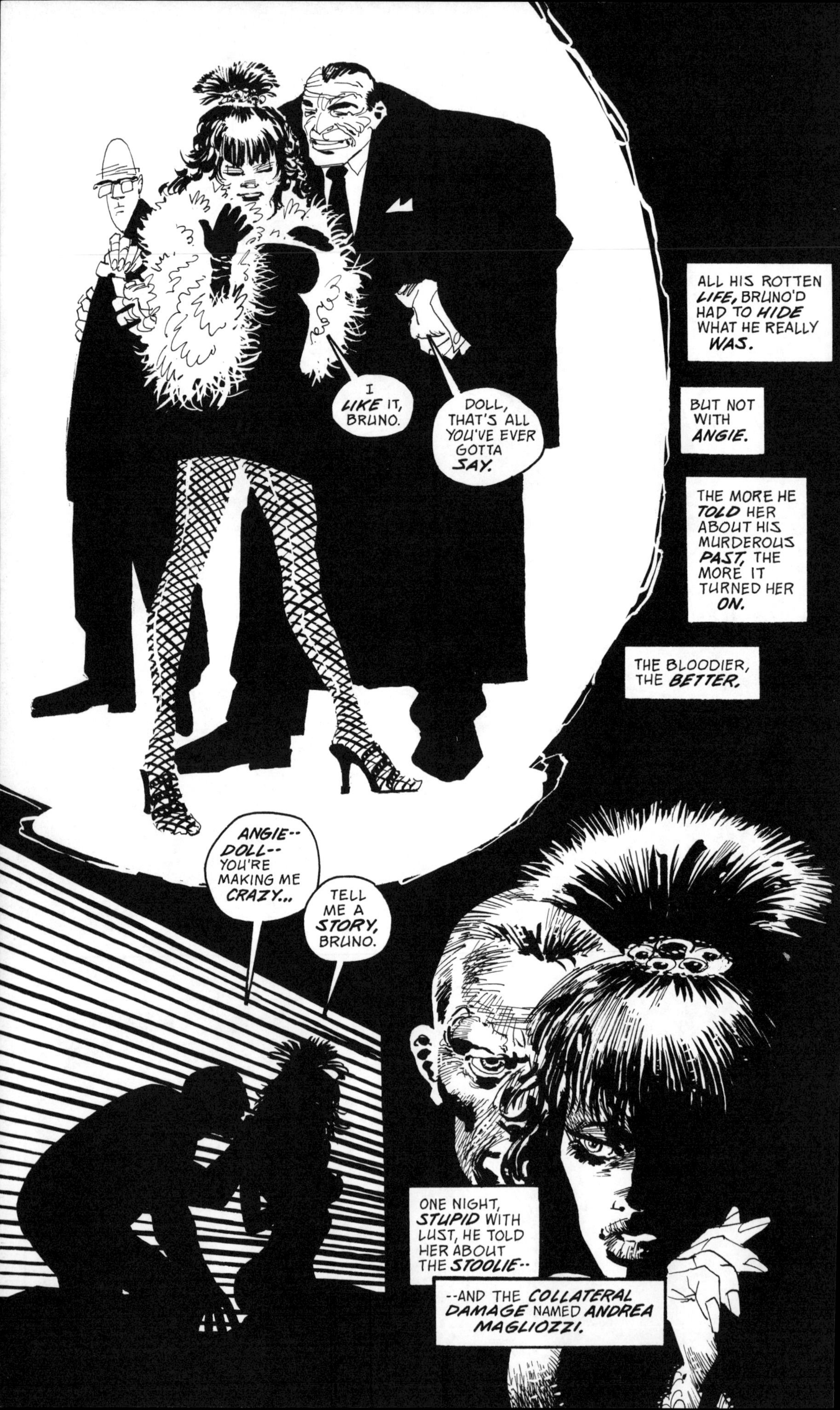

ALL HIS ROTTEN LIFE, BRUNO'D HAD TO HIDE WHAT HE REALLY WAS.
I LIKE IT, BRUNO.
DOLL, THAT'S ALL YOU'VE EVER GOTTA SAY.
BUT NOT WITH ANGIE.
THE MORE HE TOLD HER ABOUT HIS MURDEROUS PAST, THE MORE IT TURNED HER ON.
THE BLOODIER, THE BETTER.
ANGIE-- DOLL-- YOU'RE MAKING ME CRAZY...
TELL ME A STORY, BRUNO.
ONE NIGHT, STUPID WITH LUST, HE TOLD HER ABOUT THE STOOLIE--
--AND THE COLLATERAL DAMAGE NAMED ANDREA MAGLIOZZI.

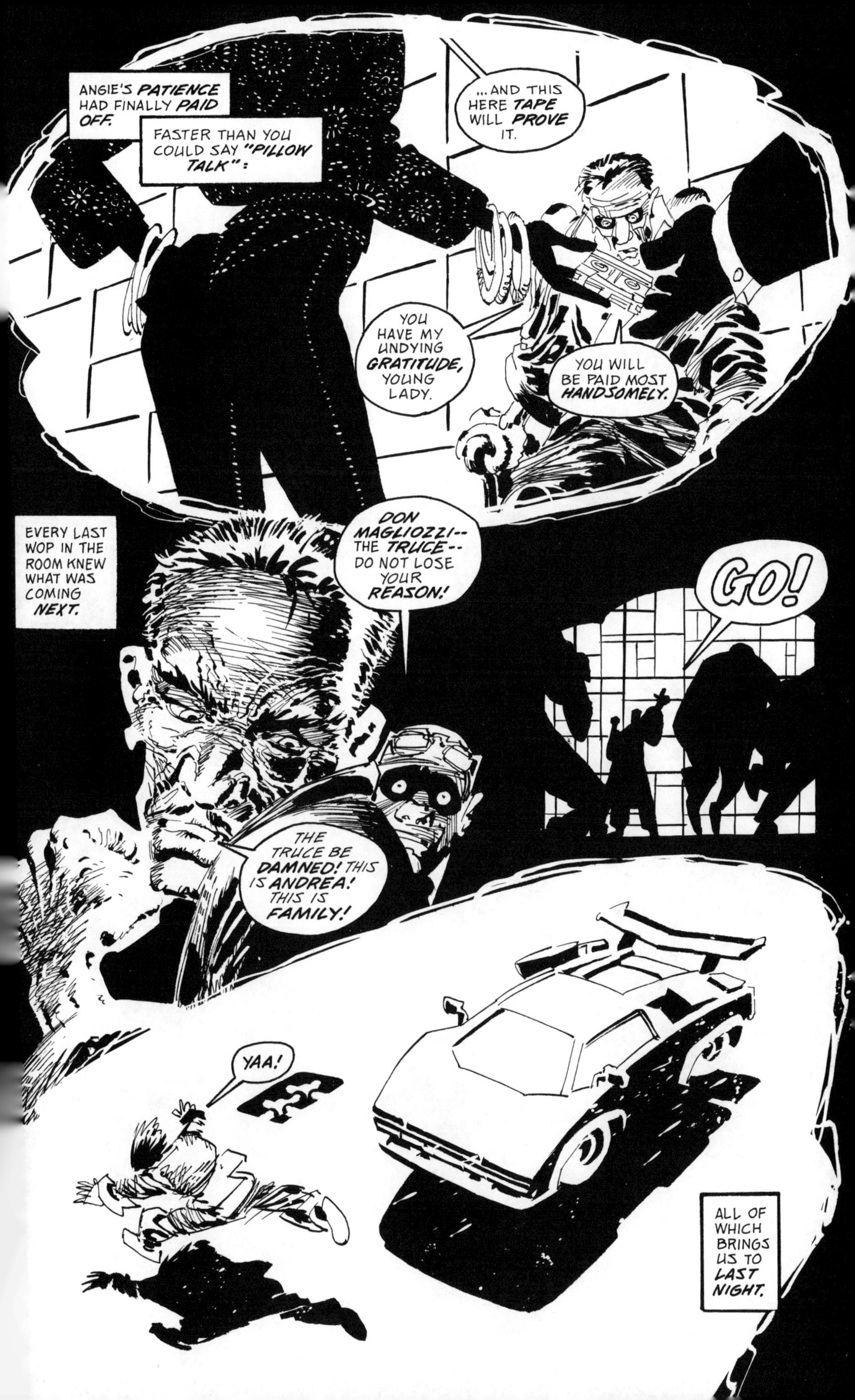
ANGIE'S PATIENCE HAD FINALLY PAID OFF.
FASTER THAN YOU COULD SAY "PILLOW TALK":
...AND THIS HERE TAPE WILL PROVE IT.
YOU HAVE MY UNDYING GRATITUDE, YOUNG LADY.
YOU WILL BE PAID MOST HANDSOMELY.
EVERY LAST WOP IN THE ROOM KNEW WHAT WAS COMING NEXT.
DON MAGLIOZZI-- THE TRUCE-- DO NOT LOSE YOUR REASON!
THE TRUCE BE DAMNED! THIS IS ANDREA! THIS IS FAMILY!
GO!
YAA!
ALL OF WHICH BRINGS US TO LAST NIGHT.

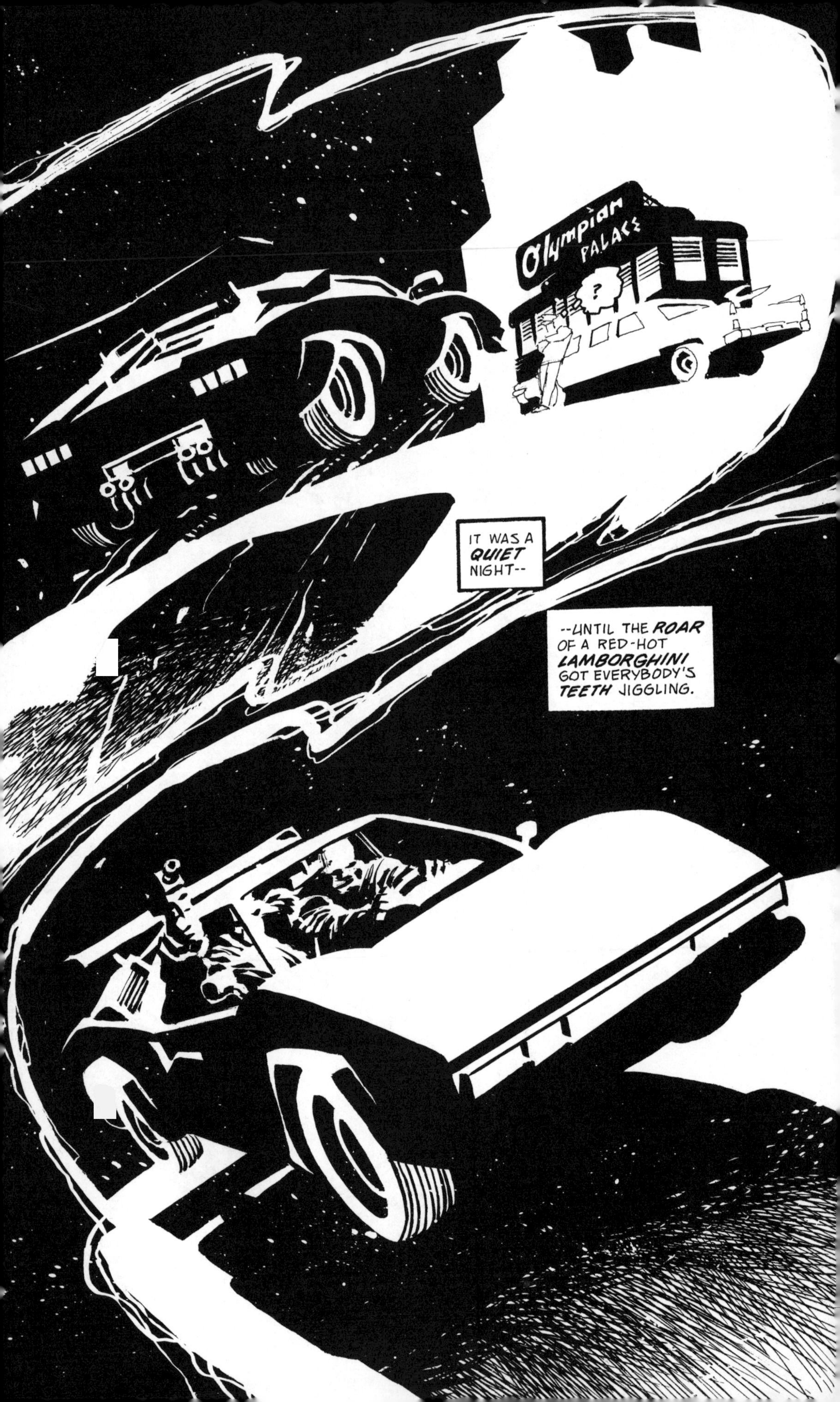
Olympian
PALACE
IT WAS A QUIET NIGHT--
--UNTIL THE ROAR OF A RED-HOT LAMBORGHINI GOT EVERYBODY'S TEETH JIGGLING.

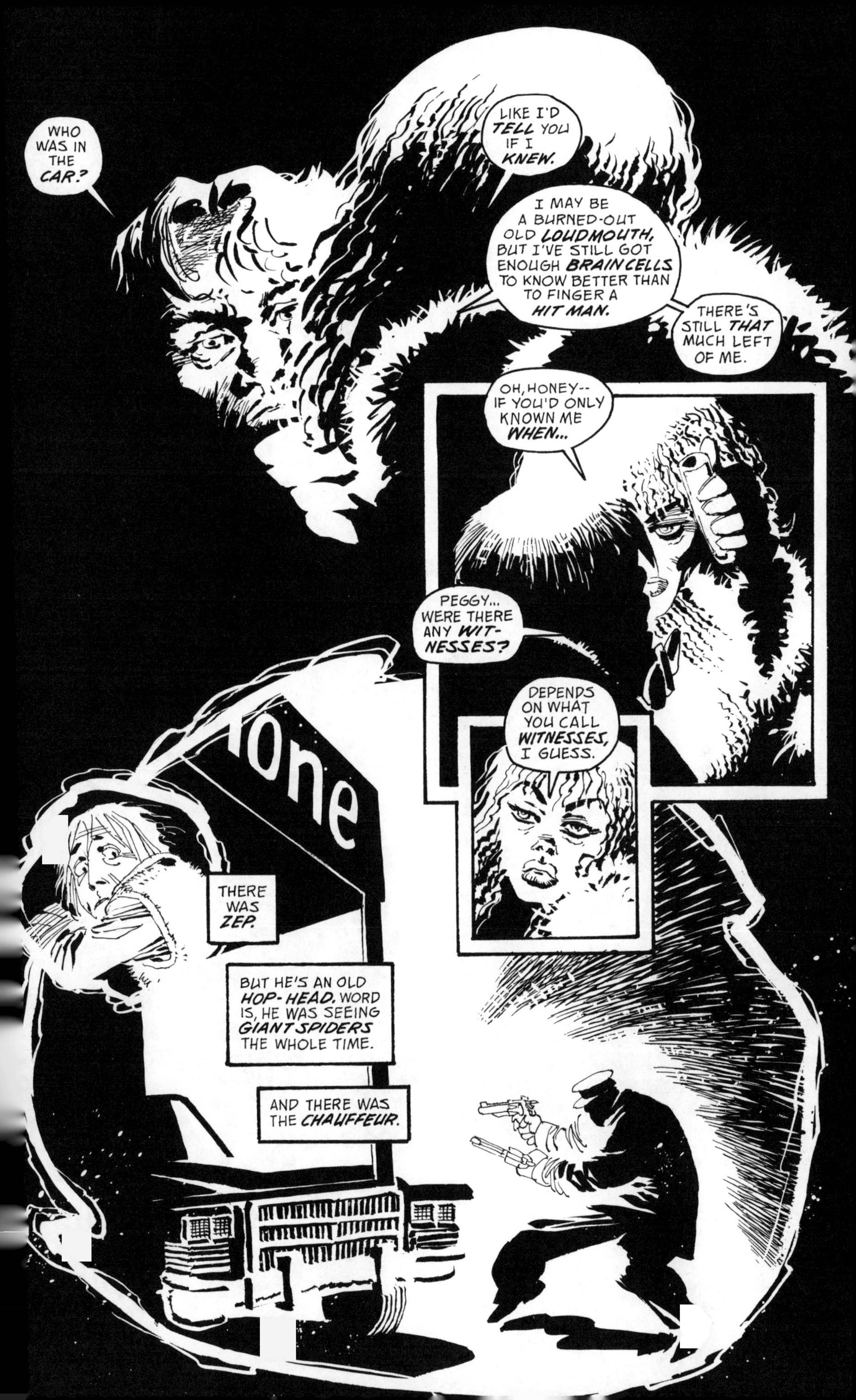
WHO WAS IN THE CAR?
LIKE I'D TELL YOU IF I KNEW.
I MAY BE A BURNED-OUT OLD LOUDMOUTH, BUT I'VE STILL GOT ENOUGH BRAIN CELLS TO KNOW BETTER THAN TO FINGER A HIT MAN.
THERE'S STILL THAT MUCH LEFT OF ME.
OH, HONEY-- IF YOU'D ONLY KNOWN ME WHEN...
PEGGY... WERE THERE ANY WITNESSES?
DEPENDS ON WHAT YOU CALL WITNESSES, I GUESS.
one
THERE WAS ZEP.
BUT HE'S AN OLD HOP-HEAD. WORD IS, HE WAS SEEING GIANT SPIDERS THE WHOLE TIME.
AND THERE WAS THE CHAUFFEUR.

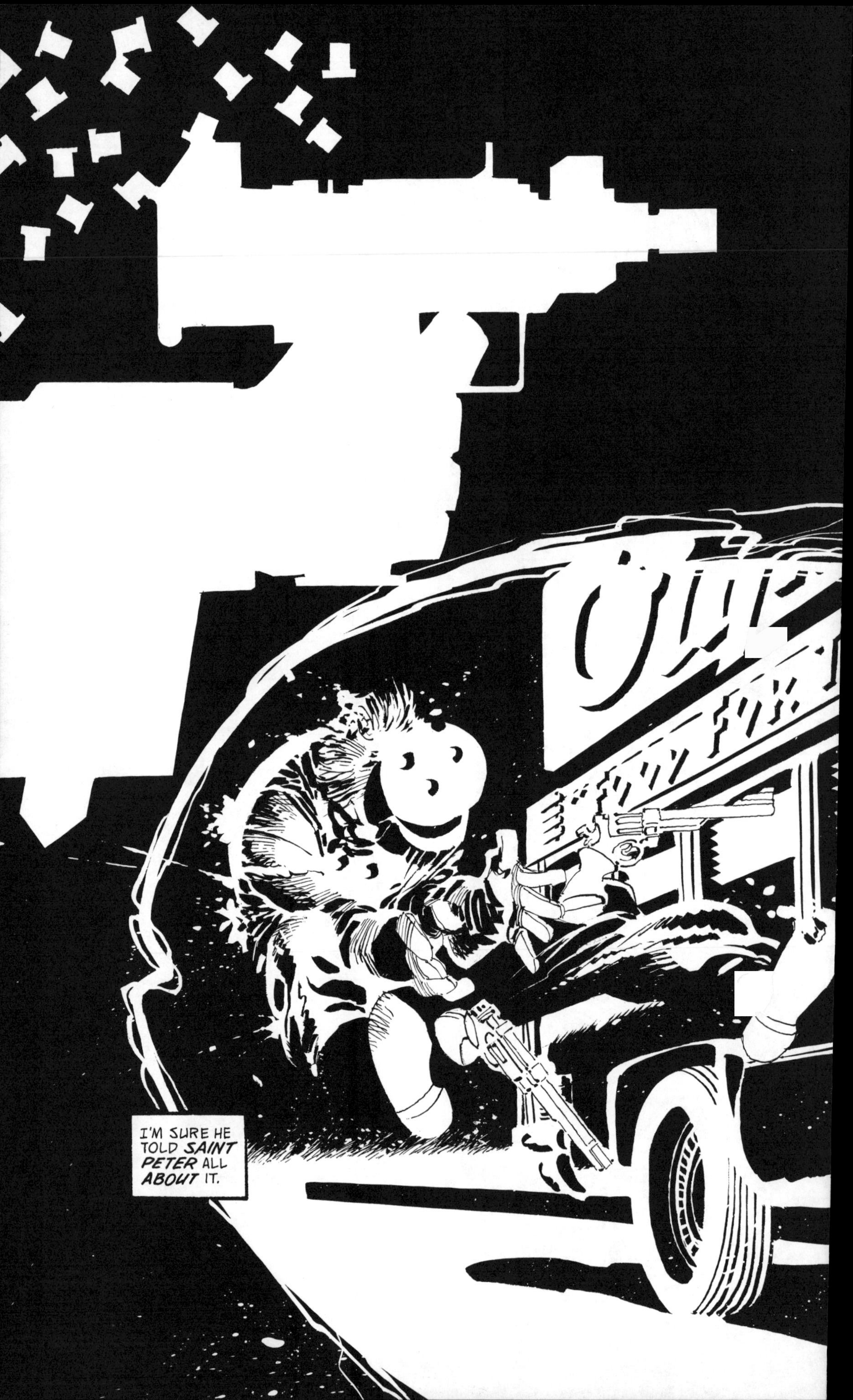
I'M SURE HE TOLD SAINT PETER ALL ABOUT IT.

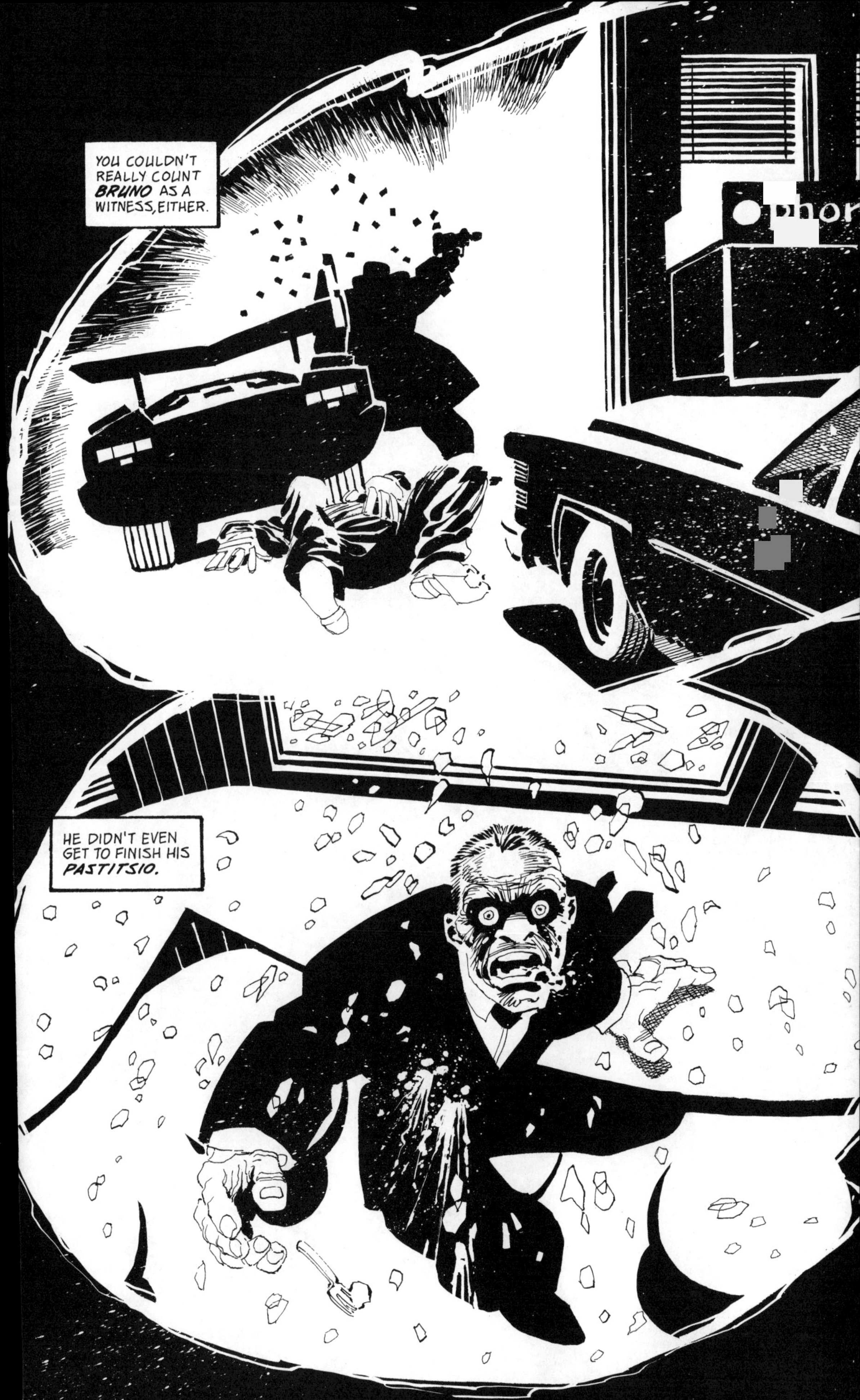
YOU COULDN'T REALLY COUNT BRUNO AS A WITNESS, EITHER.
HE DIDN'T EVEN GET TO FINISH HIS PASTITSIO.

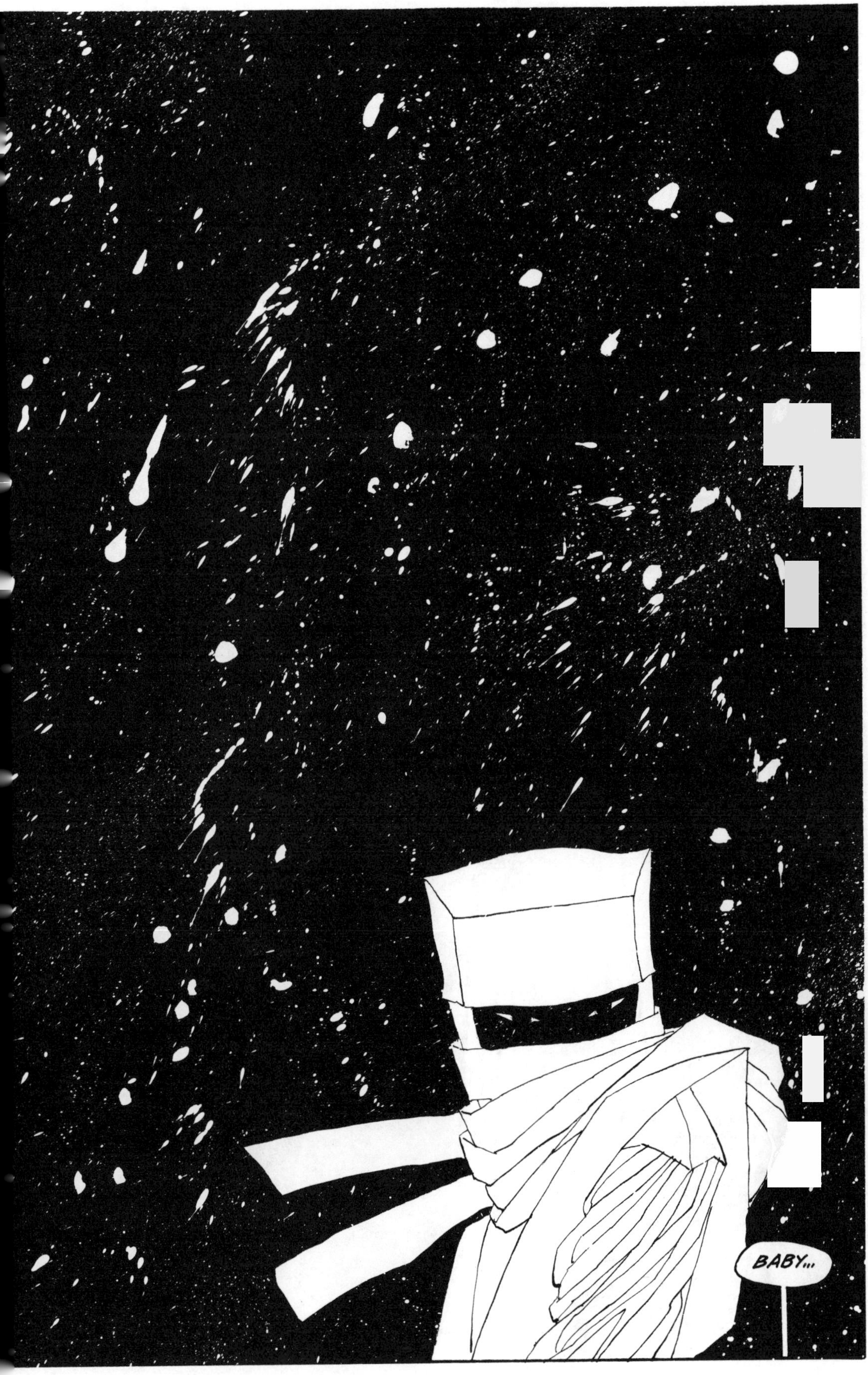
BABY...

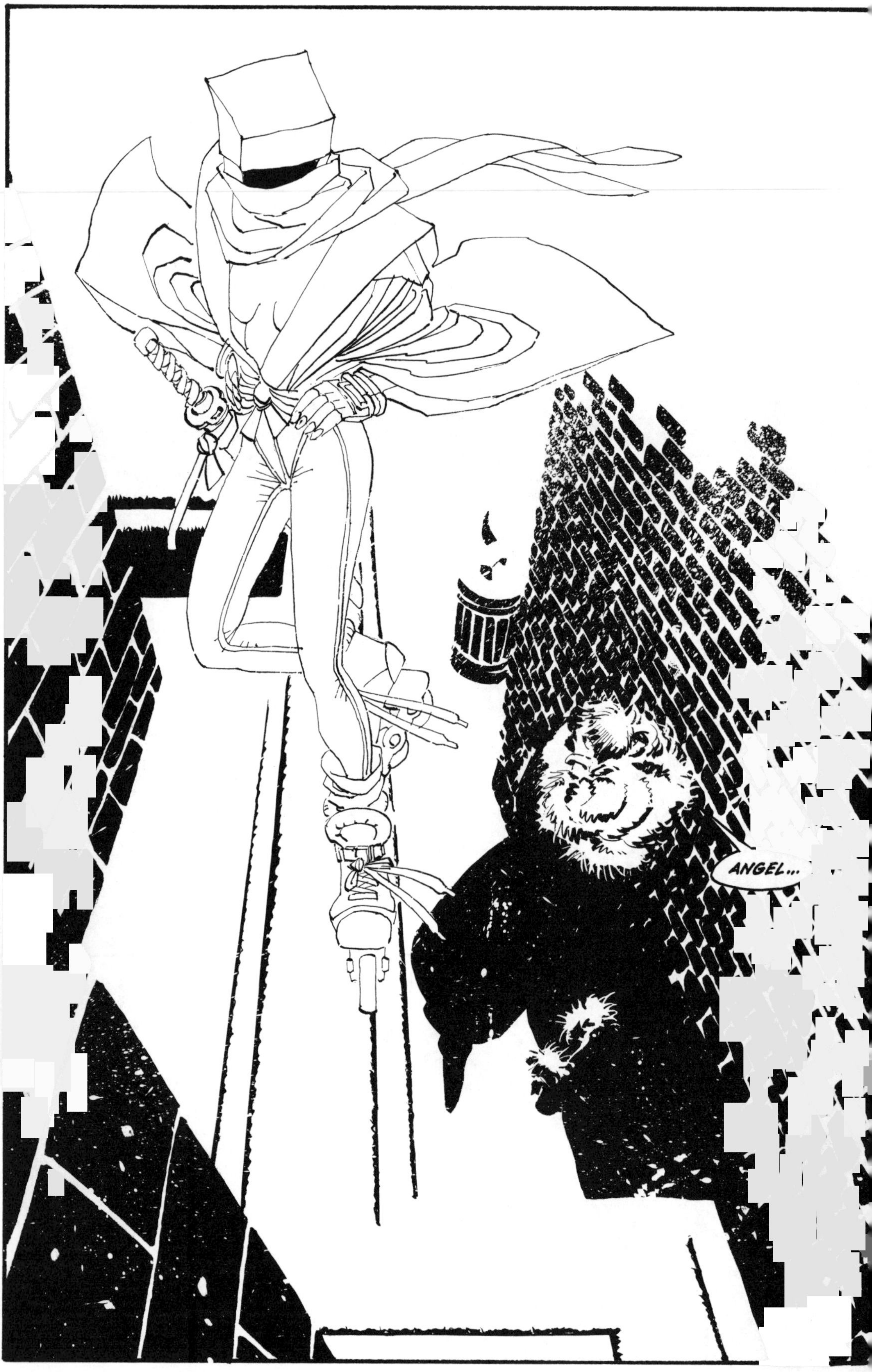
ANGEL...

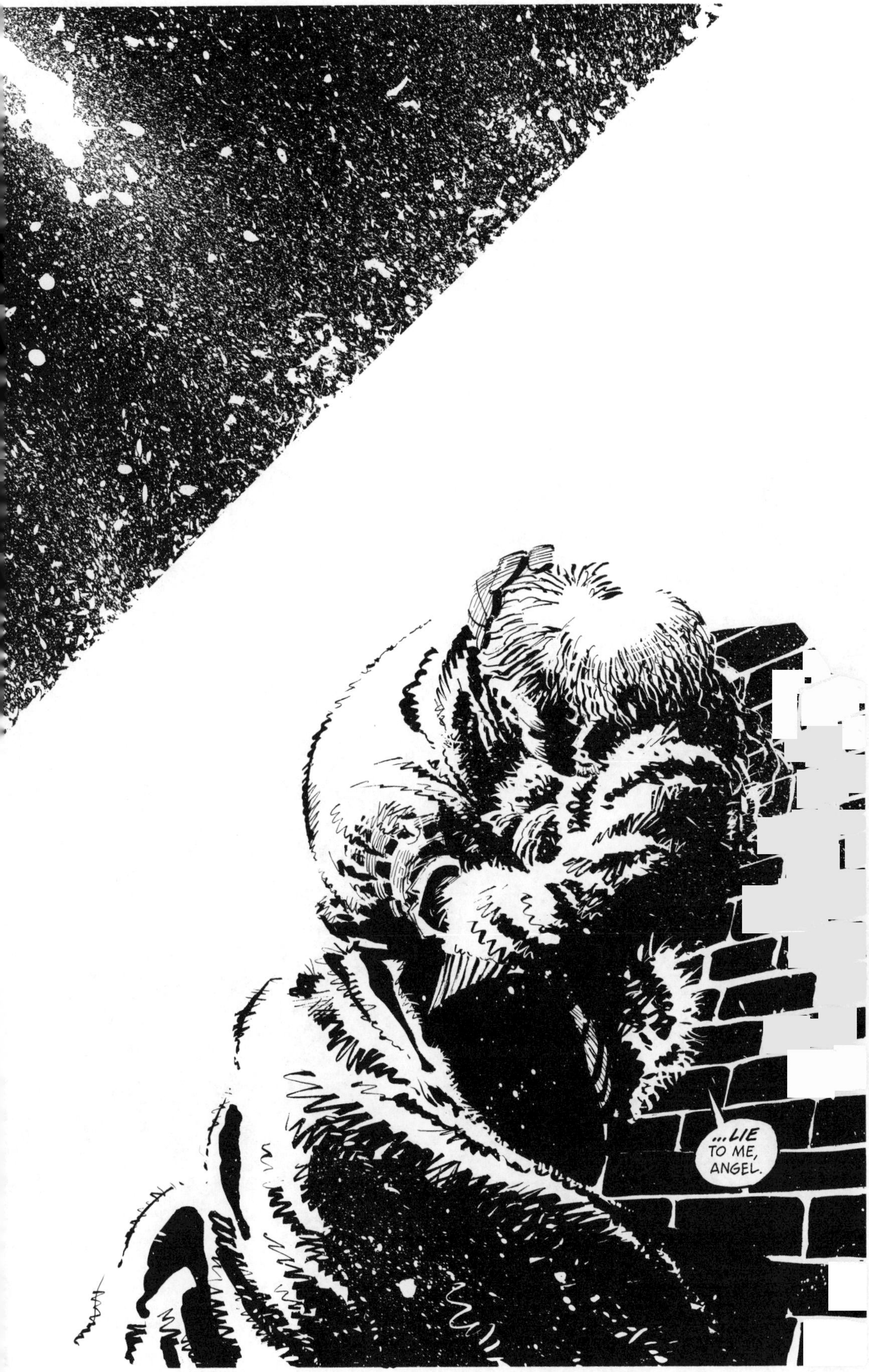
...LIE TO ME, ANGEL.

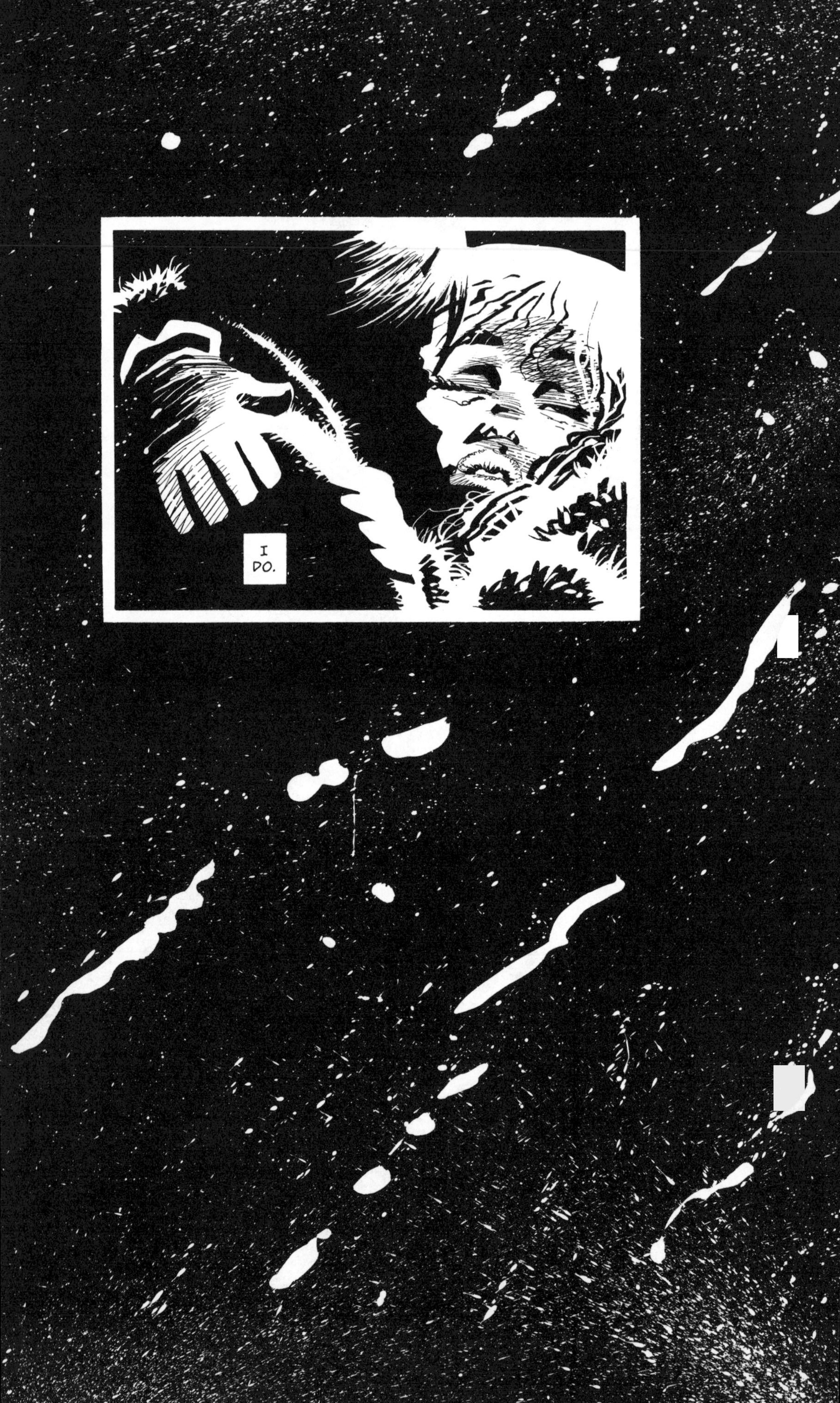
I DO.

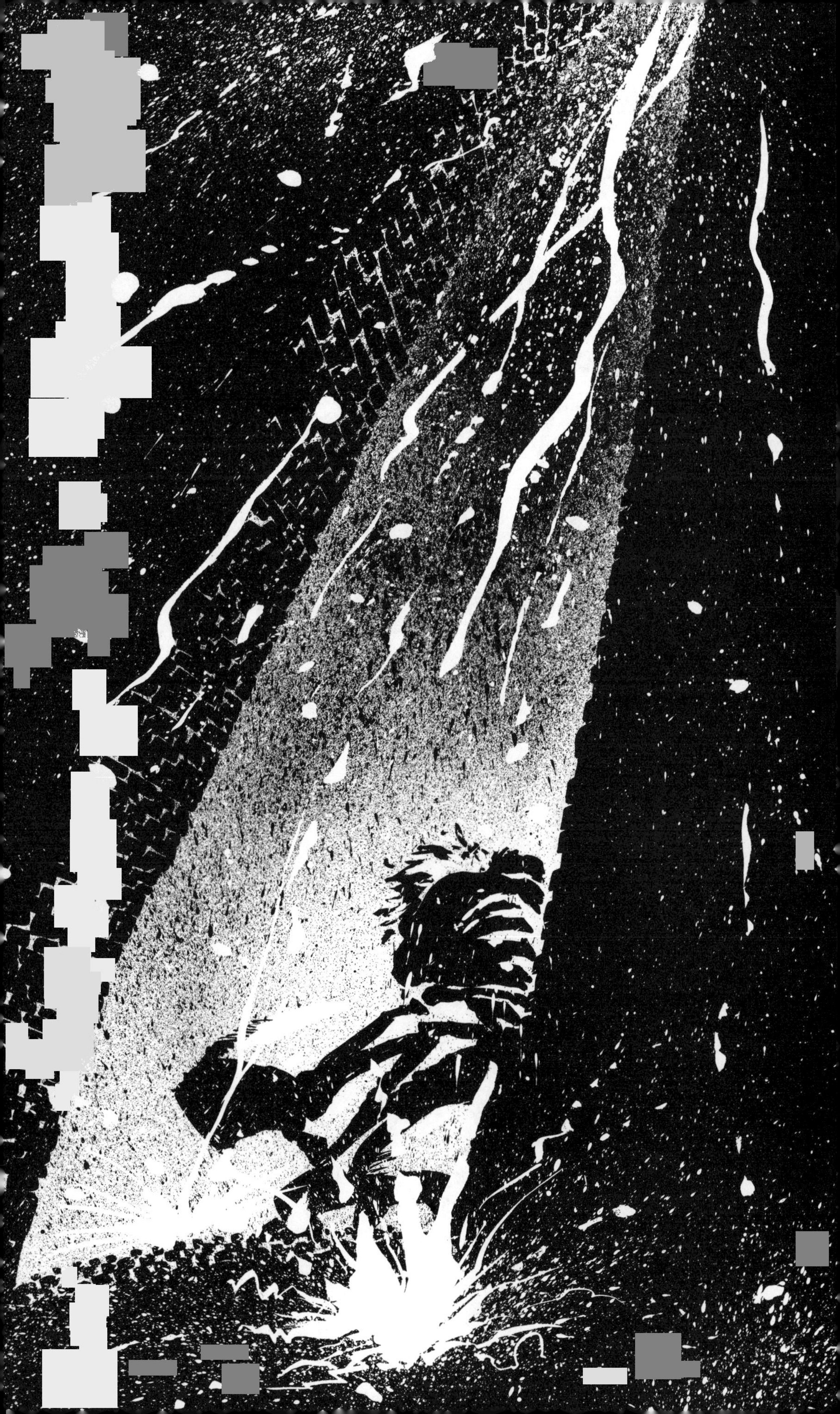

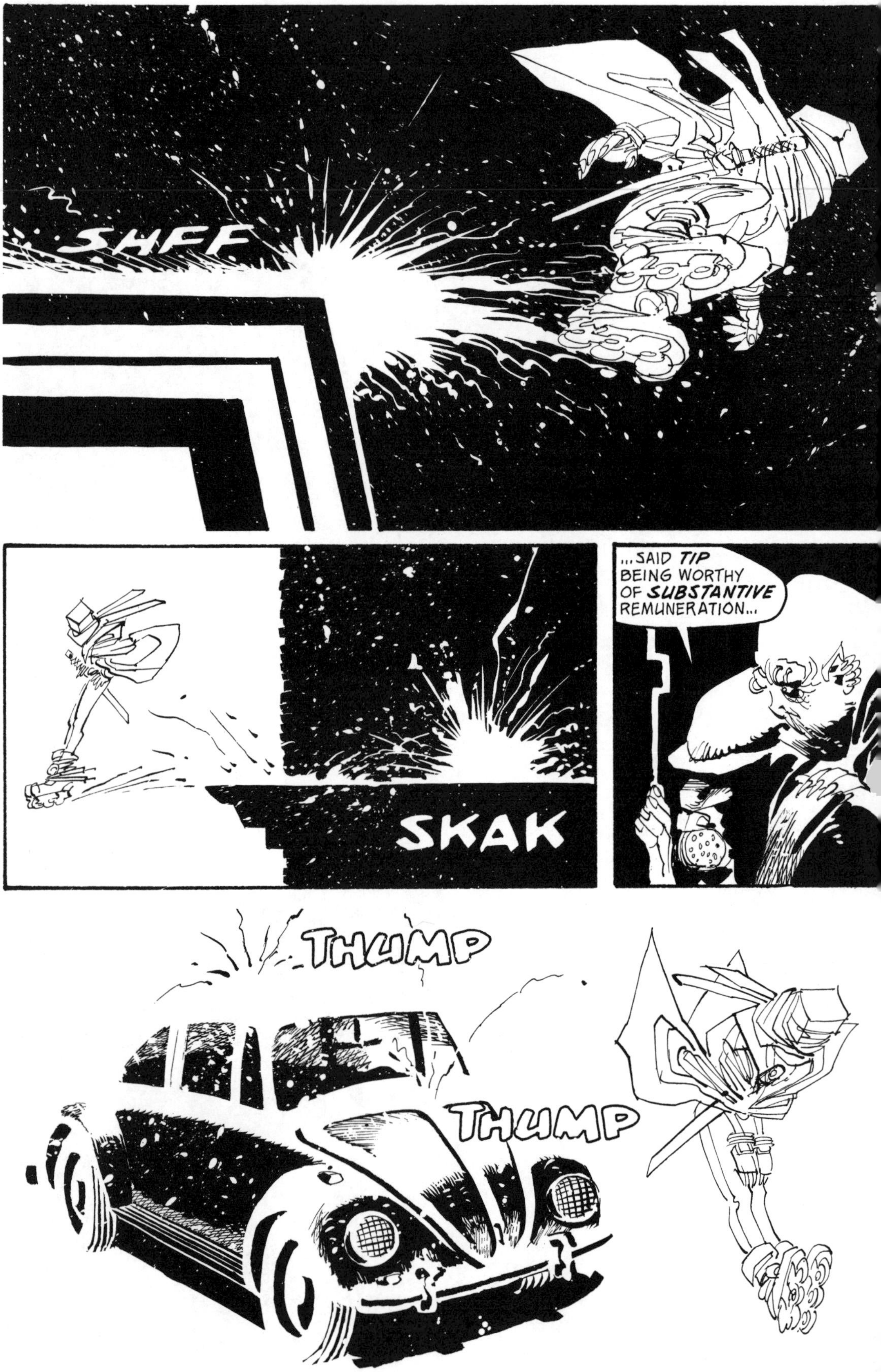
SHFF
SKAK
...SAID TIP BEING WORTHY OF SUBSTANTIVE REMUNERATION...
THUMP
THUMP

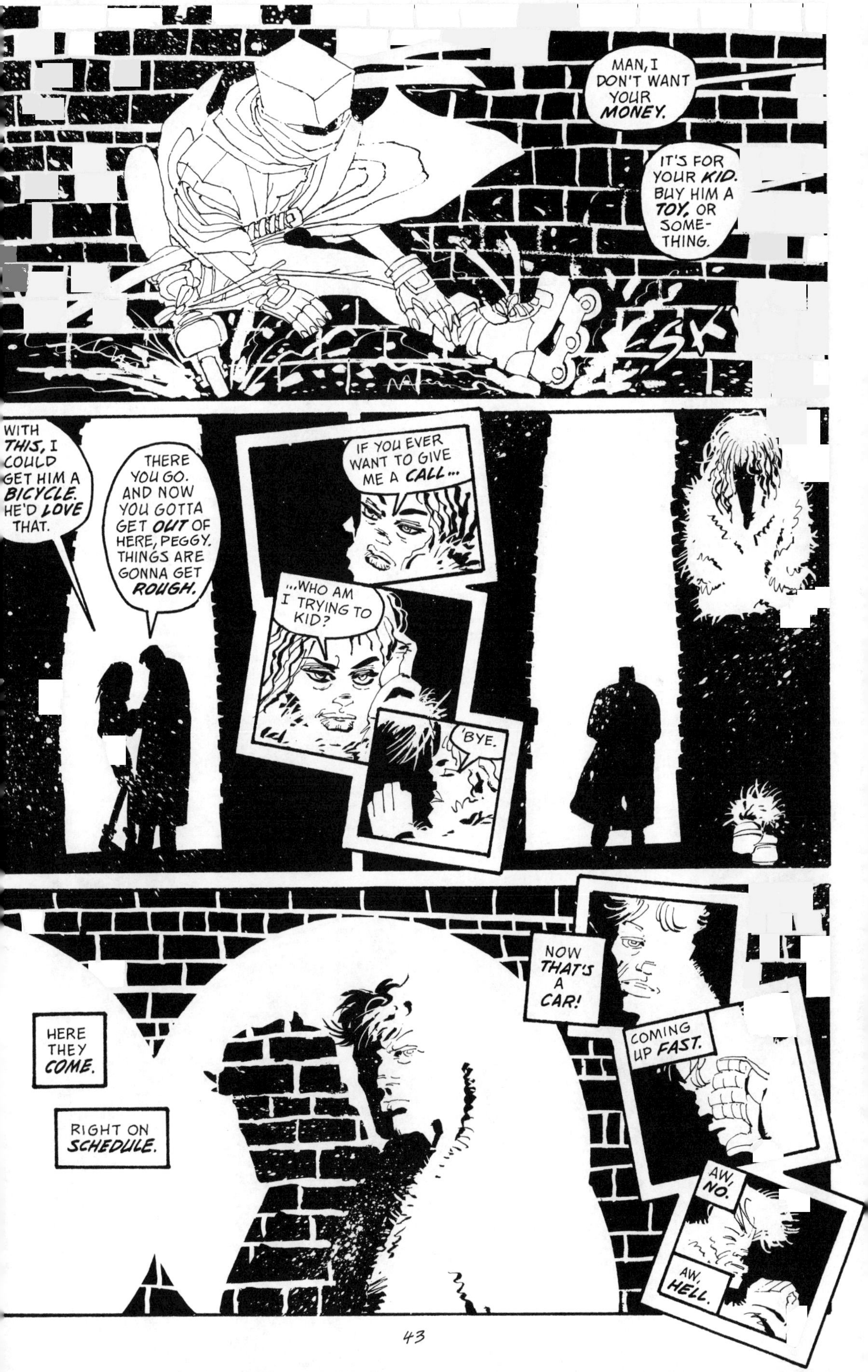
MAN, I DON'T WANT YOUR MONEY.
IT'S FOR YOUR KID. BUY HIM A TOY, OR SOME- THING.
WITH THIS, I COULD GET HIM A BICYCLE. HE'D LOVE THAT.
THERE YOU GO. AND NOW YOU GOTTA GET OUT OF HERE, PEGGY. THINGS ARE GONNA GET ROUGH.
IF YOU EVER WANT TO GIVE ME A CALL...
...WHO AM I TRYING TO KID?
'BYE.
HERE THEY COME.
RIGHT ON SCHEDULE.
NOW THAT'S A CAR!
COMING UP FAST.
AW, NO.
AW, HELL.

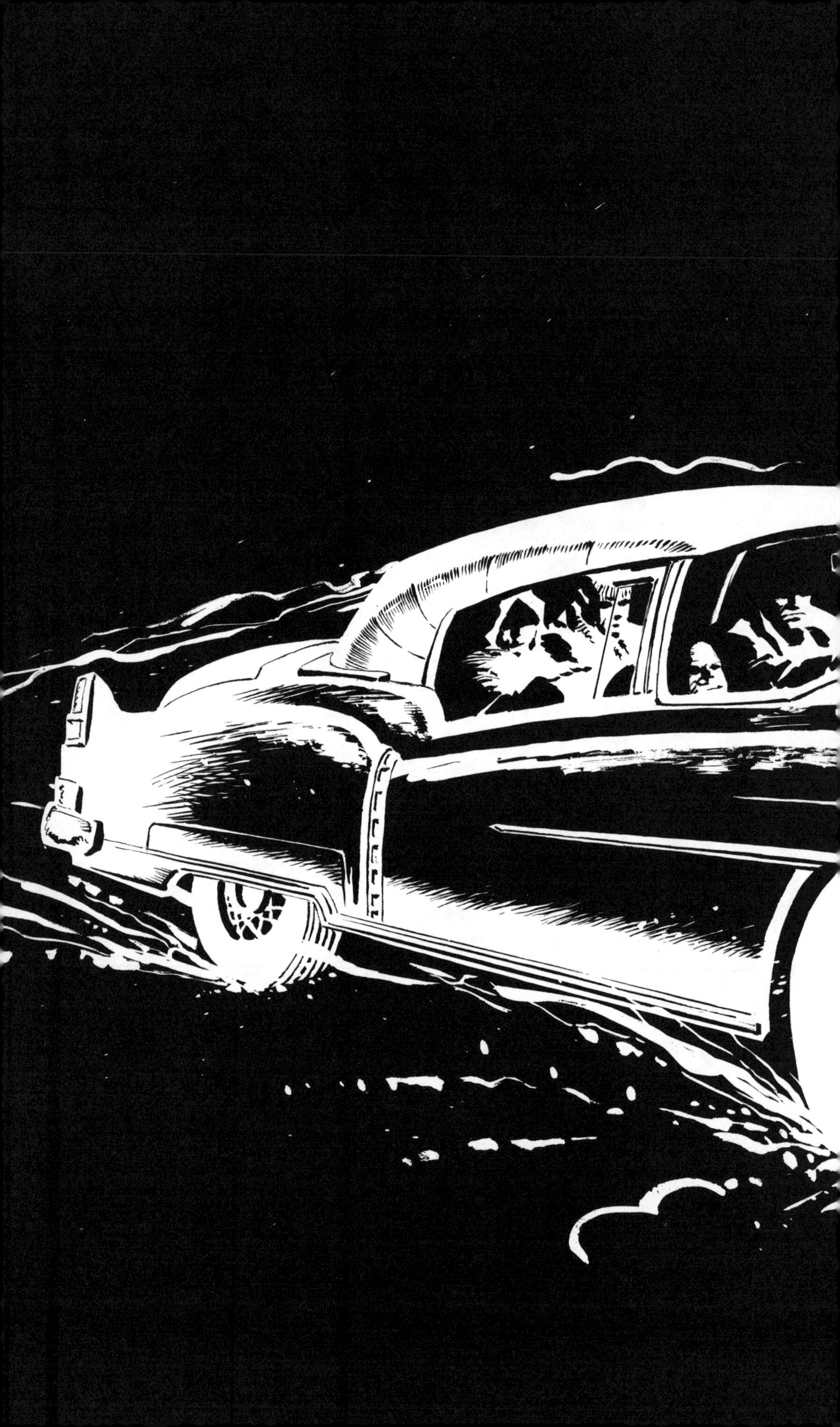

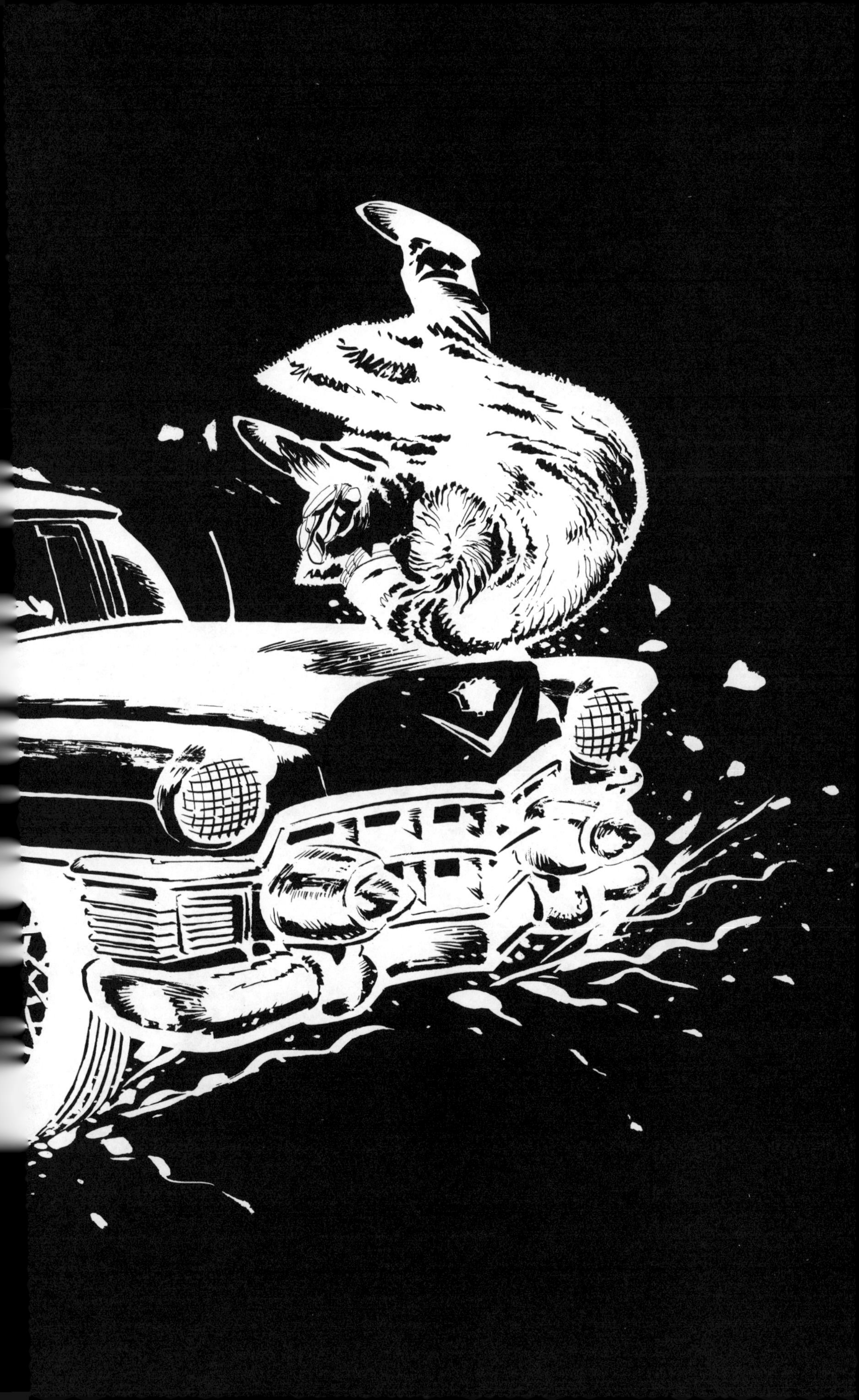

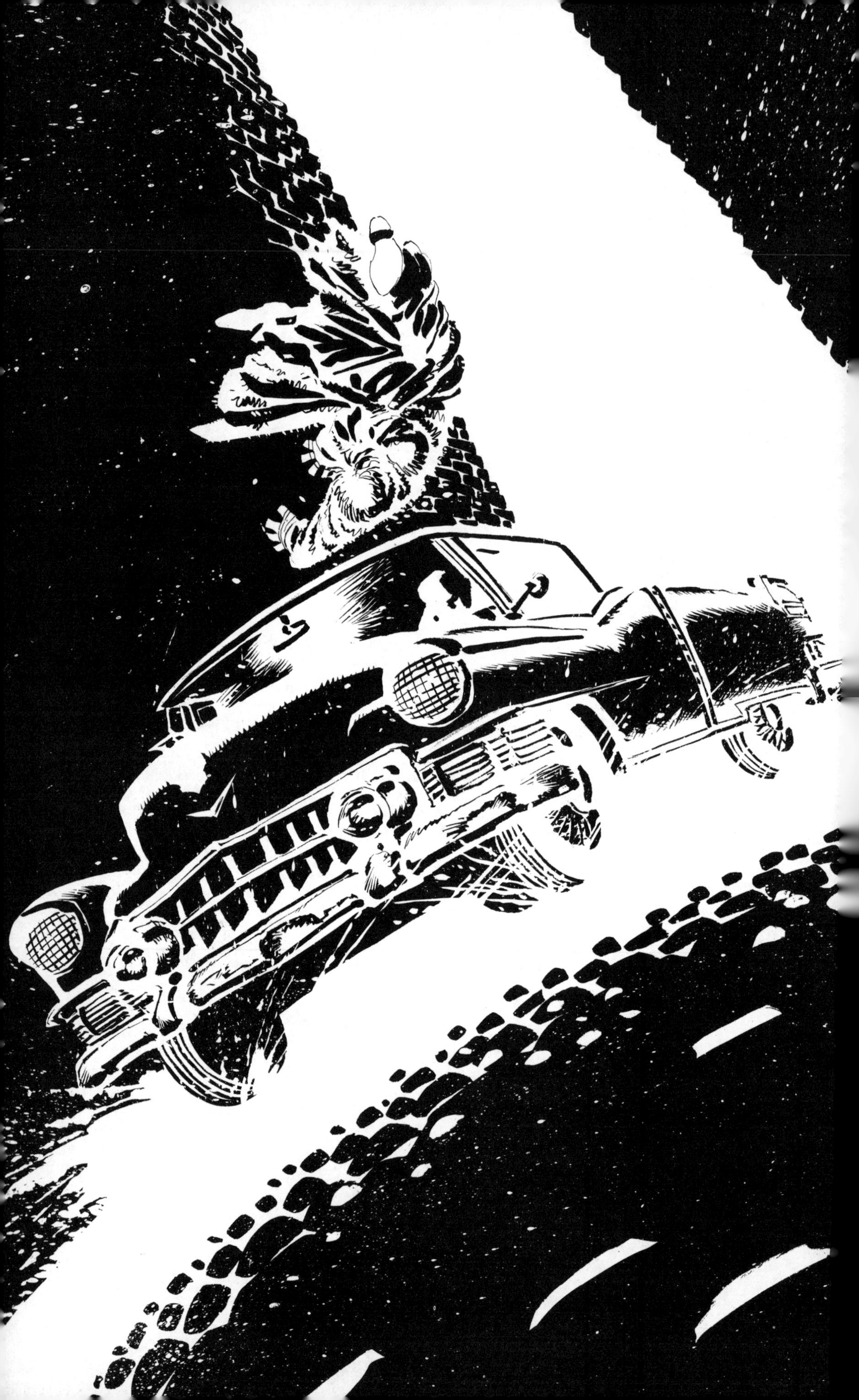

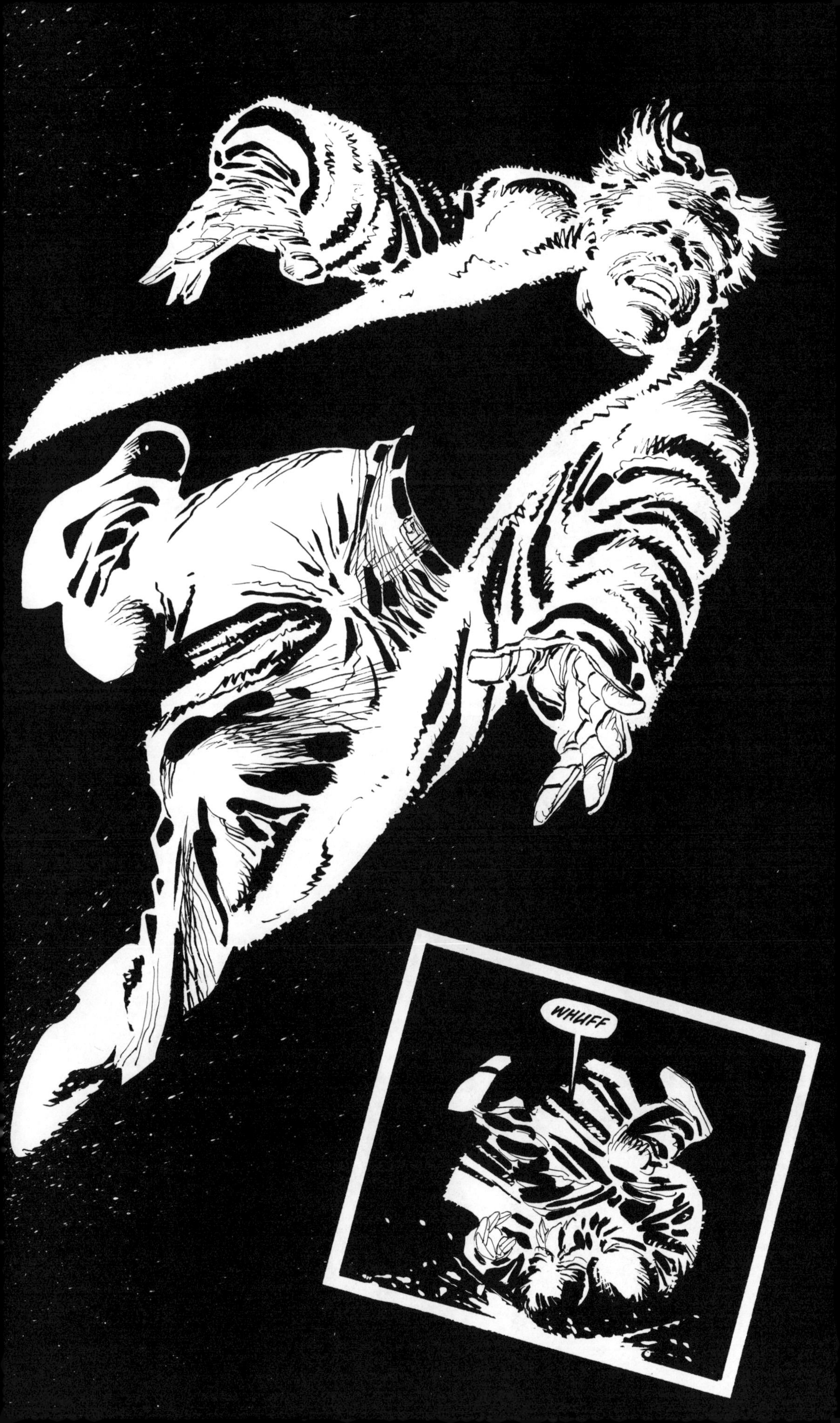
WHUFF

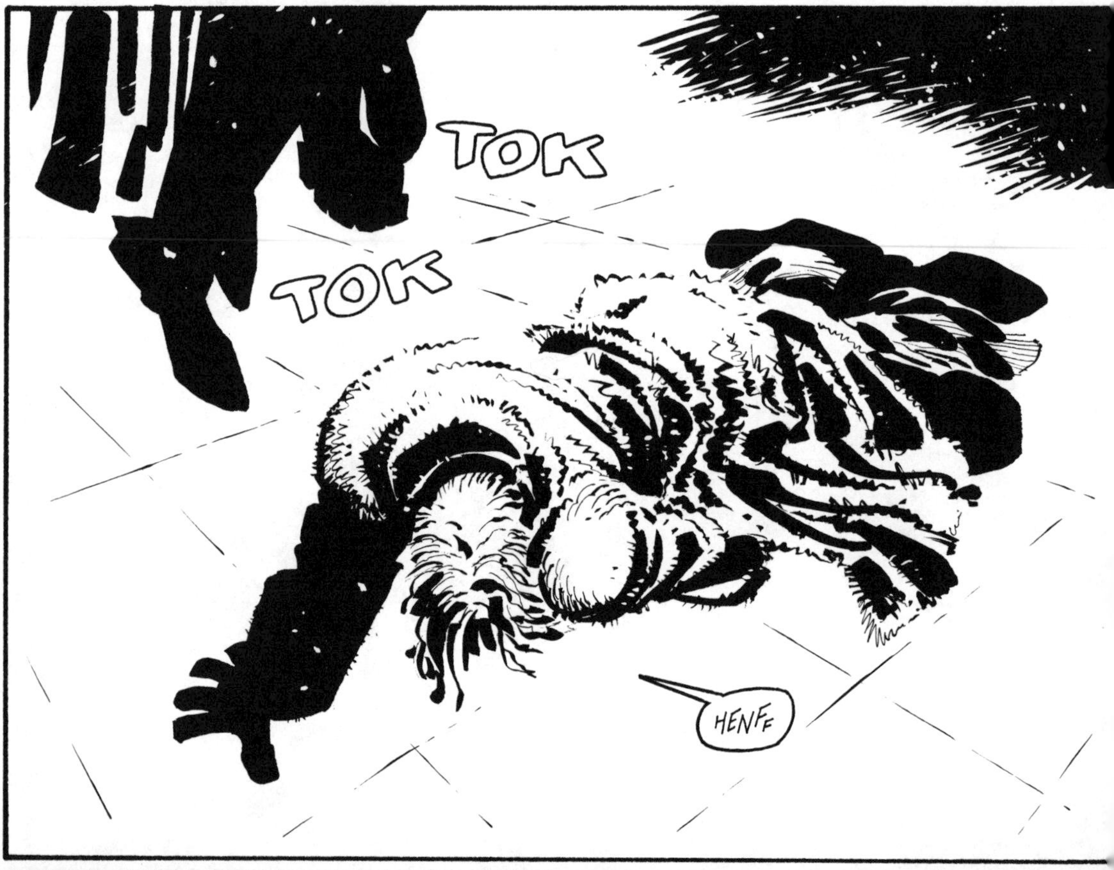
TOK
TOK
HENFF

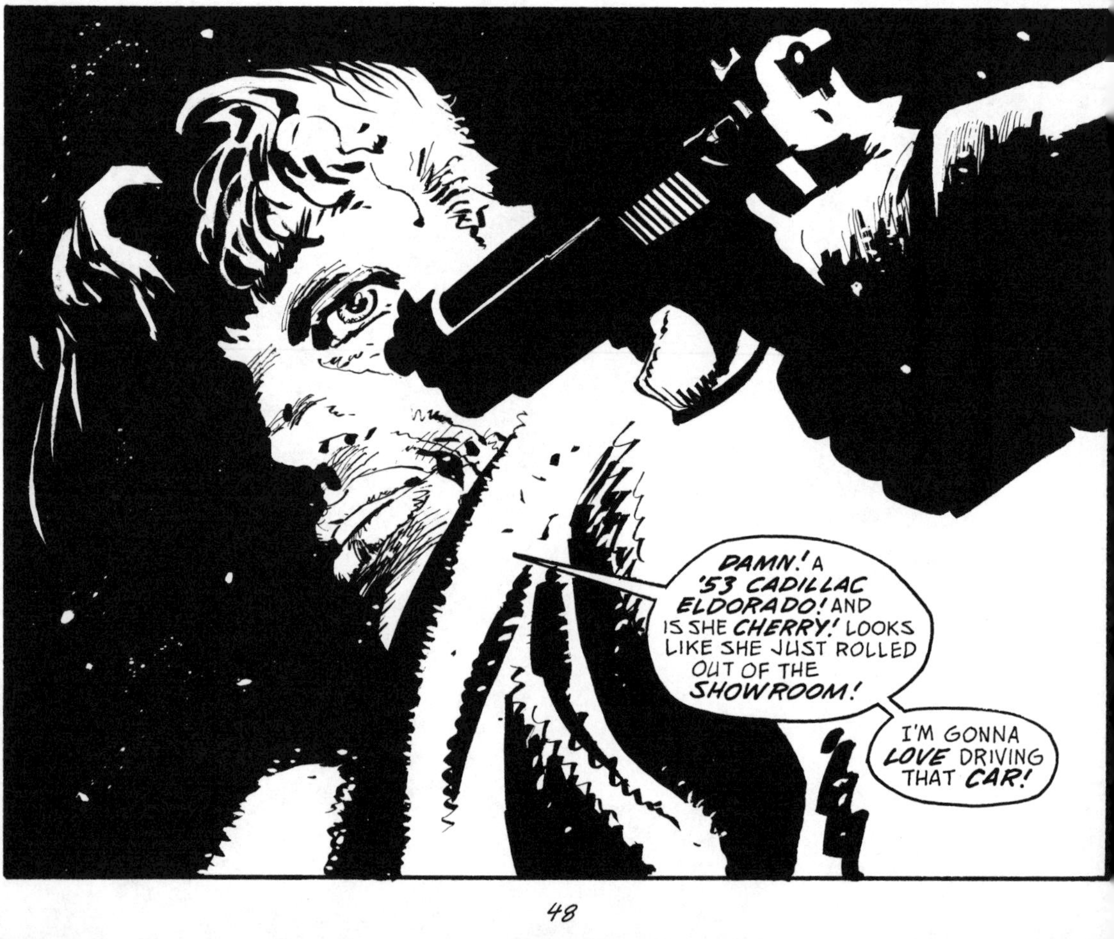
DAMN! A '53 CADILLAC ELDORADO! AND IS SHE CHERRY! LOOKS LIKE SHE JUST ROLLED OUT OF THE SHOWROOM!
I'M GONNA LOVE DRIVING THAT CAR!

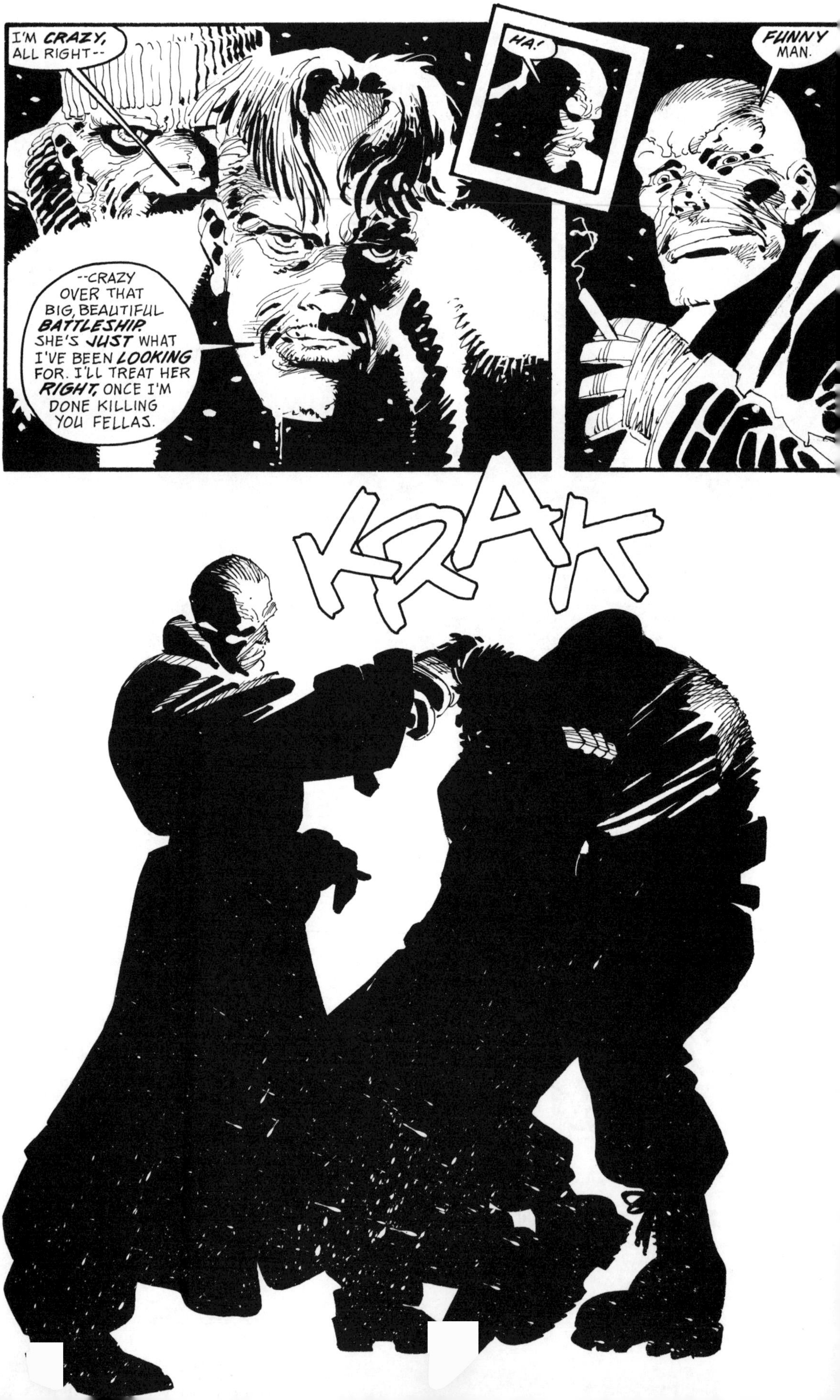

I'M CRAZY, ALL RIGHT--
--CRAZY OVER THAT BIG, BEAUTIFUL BATTLESHIP. SHE'S JUST WHAT I'VE BEEN LOOKING FOR. I'LL TREAT HER RIGHT, ONCE I'M DONE KILLING YOU FELLAS.
HA!
FUNNY MAN.
KRAK

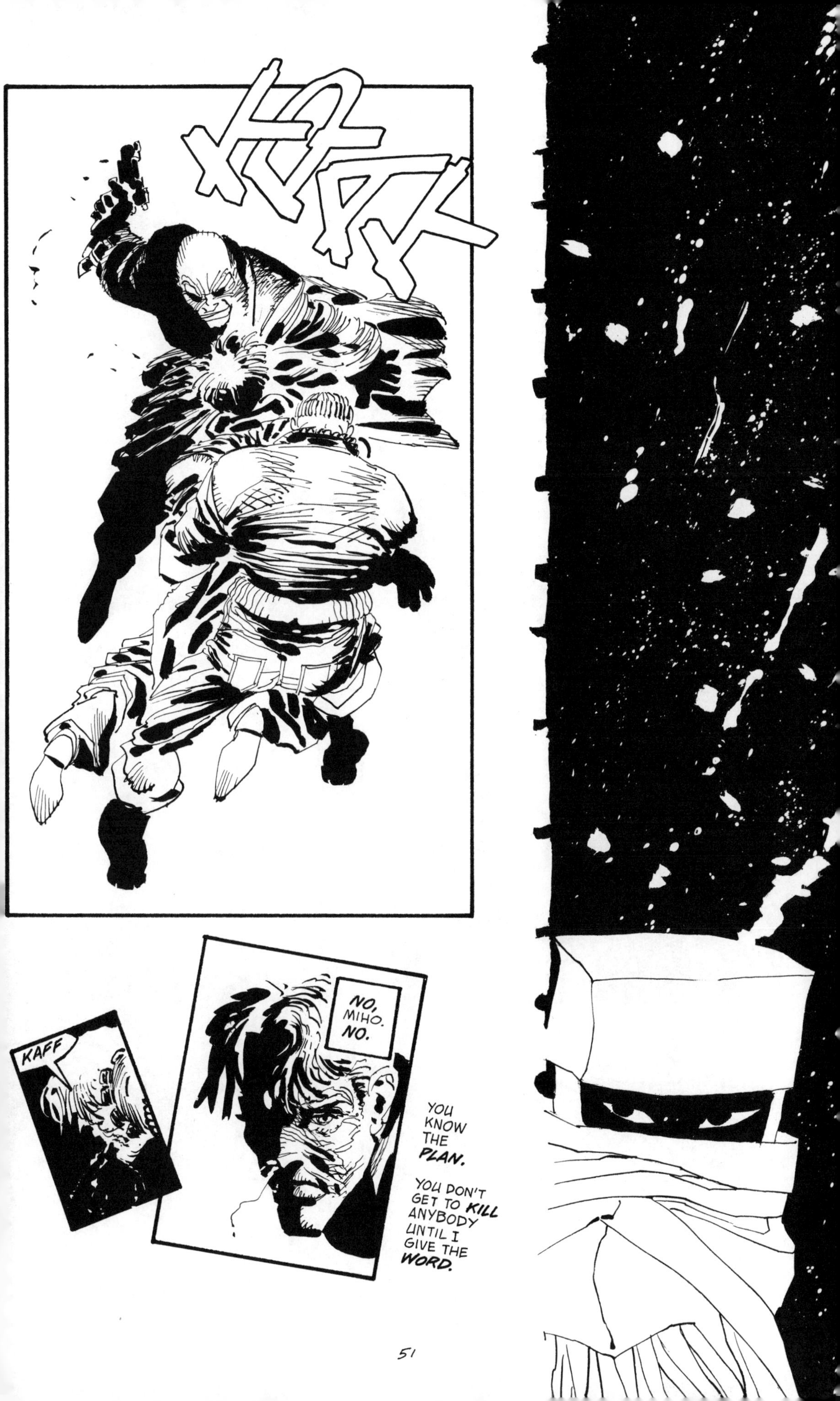
KAFF
NO, MIHO. NO.
YOU KNOW THE PLAN.
YOU DON'T GET TO KILL ANYBODY UNTIL I GIVE THE WORD.

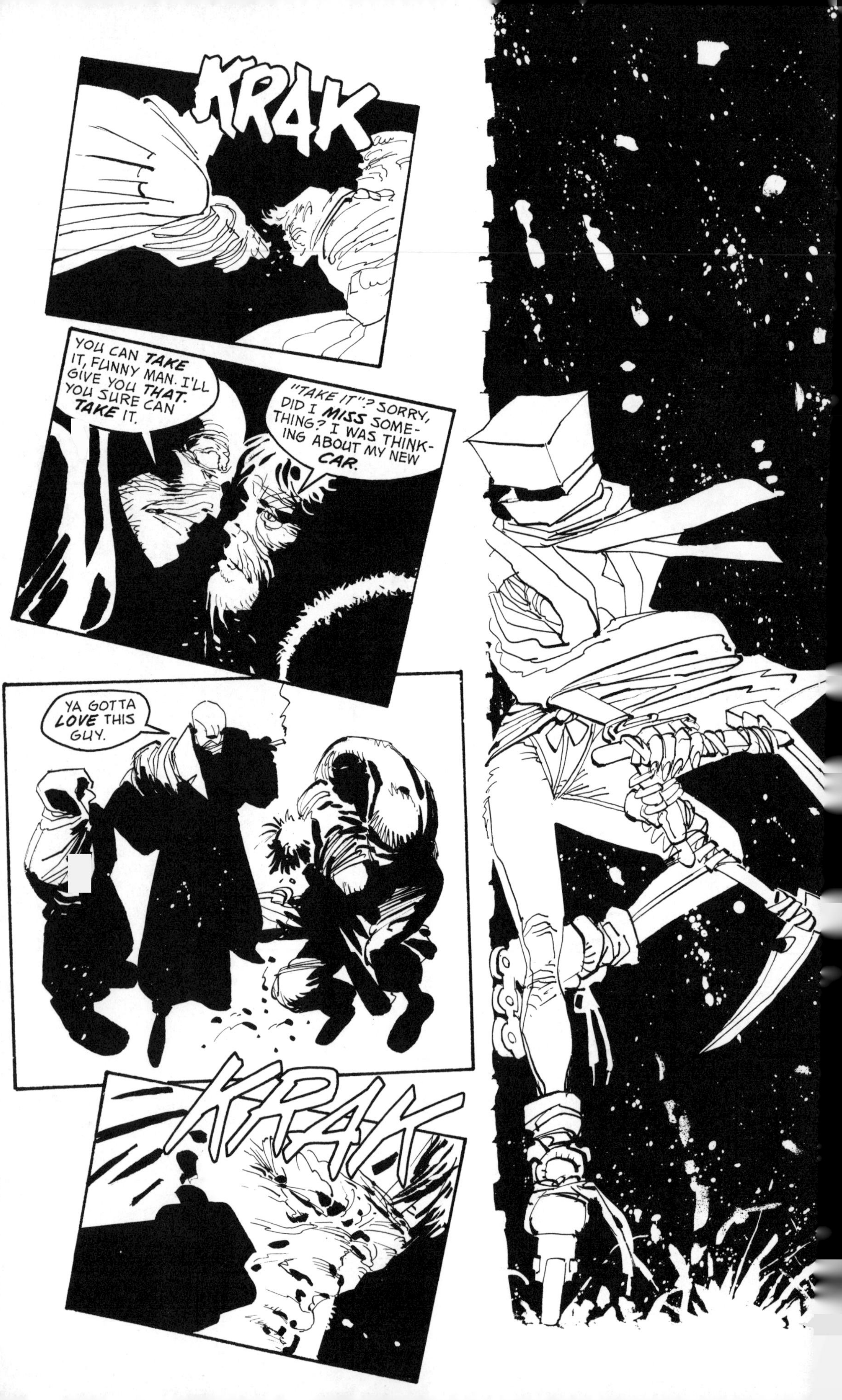
KRAK
YOU CAN TAKE IT, FUNNY MAN. I'LL GIVE YOU THAT. YOU SURE CAN TAKE IT.
"TAKE IT"? SORRY, DID I MISS SOME- THING? I WAS THINK- ING ABOUT MY NEW CAR.
YA GOTTA LOVE THIS GUY.
KRAK

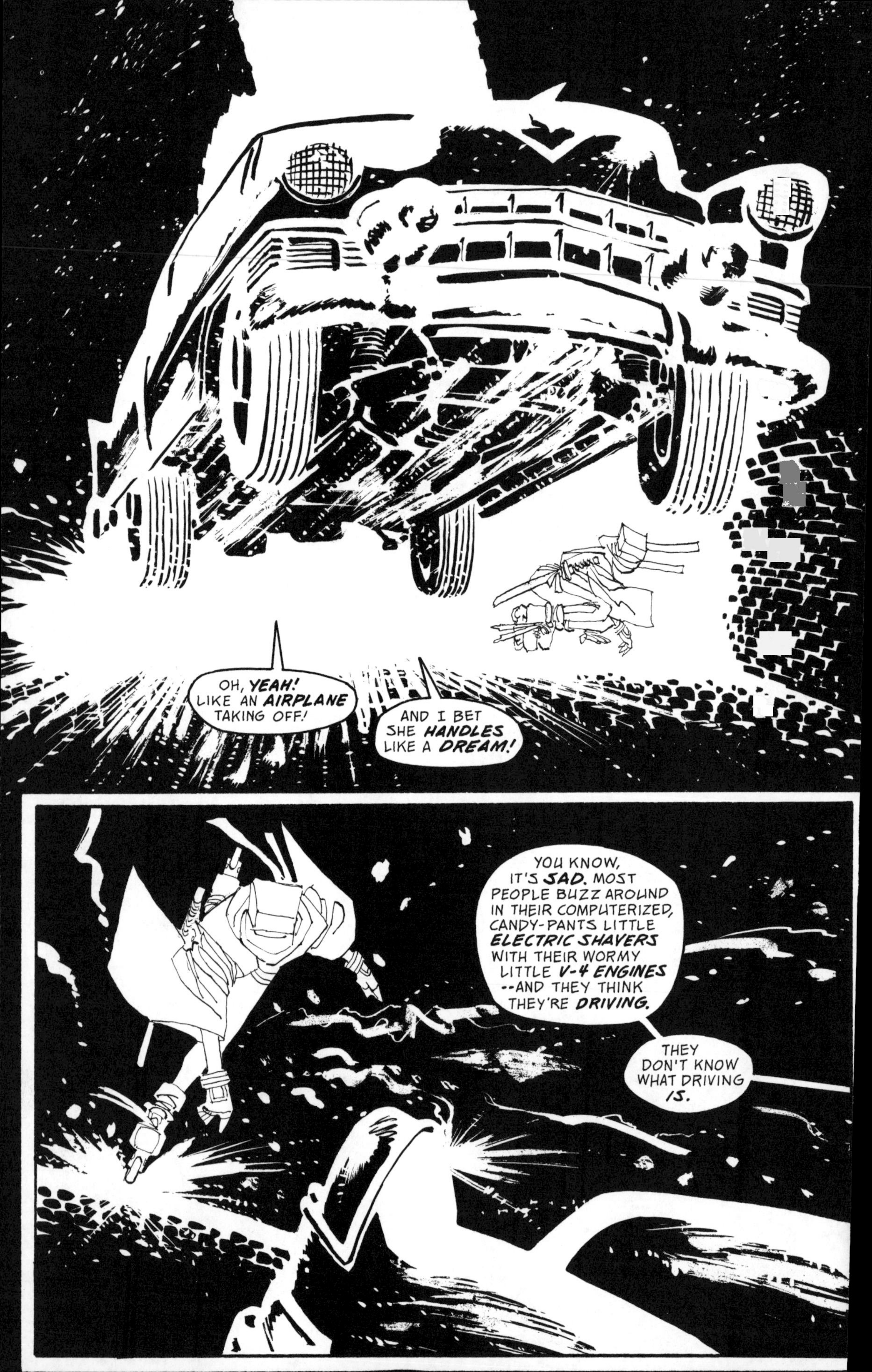
OH, YEAH! LIKE AN AIRPLANE TAKING OFF!
AND I BET SHE HANDLES LIKE A DREAM!
YOU KNOW, IT'S SAD. MOST PEOPLE BUZZ AROUND IN THEIR COMPUTERIZED, CANDY-PANTS LITTLE ELECTRIC SHAVERS WITH THEIR WORMY LITTLE V-4 ENGINES --AND THEY THINK THEY'RE DRIVING.
THEY DON'T KNOW WHAT DRIVING IS.

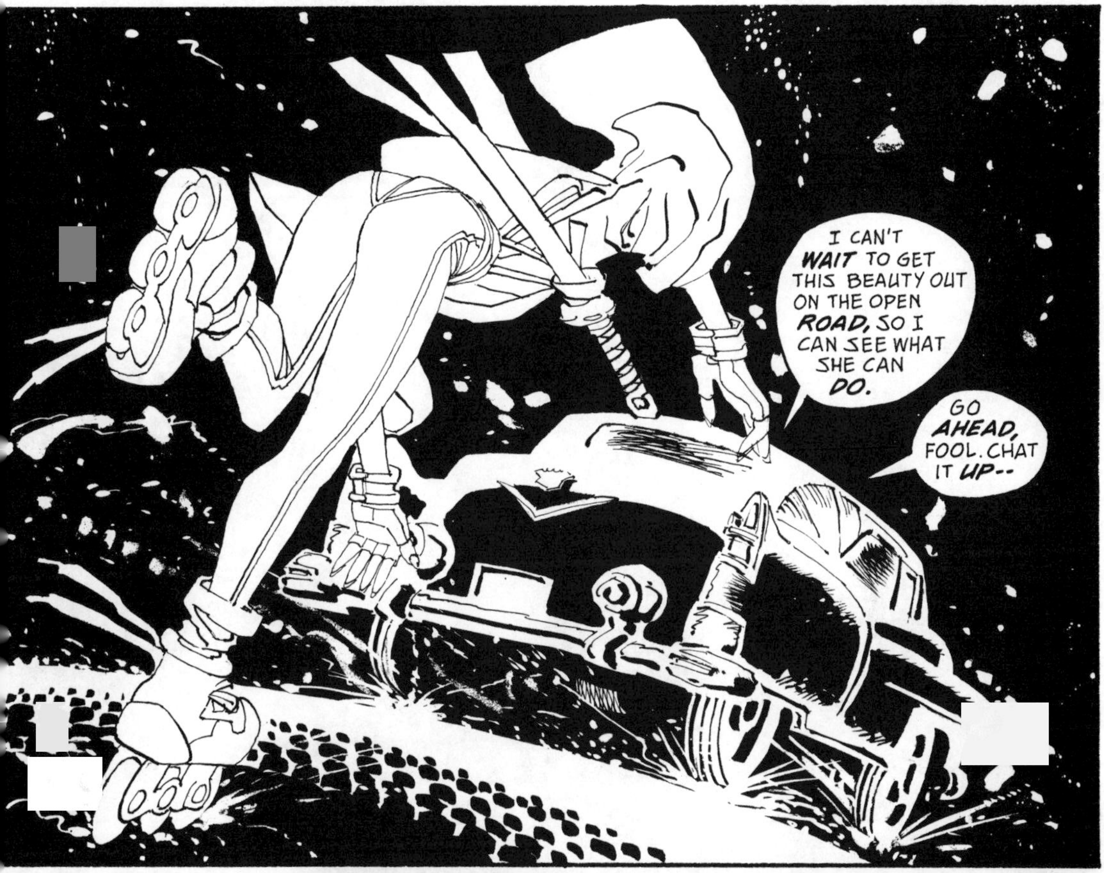
I CAN'T WAIT TO GET THIS BEAUTY OUT ON THE OPEN ROAD, SO I CAN SEE WHAT SHE CAN DO.
GO AHEAD, FOOL. CHAT IT UP--

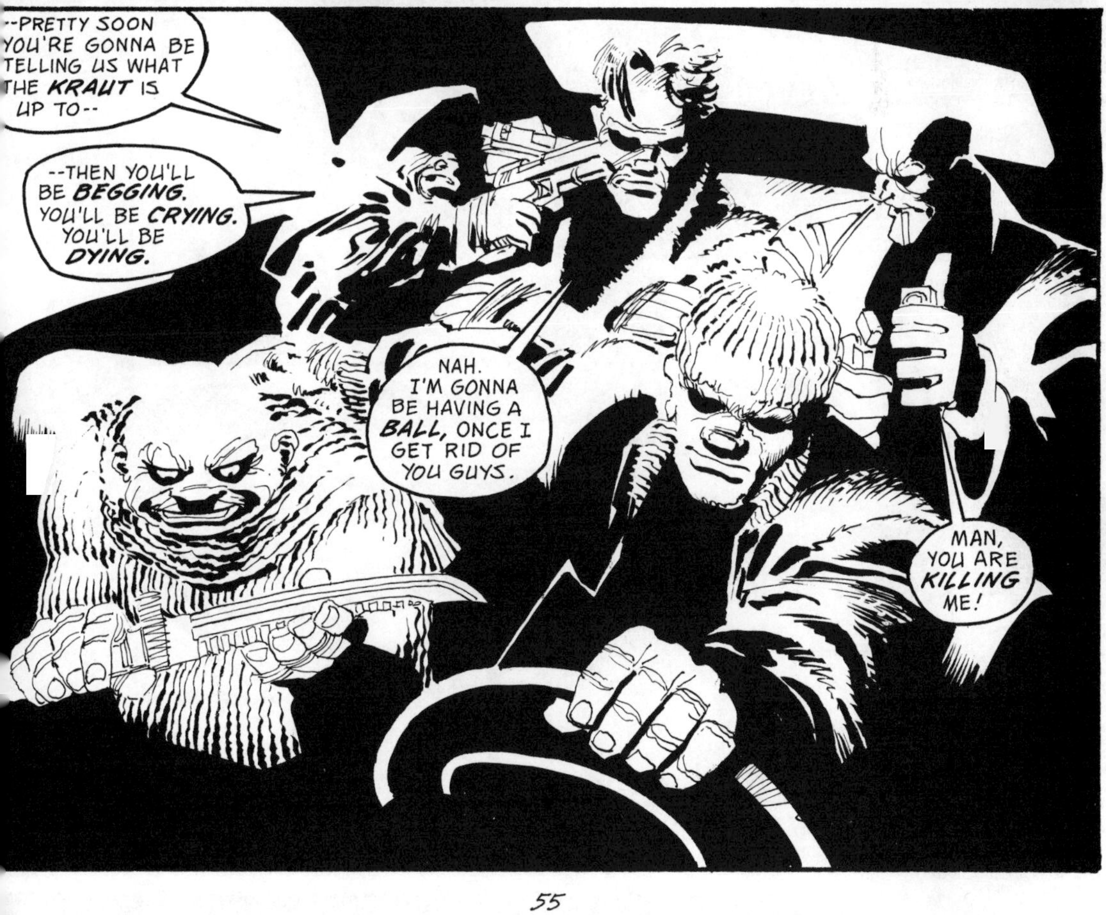
--PRETTY SOON YOU'RE GONNA BE TELLING US WHAT THE KRAUT IS UP TO--
--THEN YOU'LL BE BEGGING. YOU'LL BE CRYING. YOU'LL BE DYING.
NAH. I'M GONNA BE HAVING A BALL, ONCE I GET RID OF YOU GUYS.
MAN, YOU ARE KILLING ME!

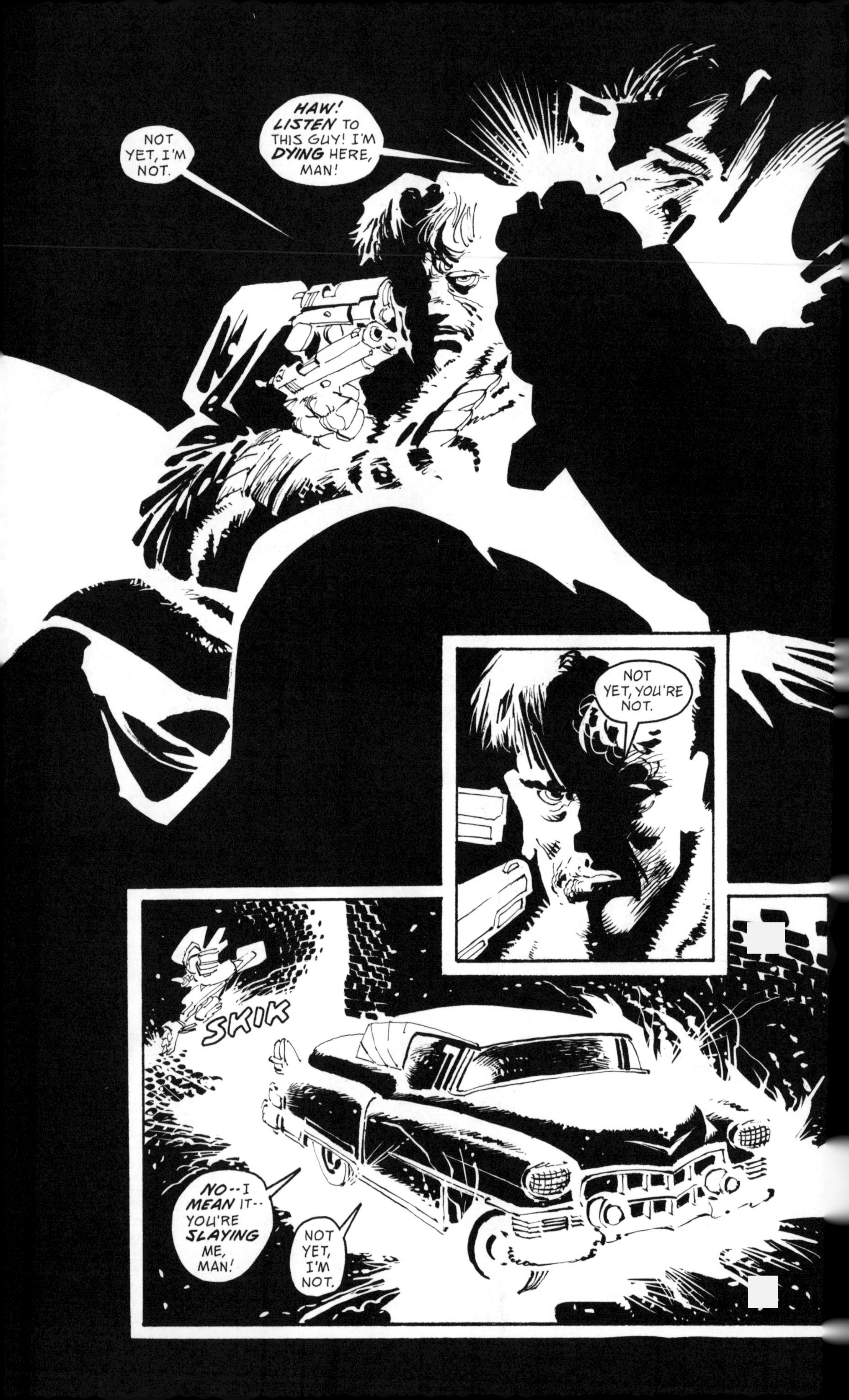
NOT YET, I'M NOT.
HAW! LISTEN TO THIS GUY! I'M DYING HERE, MAN!
NOT YET, YOU'RE NOT.
SKIK
NO--I MEAN IT--YOU'RE SLAYING ME, MAN!
NOT YET, I'M NOT.

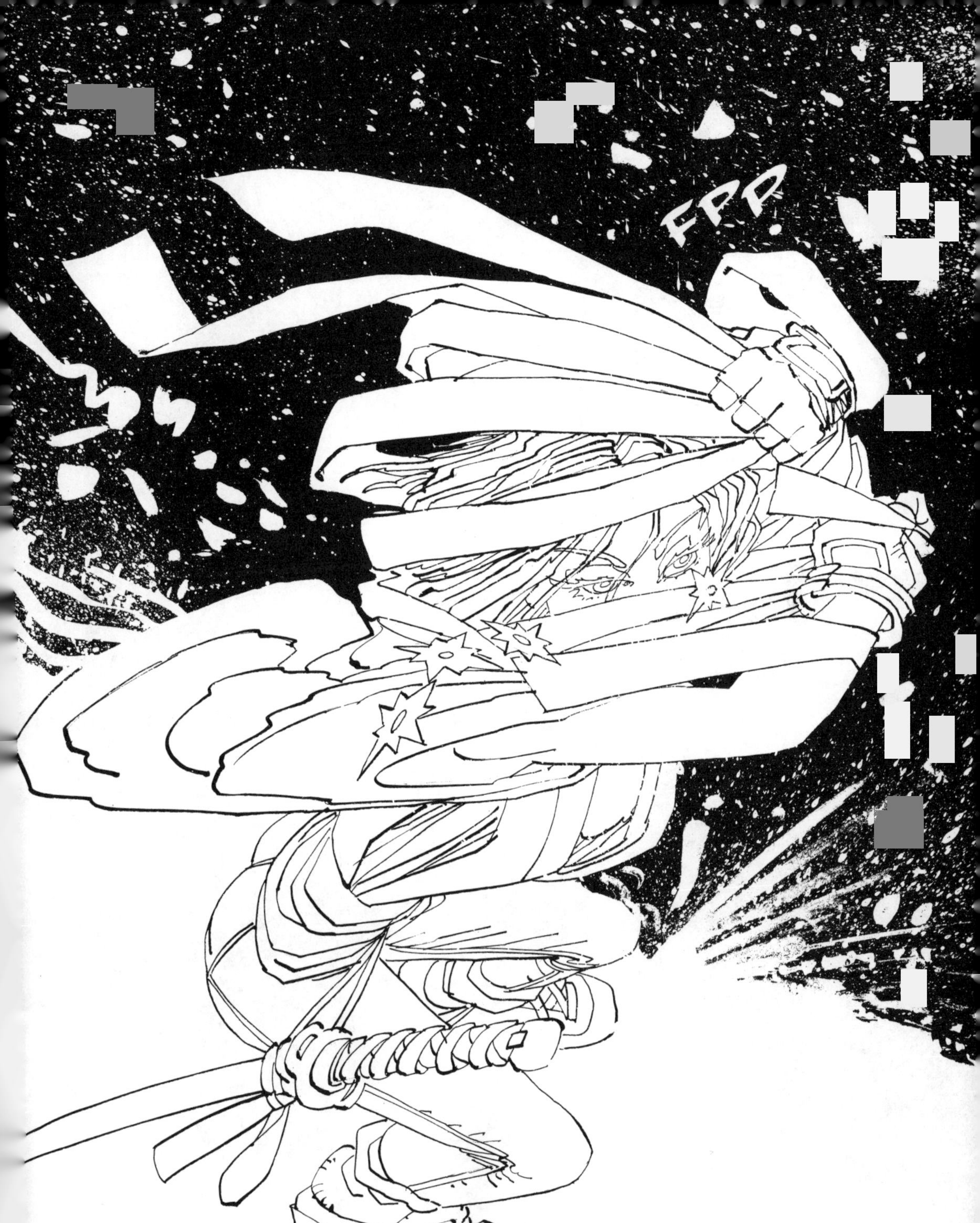
FPP
SKEEEE

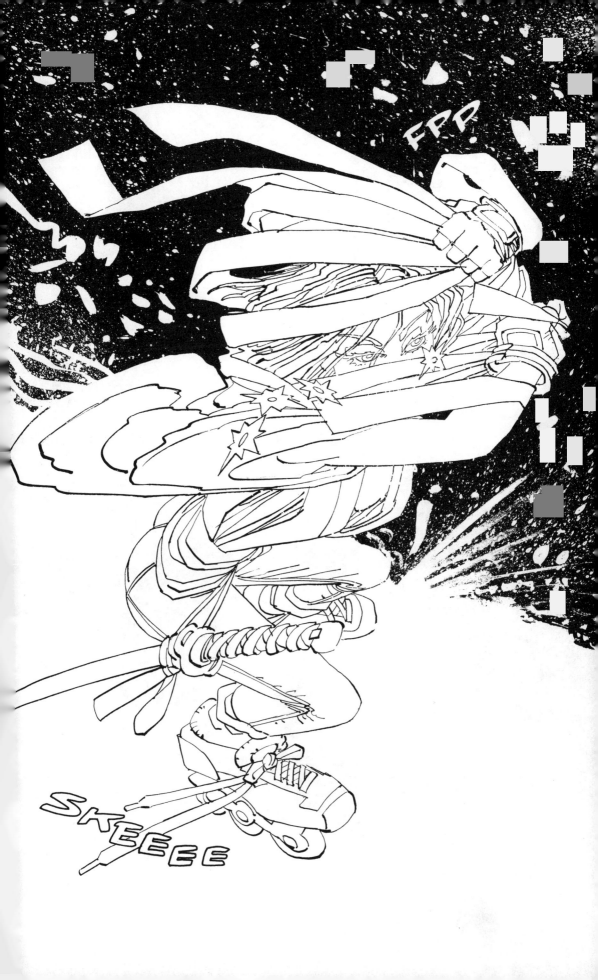

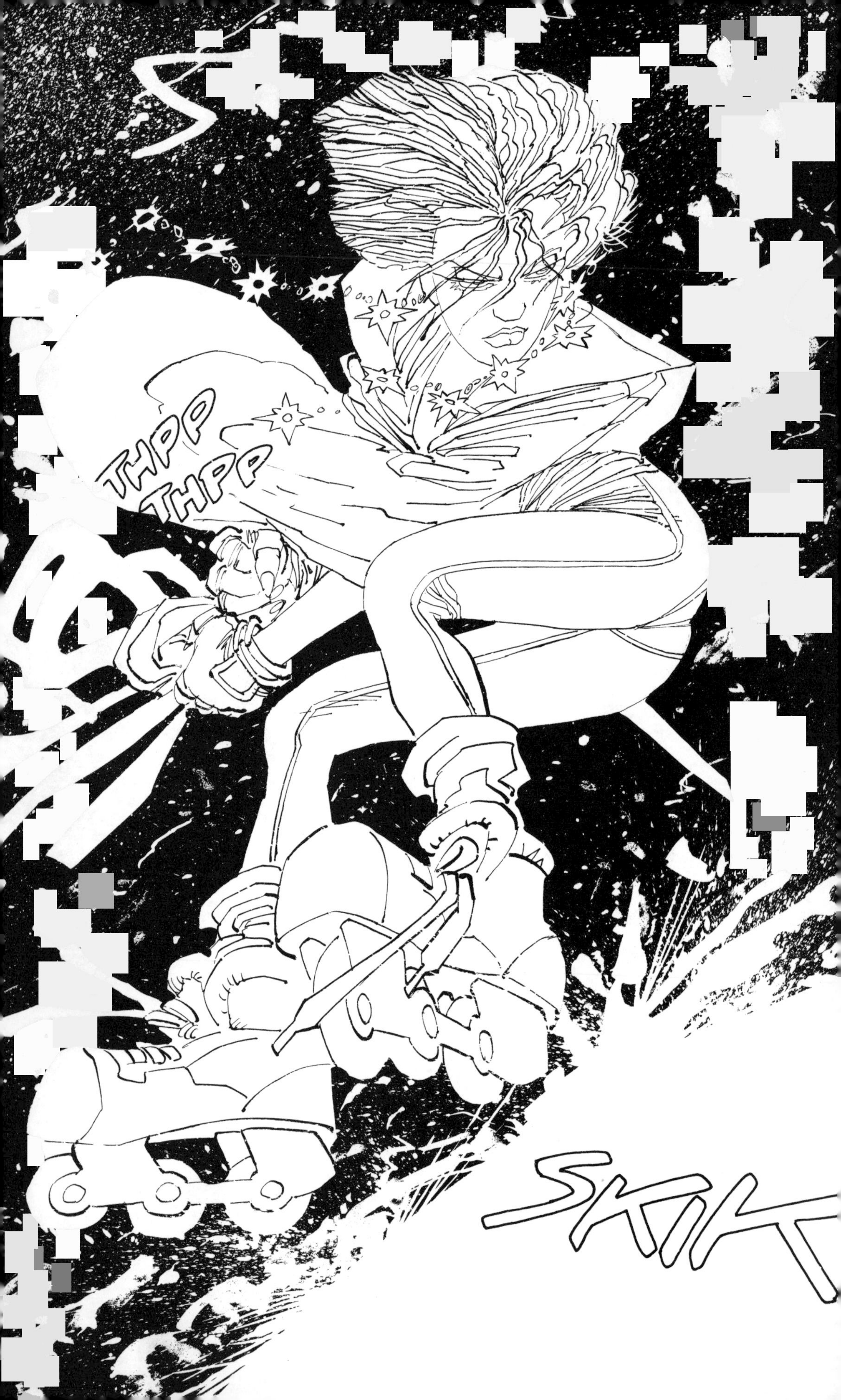
THPP
THPP
SKIK

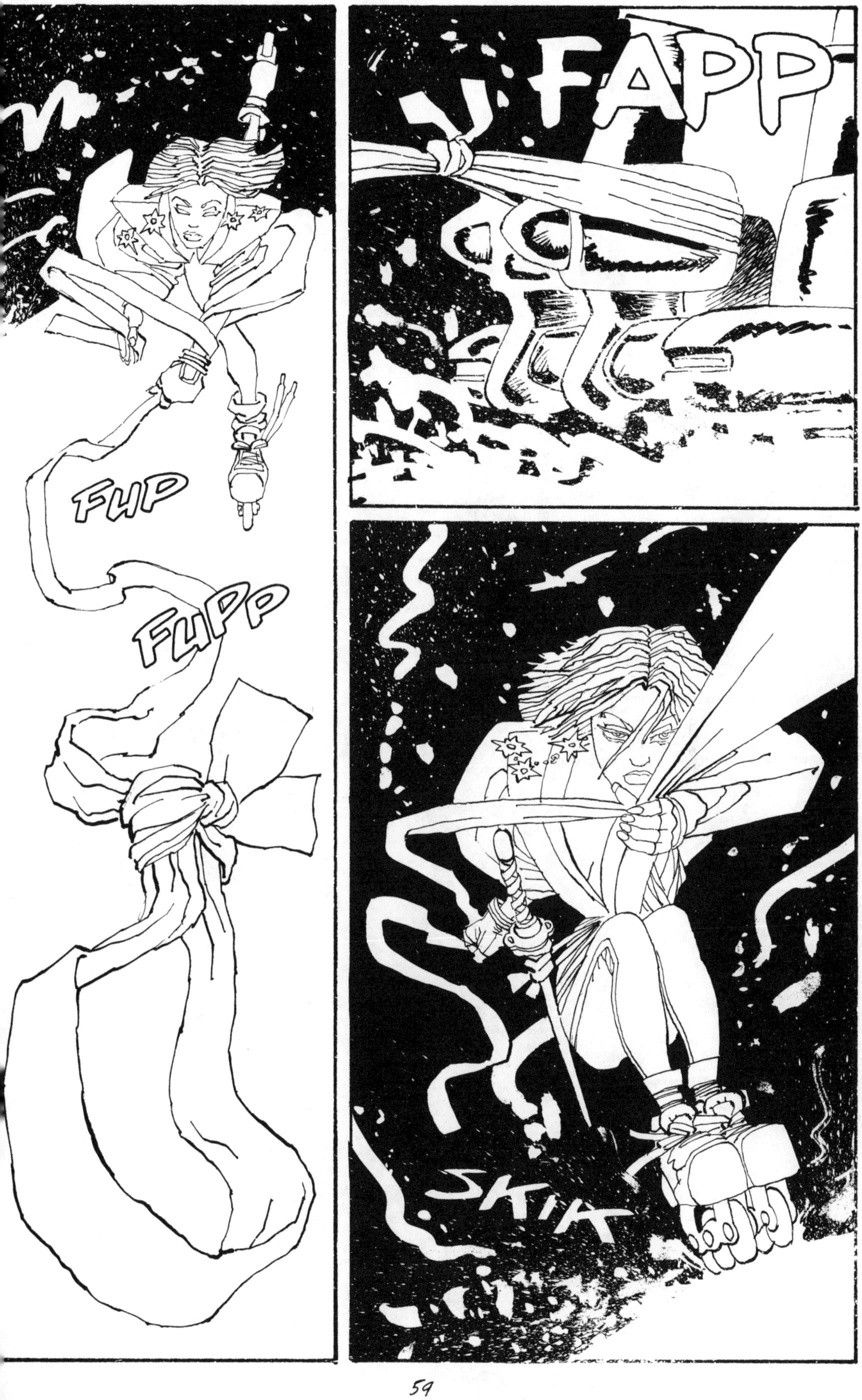
FAPP
FUP
FUPP
SKIA

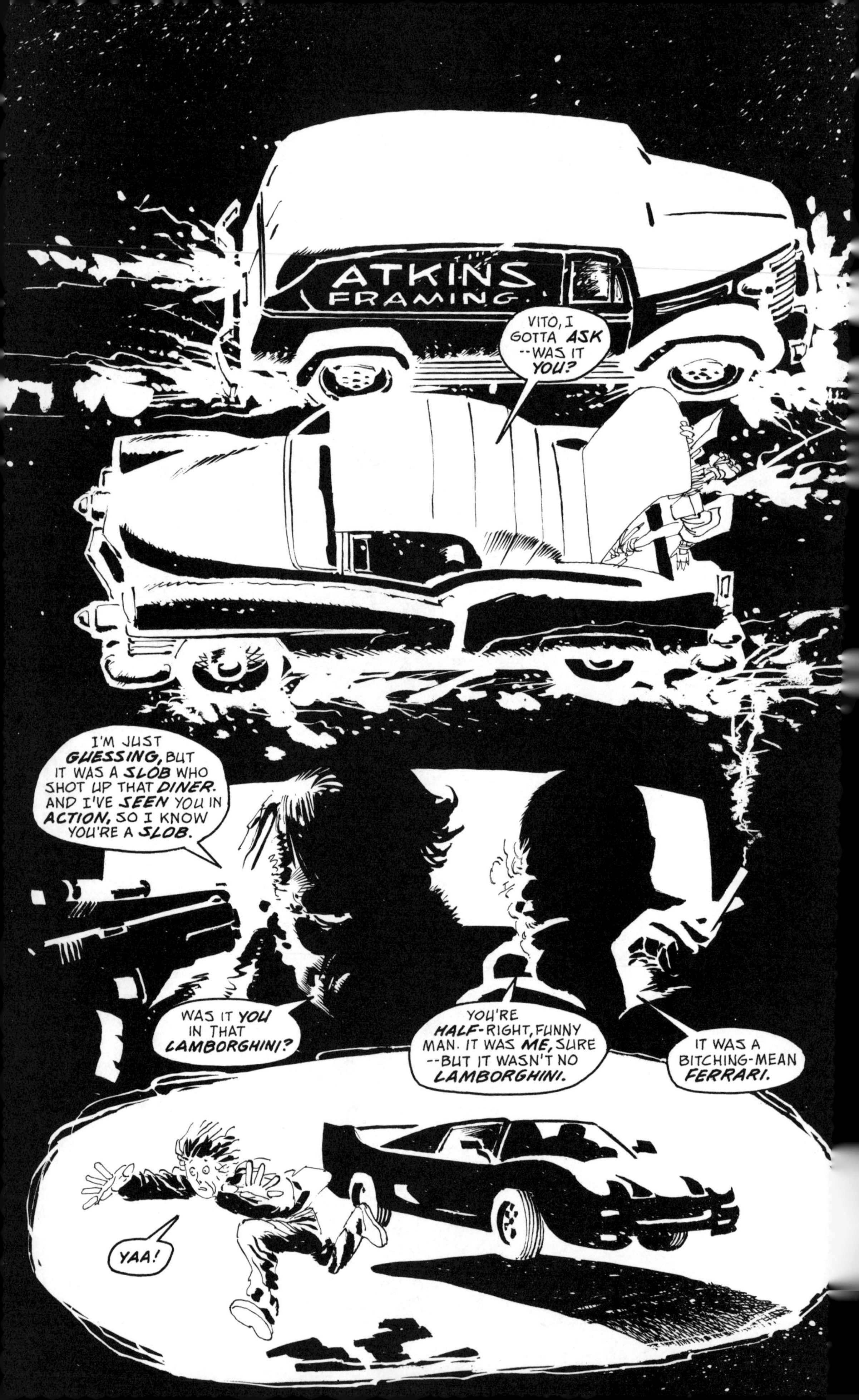
ATKINS FRAMING
VITO, I GOTTA ASK --WAS IT YOU?
I'M JUST GUESSING, BUT IT WAS A SLOB WHO SHOT UP THAT DINER. AND I'VE SEEN YOU IN ACTION, SO I KNOW YOU'RE A SLOB.
WAS IT YOU IN THAT LAMBORGHINI?
YOU'RE HALF-RIGHT, FUNNY MAN. IT WAS ME, SURE --BUT IT WASN'T NO LAMBORGHINI.
IT WAS A BITCHING-MEAN FERRARI.
YAA!

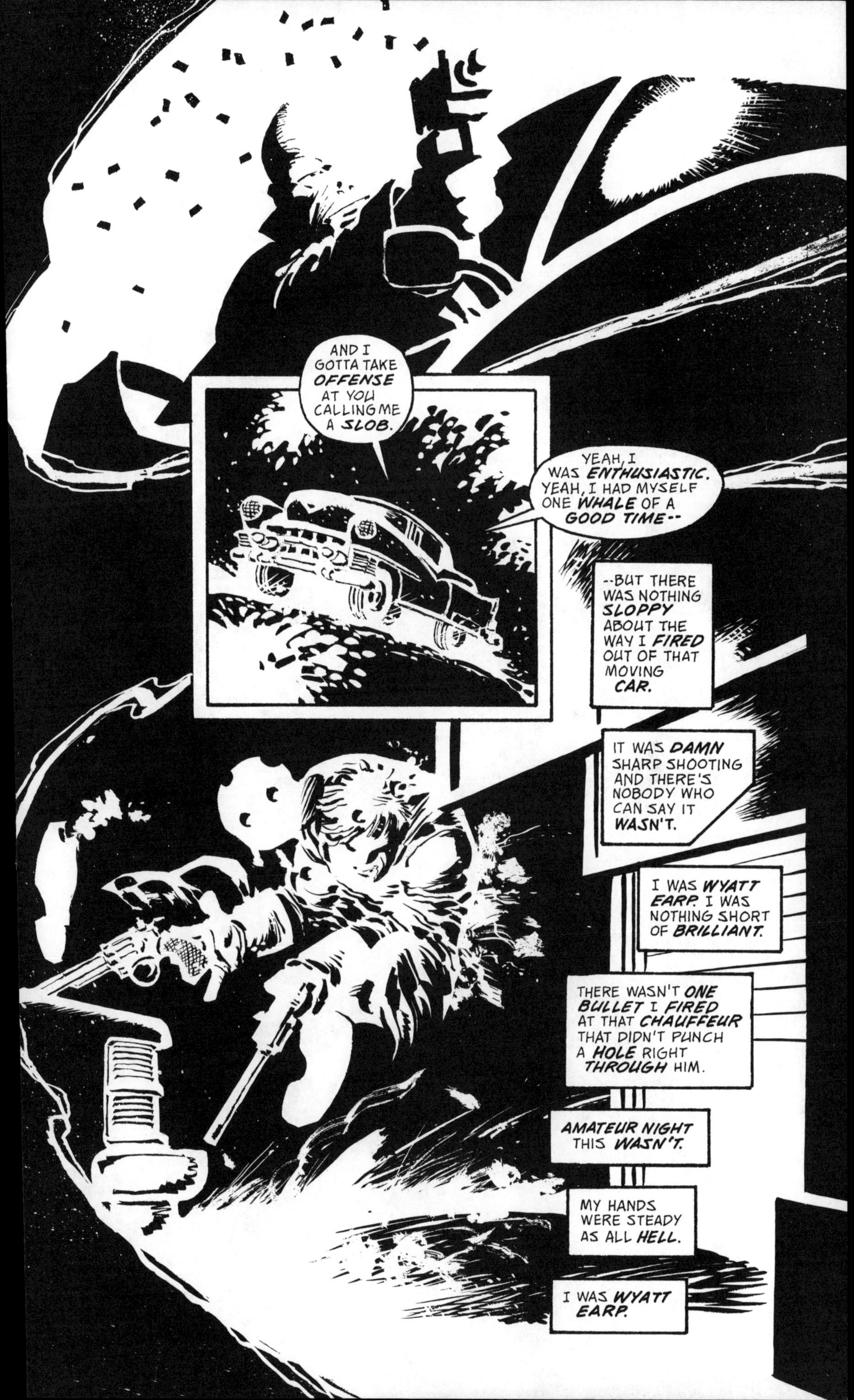
AND I GOTTA TAKE OFFENSE AT YOU CALLING ME A SLOB.
YEAH, I WAS ENTHUSIASTIC. YEAH, I HAD MYSELF ONE WHALE OF A GOOD TIME--
--BUT THERE WAS NOTHING SLOPPY ABOUT THE WAY I FIRED OUT OF THAT MOVING CAR.
IT WAS DAMN SHARP SHOOTING AND THERE'S NOBODY WHO CAN SAY IT WASN'T.
I WAS WYATT EARP. I WAS NOTHING SHORT OF BRILLIANT.
THERE WASN'T ONE BULLET I FIRED AT THAT CHAUFFEUR THAT DIDN'T PUNCH A HOLE RIGHT THROUGH HIM.
AMATEUR NIGHT THIS WASN'T.
MY HANDS WERE STEADY AS ALL HELL.
I WAS WYATT EARP.

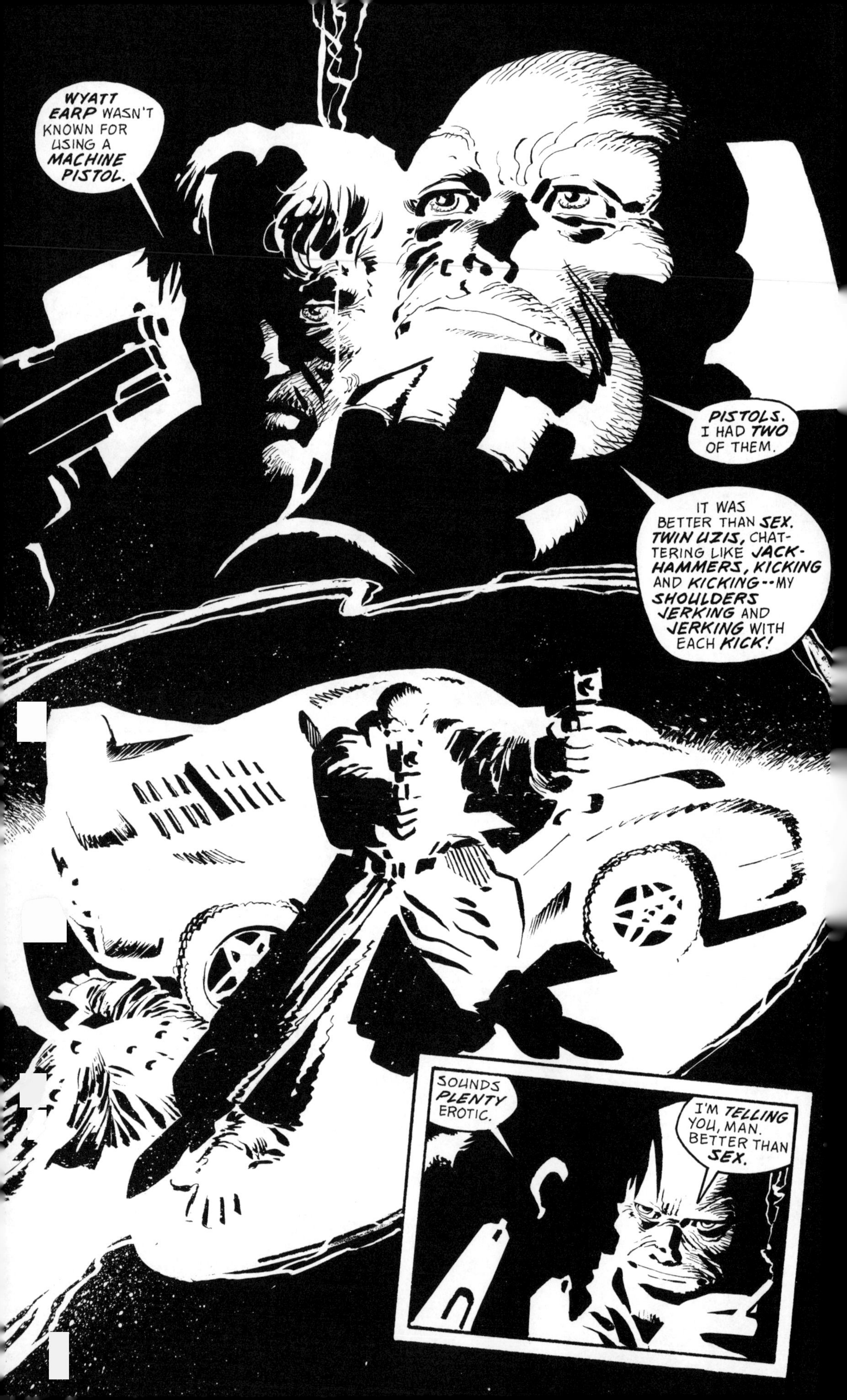
WYATT EARP WASN'T KNOWN FOR USING A MACHINE PISTOL.
PISTOLS. I HAD TWO OF THEM.
IT WAS BETTER THAN SEX. TWIN UZIS, CHATTERING LIKE JACKHAMMERS, KICKING AND KICKING--MY SHOULDERS JERKING AND JERKING WITH EACH KICK!
SOUNDS PLENTY EROTIC.
I'M TELLING YOU, MAN. BETTER THAN SEX.

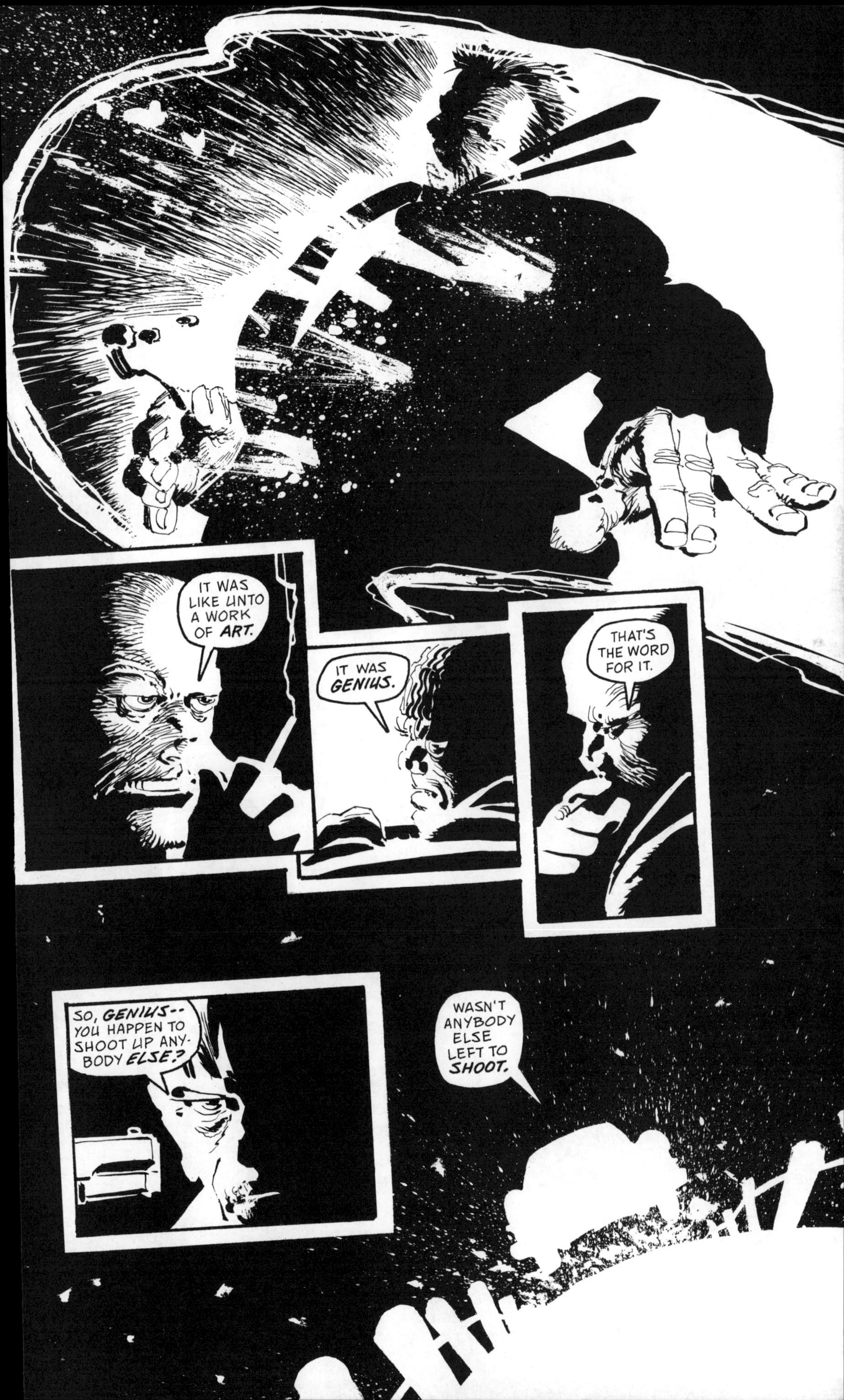
IT WAS LIKE UNTO A WORK OF ART.
IT WAS GENIUS.
THAT'S THE WORD FOR IT.
SO, GENIUS-- YOU HAPPEN TO SHOOT UP ANYBODY ELSE?
WASN'T ANYBODY ELSE LEFT TO SHOOT.

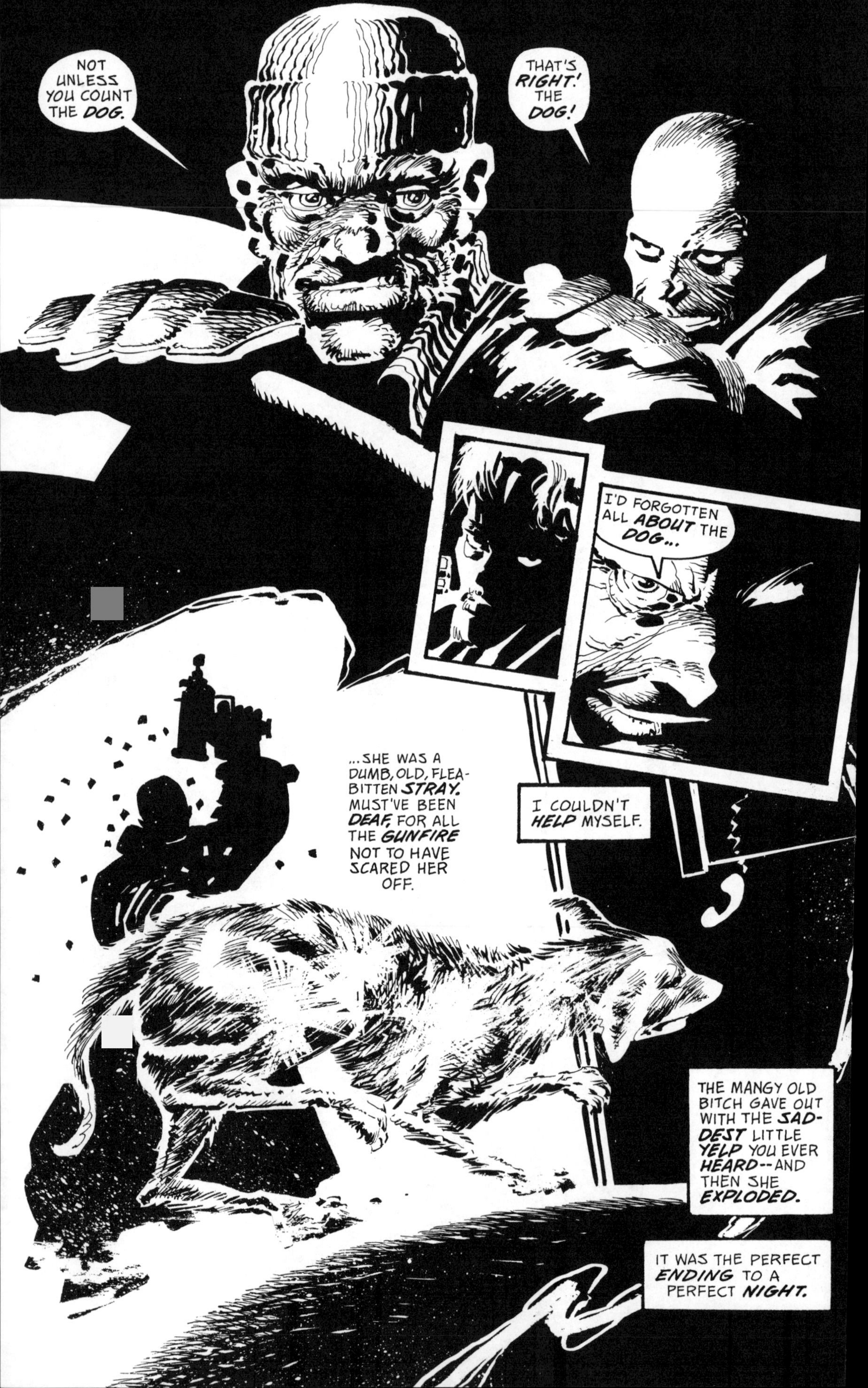

NOT UNLESS YOU COUNT THE DOG.
THAT'S RIGHT! THE DOG!
I'D FORGOTTEN ALL ABOUT THE DOG...
...SHE WAS A DUMB, OLD, FLEA-BITTEN STRAY. MUST'VE BEEN DEAF, FOR ALL THE GUNFIRE NOT TO HAVE SCARED HER OFF.
I COULDN'T HELP MYSELF.
THE MANGY OLD BITCH GAVE OUT WITH THE SAD-DEST LITTLE YELP YOU EVER HEARD--AND THEN SHE EXPLODED.
IT WAS THE PERFECT ENDING TO A PERFECT NIGHT.

65

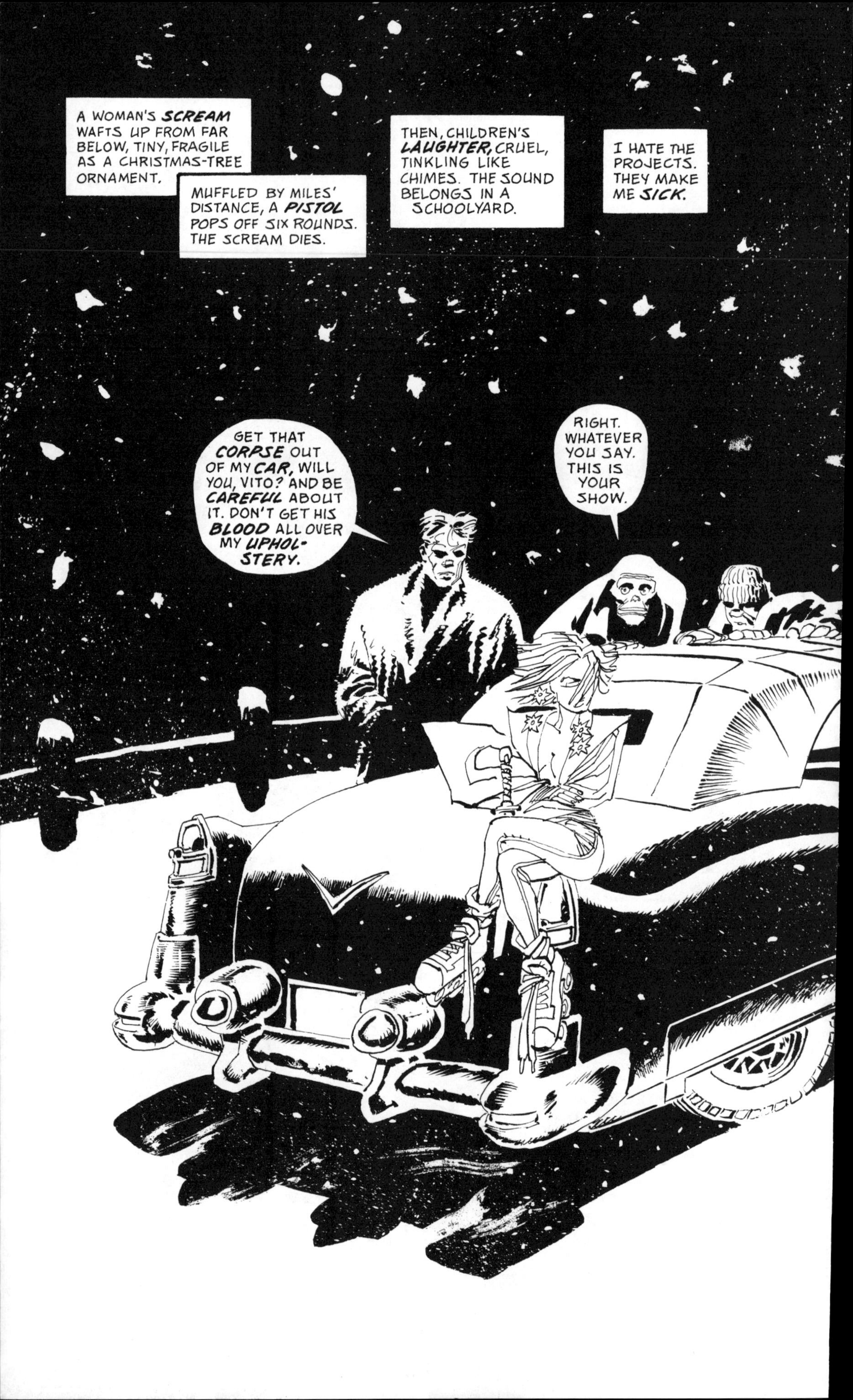
A WOMAN'S SCREAM WAFTS UP FROM FAR BELOW, TINY, FRAGILE AS A CHRISTMAS-TREE ORNAMENT.
MUFFLED BY MILES' DISTANCE, A PISTOL POPS OFF SIX ROUNDS. THE SCREAM DIES.
THEN, CHILDREN'S LAUGHTER, CRUEL, TINKLING LIKE CHIMES. THE SOUND BELONGS IN A SCHOOLYARD.
I HATE THE PROJECTS. THEY MAKE ME SICK.
GET THAT CORPSE OUT OF MY CAR, WILL YOU, VITO? AND BE CAREFUL ABOUT IT. DON'T GET HIS BLOOD ALL OVER MY UPHOL-STERY.
RIGHT. WHATEVER YOU SAY. THIS IS YOUR SHOW.

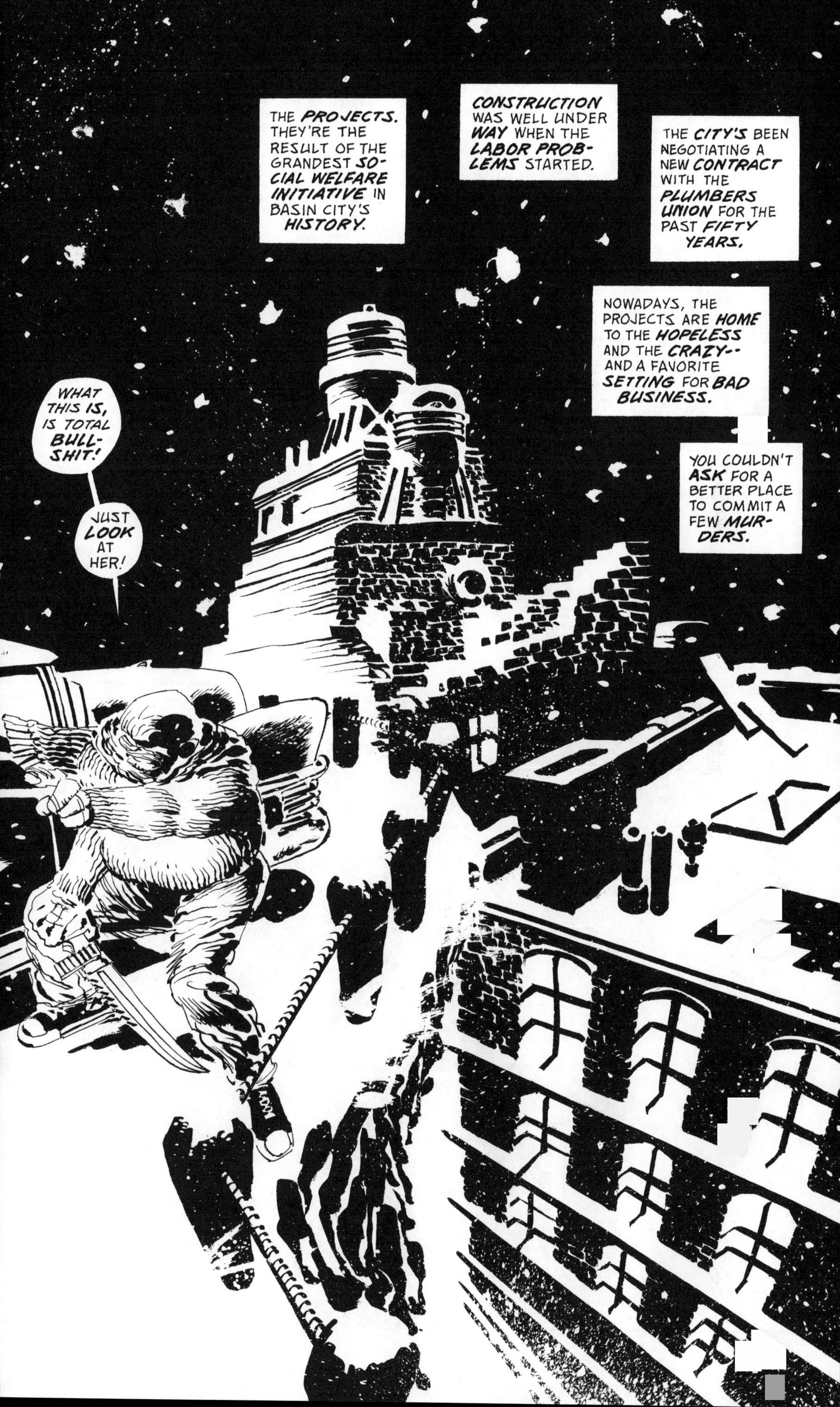
THE PROJECTS. THEY'RE THE RESULT OF THE GRANDEST SOCIAL WELFARE INITIATIVE IN BASIN CITY'S HISTORY.
CONSTRUCTION WAS WELL UNDER WAY WHEN THE LABOR PROBLEMS STARTED.
THE CITY'S BEEN NEGOTIATING A NEW CONTRACT WITH THE PLUMBERS UNION FOR THE PAST FIFTY YEARS.
NOWADAYS, THE PROJECTS ARE HOME TO THE HOPELESS AND THE CRAZY-- AND A FAVORITE SETTING FOR BAD BUSINESS.
YOU COULDN'T ASK FOR A BETTER PLACE TO COMMIT A FEW MURDERS.
WHAT THIS IS, IS TOTAL BULLSHIT!
JUST LOOK AT HER!

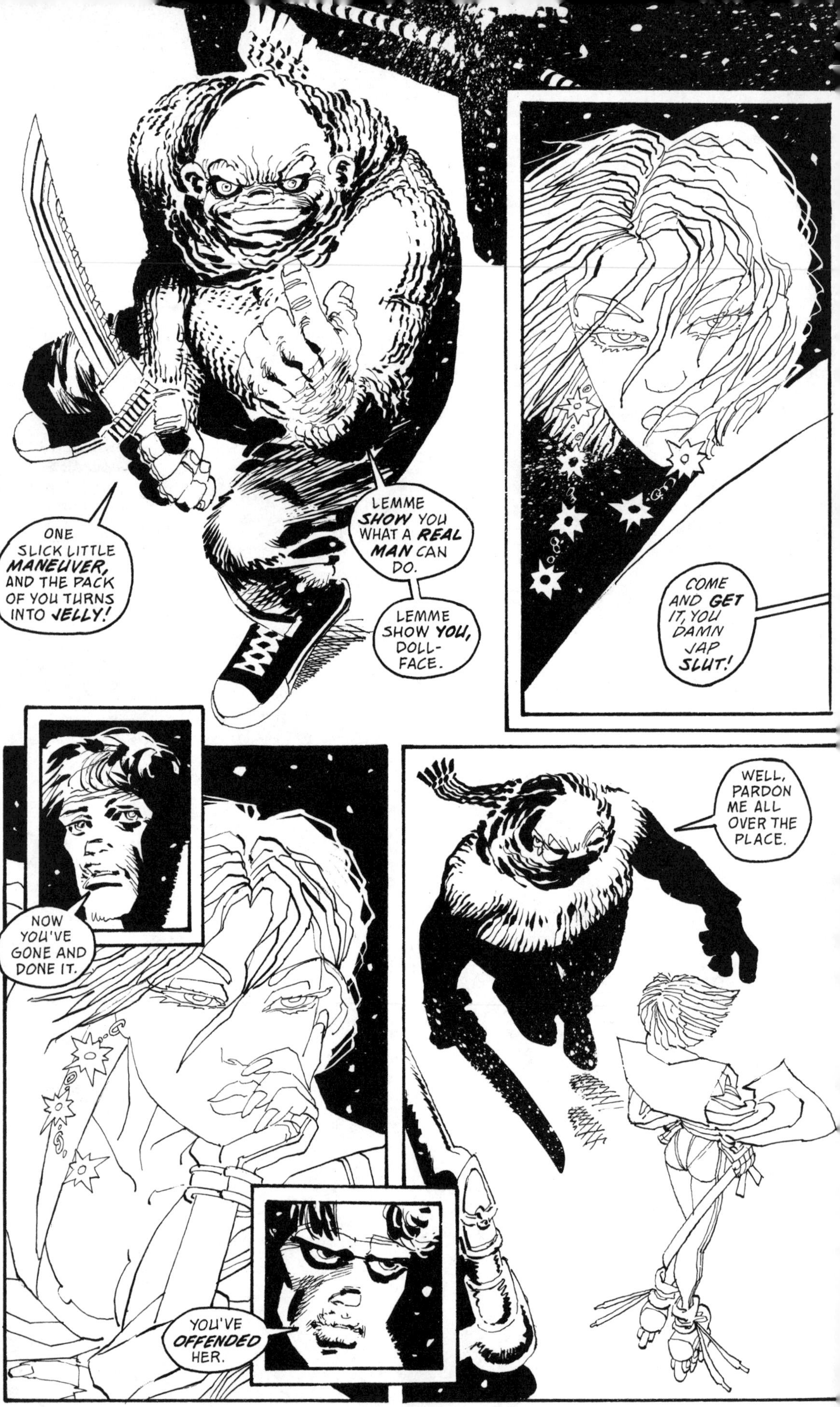
ONE SLICK LITTLE MANEUVER, AND THE PACK OF YOU TURNS INTO JELLY!
LEMME SHOW YOU WHAT A REAL MAN CAN DO.
LEMME SHOW YOU, DOLL-FACE.
COME AND GET IT, YOU DAMN JAP SLUT!
NOW YOU'VE GONE AND DONE IT.
YOU'VE OFFENDED HER.
WELL, PARDON ME ALL OVER THE PLACE.

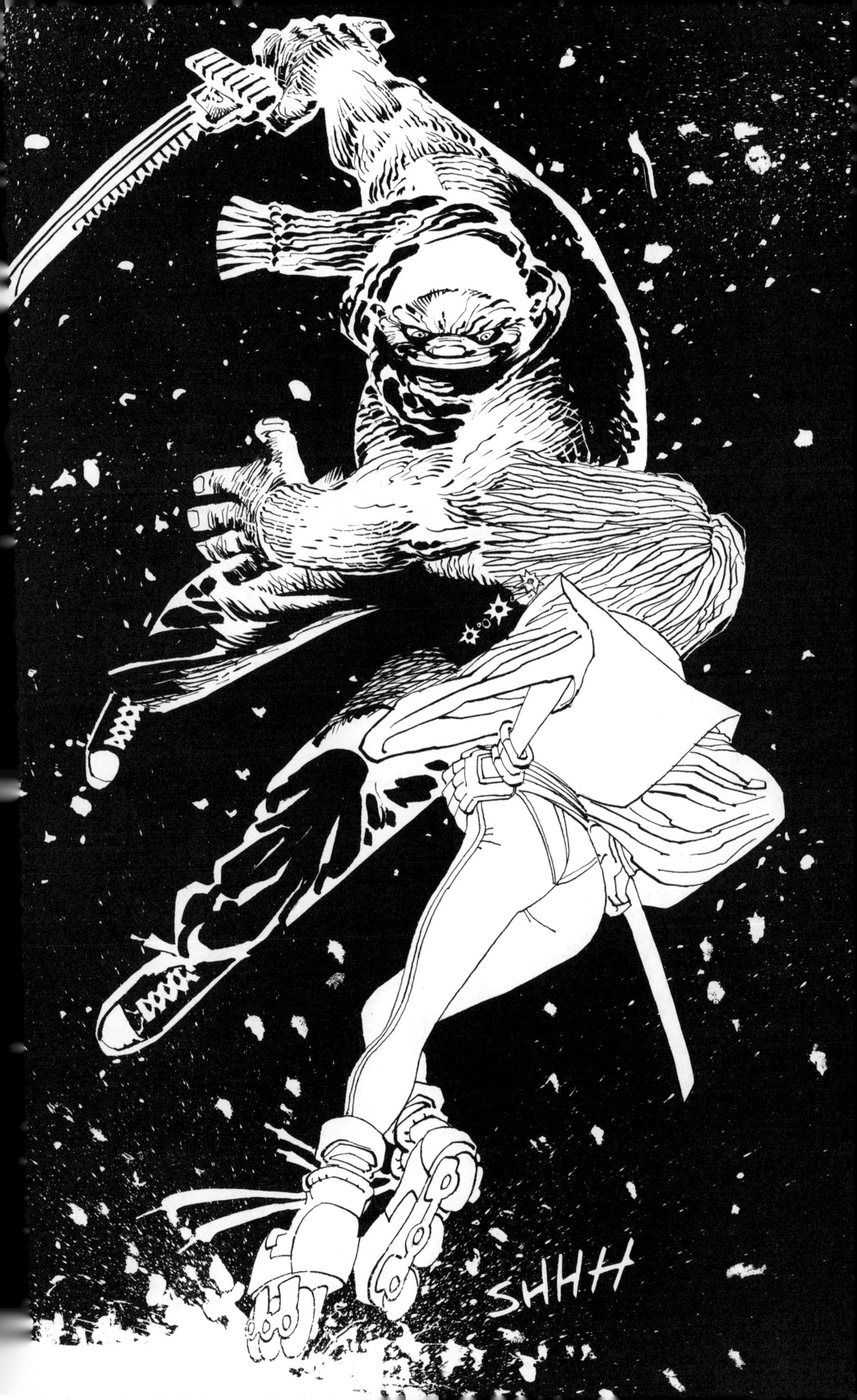
SHHH

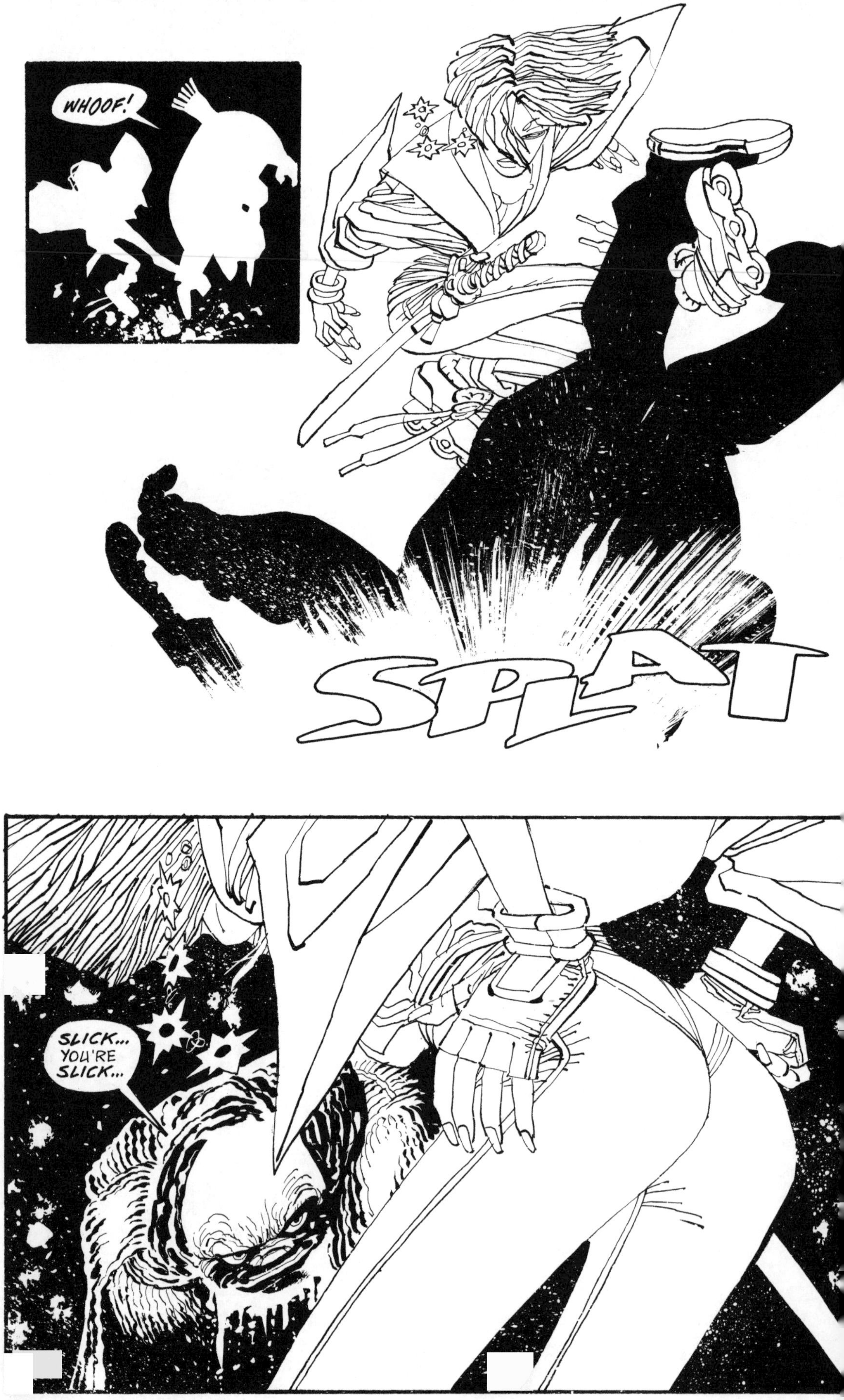
WHOOF!
SPLAT
SLICK... YOU'RE SLICK...

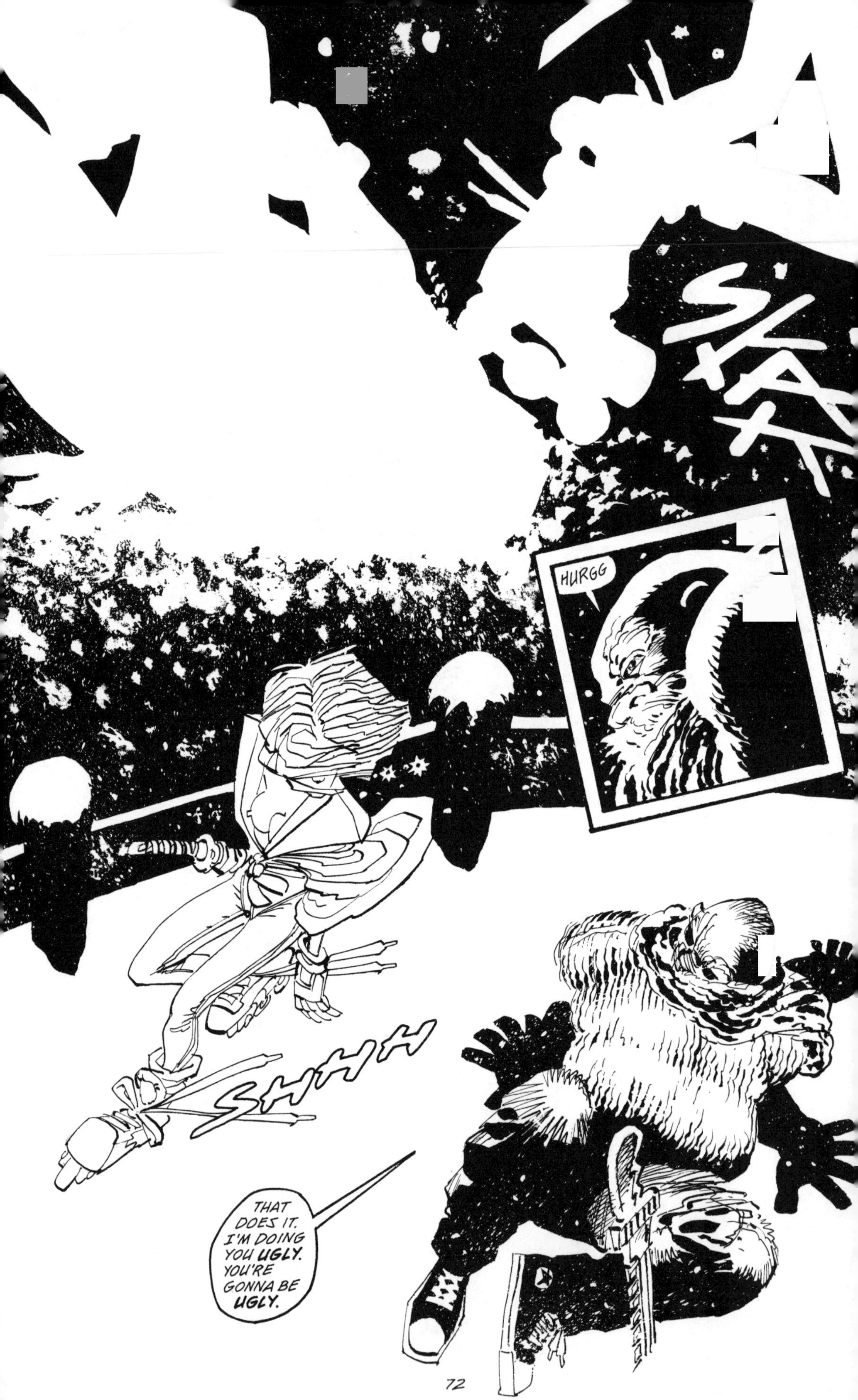
SKAK
HURGG
SHHHH
THAT DOES IT. I'M DOING YOU **UGLY**. YOU'RE GONNA BE **UGLY**.

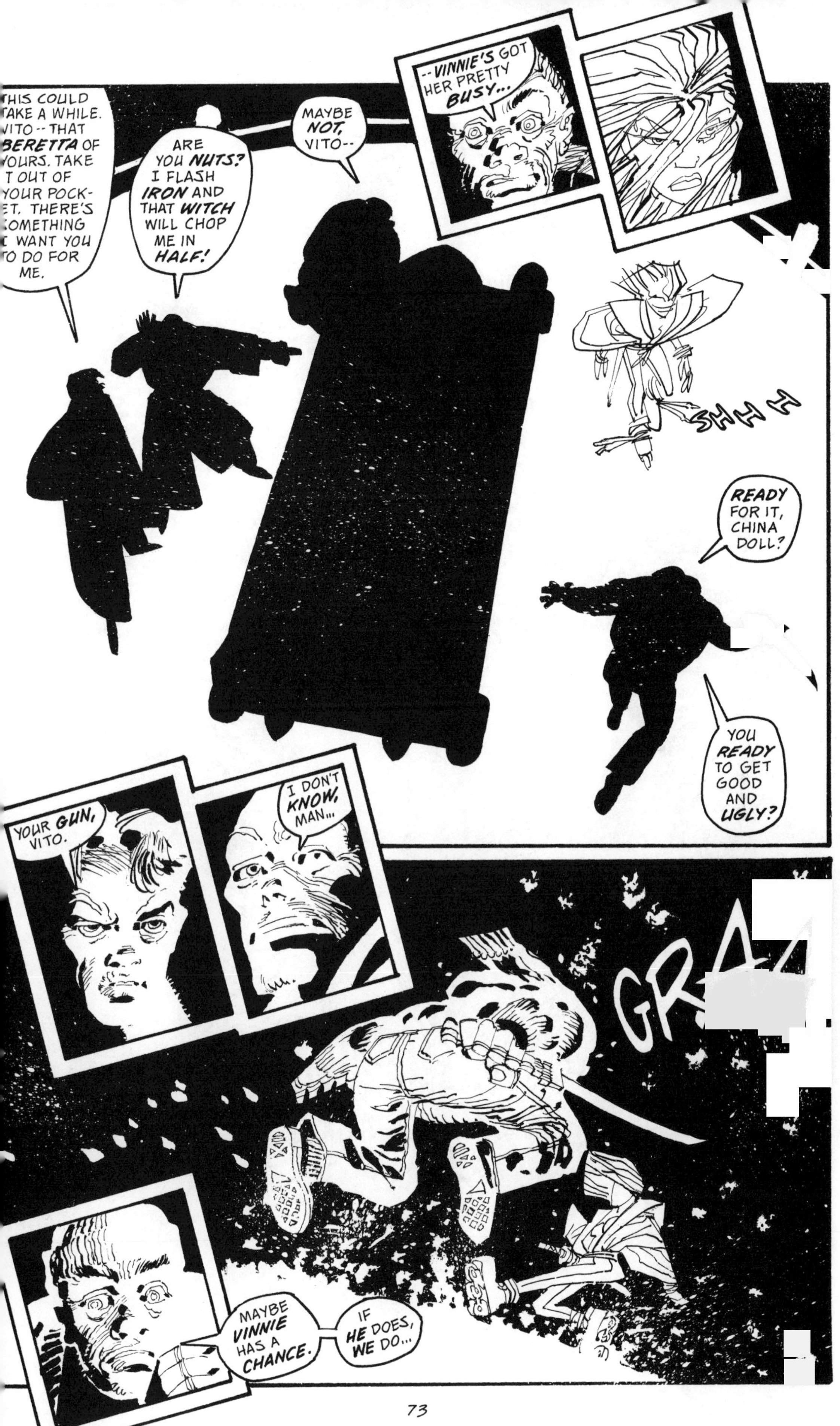

THIS COULD TAKE A WHILE. VITO -- THAT BERETTA OF YOURS. TAKE IT OUT OF YOUR POCKET. THERE'S SOMETHING I WANT YOU TO DO FOR ME.
ARE YOU NUTS? I FLASH IRON AND THAT WITCH WILL CHOP ME IN HALF!
MAYBE NOT, VITO--
--VINNIE'S GOT HER PRETTY BUSY...
SHHH
READY FOR IT, CHINA DOLL?
YOU READY TO GET GOOD AND UGLY?
YOUR GUN, VITO.
I DON'T KNOW, MAN...
GRA
MAYBE VINNIE HAS A CHANCE.
IF HE DOES, WE DO...

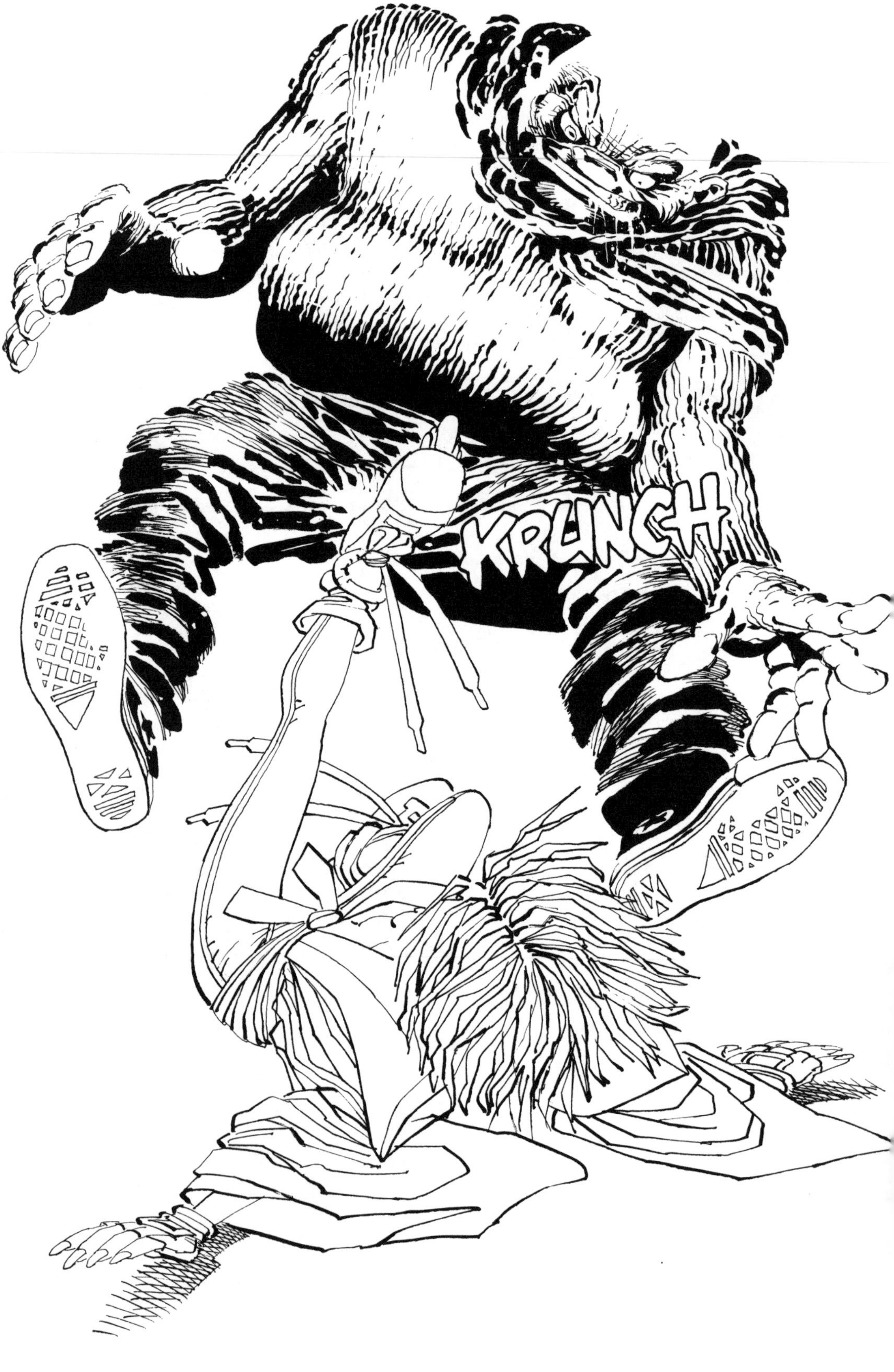
KRUNCH

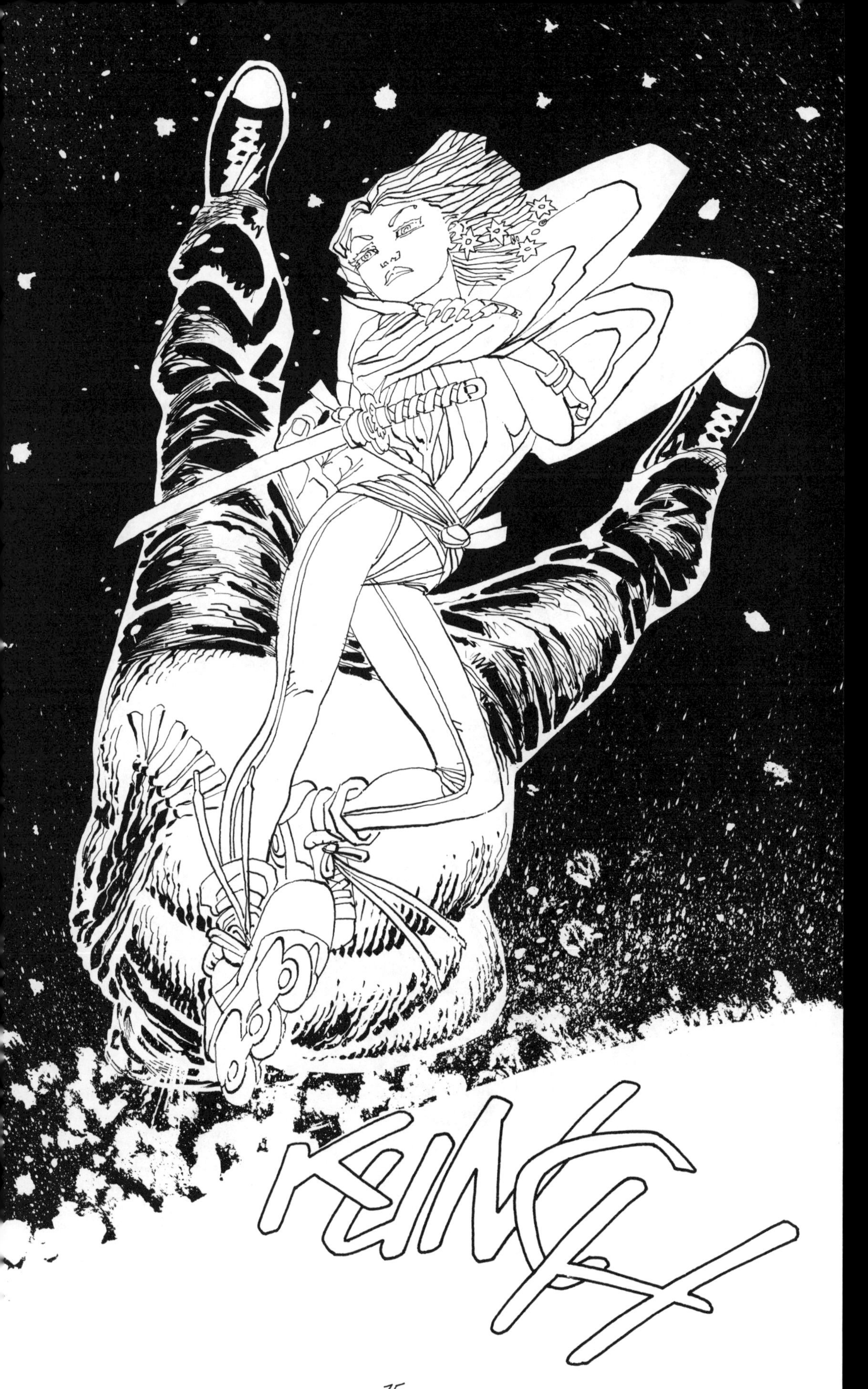
KLUNCH

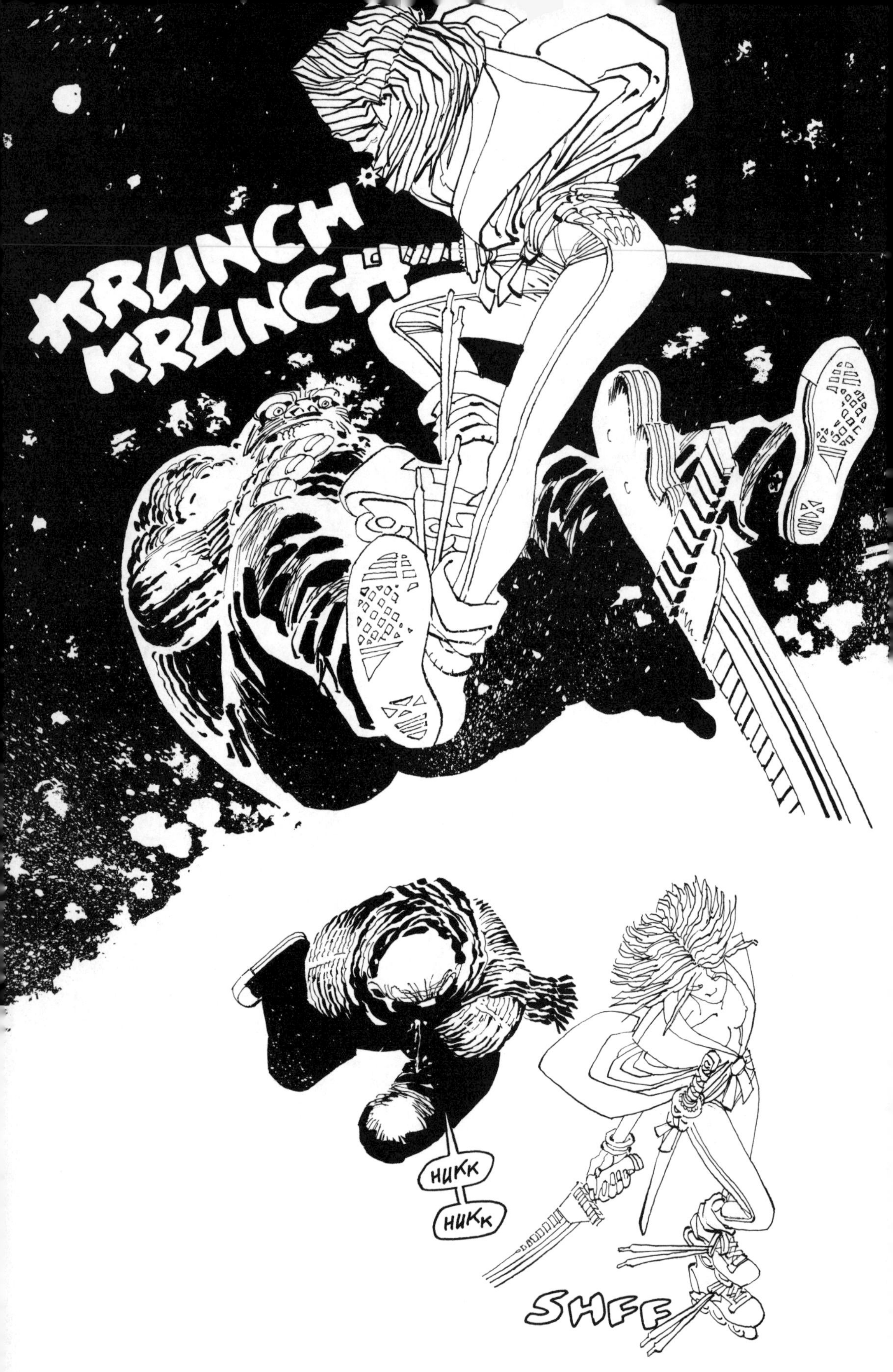
KRUNCH
KRUNCH
HUKK
HUKK
SHFF

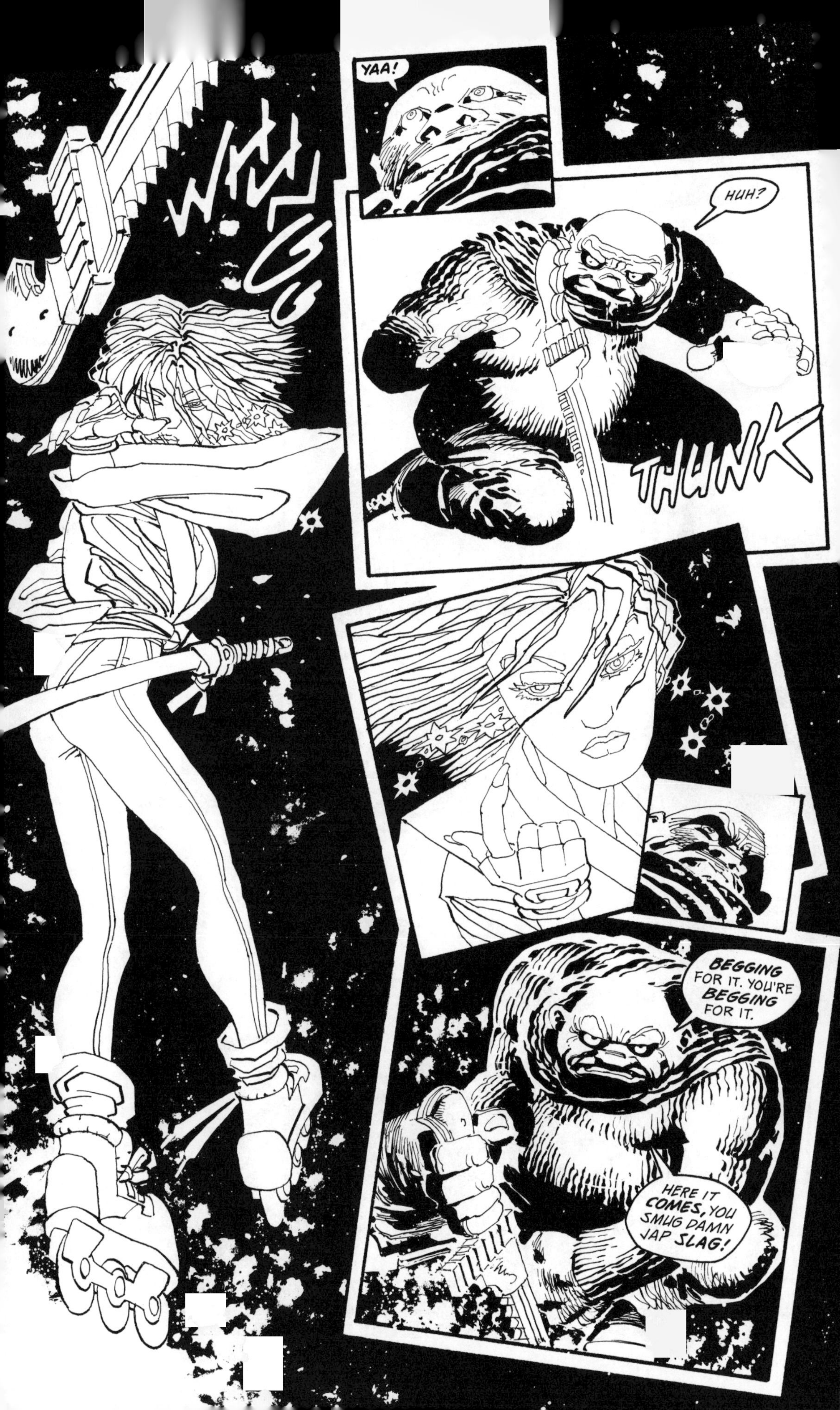
YAA!
HUH?
THUNK
BEGGING FOR IT. YOU'RE BEGGING FOR IT.
HERE IT COMES, YOU SMUG DAMN JAP SLAG!

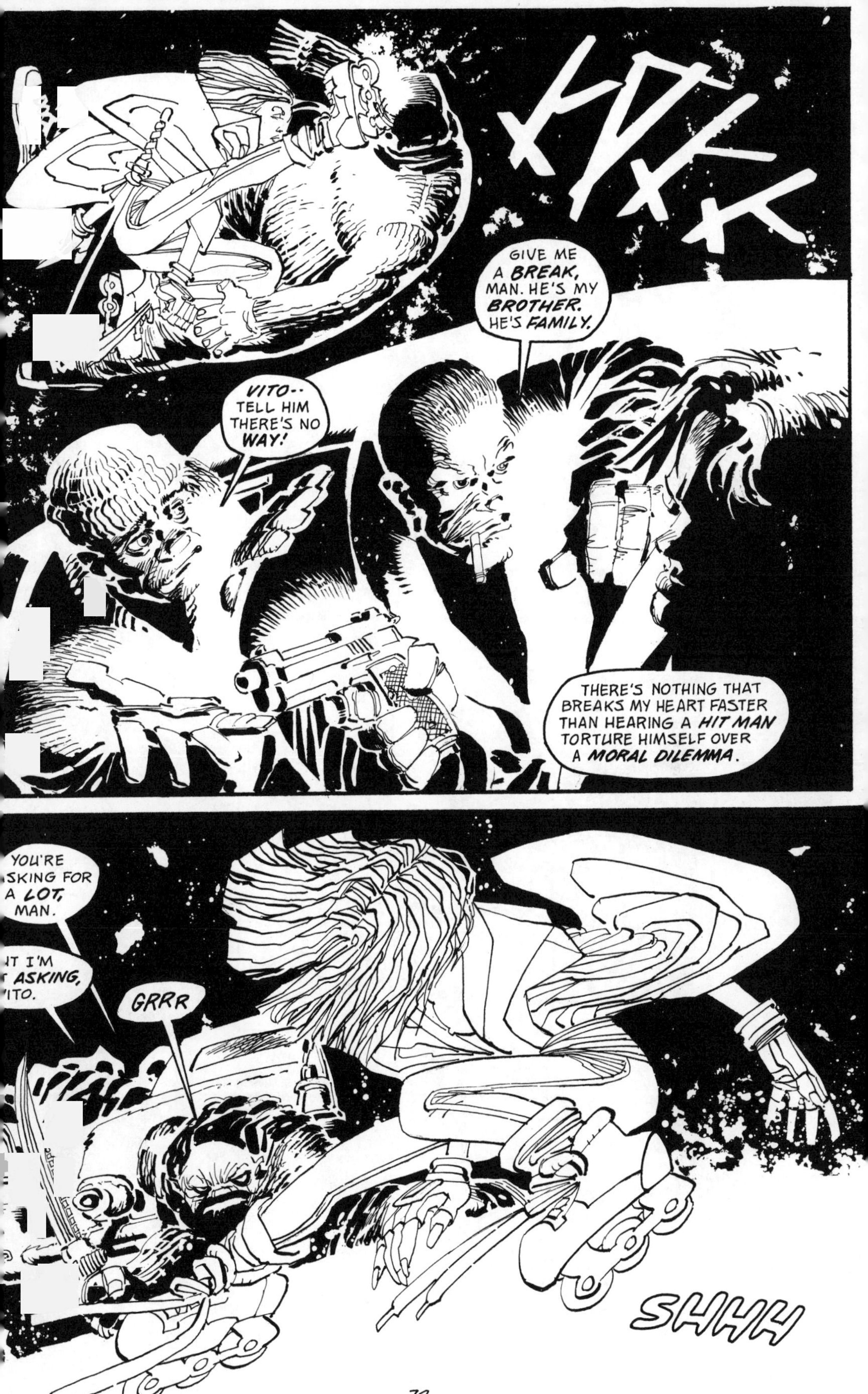
GIVE ME A BREAK, MAN. HE'S MY BROTHER. HE'S FAMILY.
VITO-- TELL HIM THERE'S NO WAY!
THERE'S NOTHING THAT BREAKS MY HEART FASTER THAN HEARING A HIT MAN TORTURE HIMSELF OVER A MORAL DILEMMA.
YOU'RE SKING FOR A LOT, MAN.
T I'M ASKING, ITO.
GRRR
SHHH

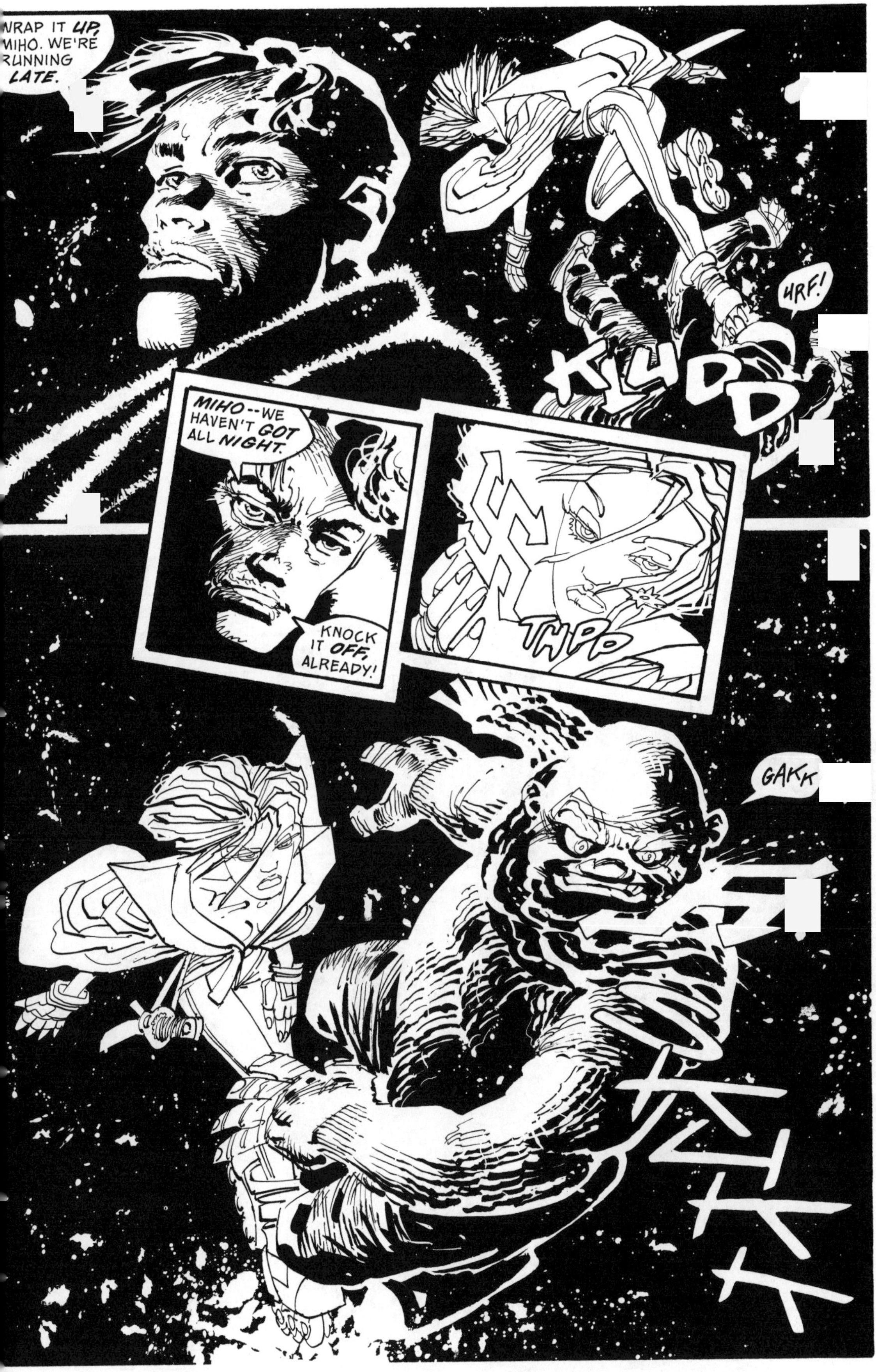
WRAP IT UP, MIHO. WE'RE RUNNING LATE.
URF!
KLUDD
MIHO--WE HAVEN'T GOT ALL NIGHT.
KNOCK IT OFF, ALREADY!
THPP
GAKK

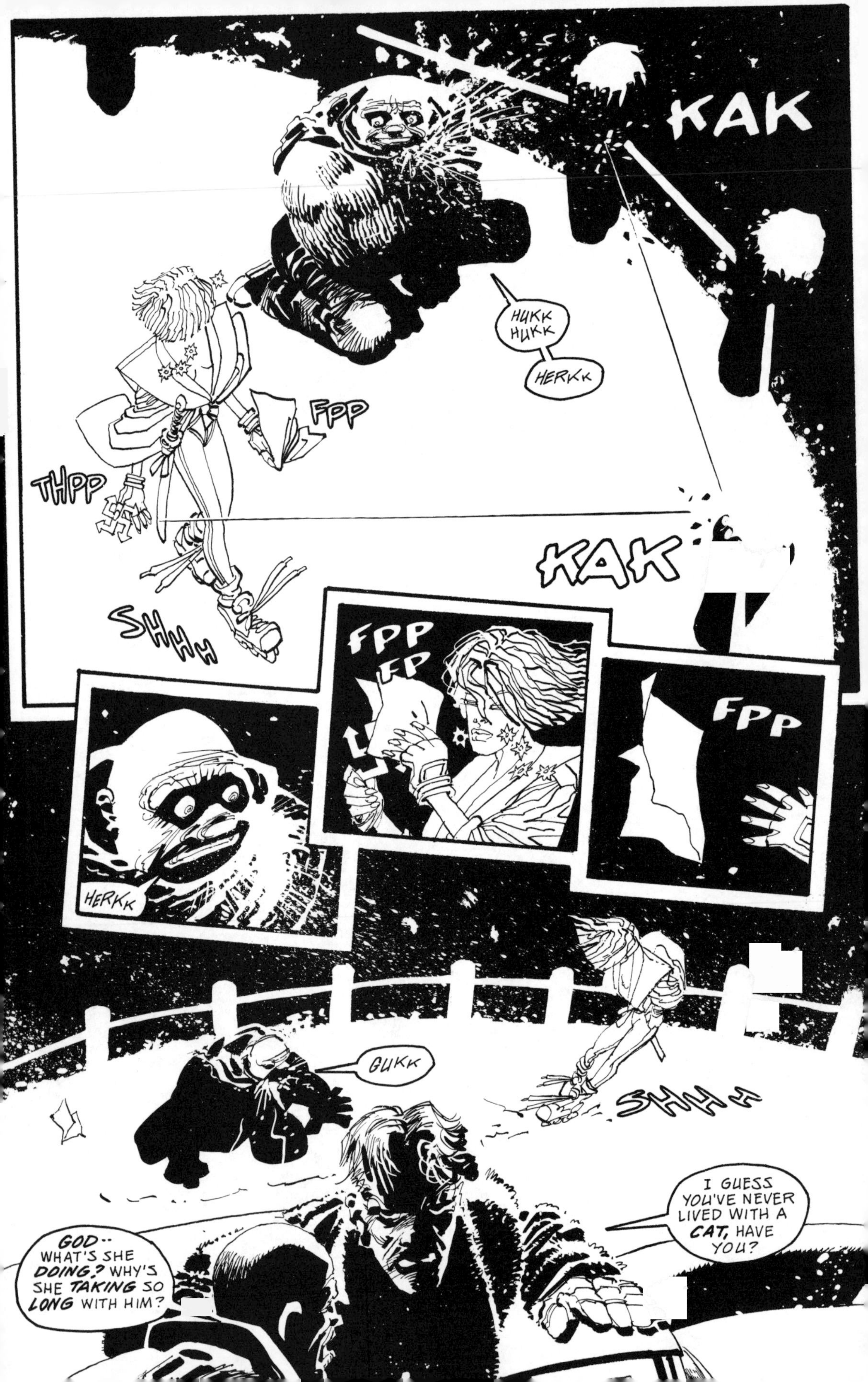
KAK
HUKK HUKK
HERKK
FPP
THPP
KAK
SHHHH
HERKK
FPP FP
FPP
GUKK
SHHHH
GOD -- WHAT'S SHE DOING? WHY'S SHE TAKING SO LONG WITH HIM?
I GUESS YOU'VE NEVER LIVED WITH A CAT, HAVE YOU?

HRNH?

PUNT

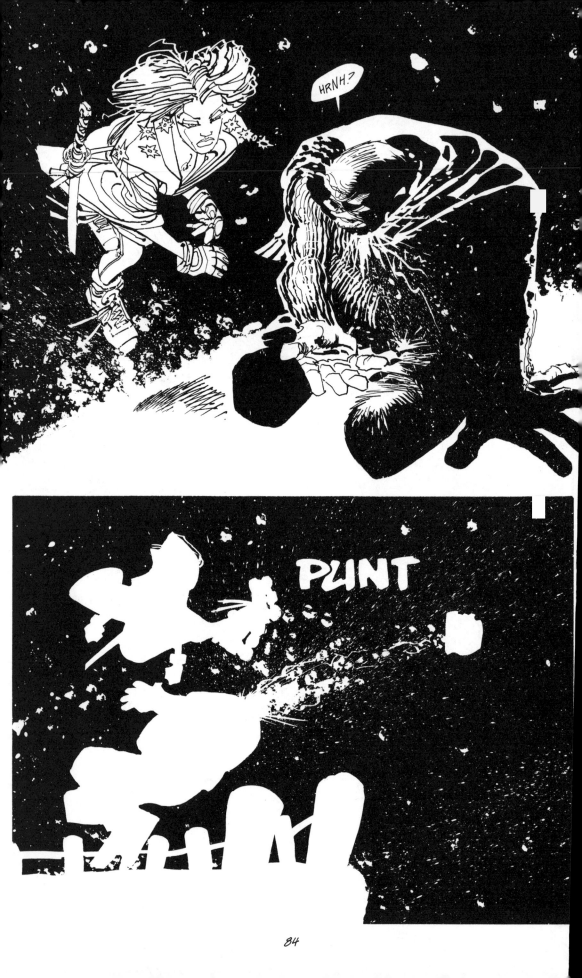

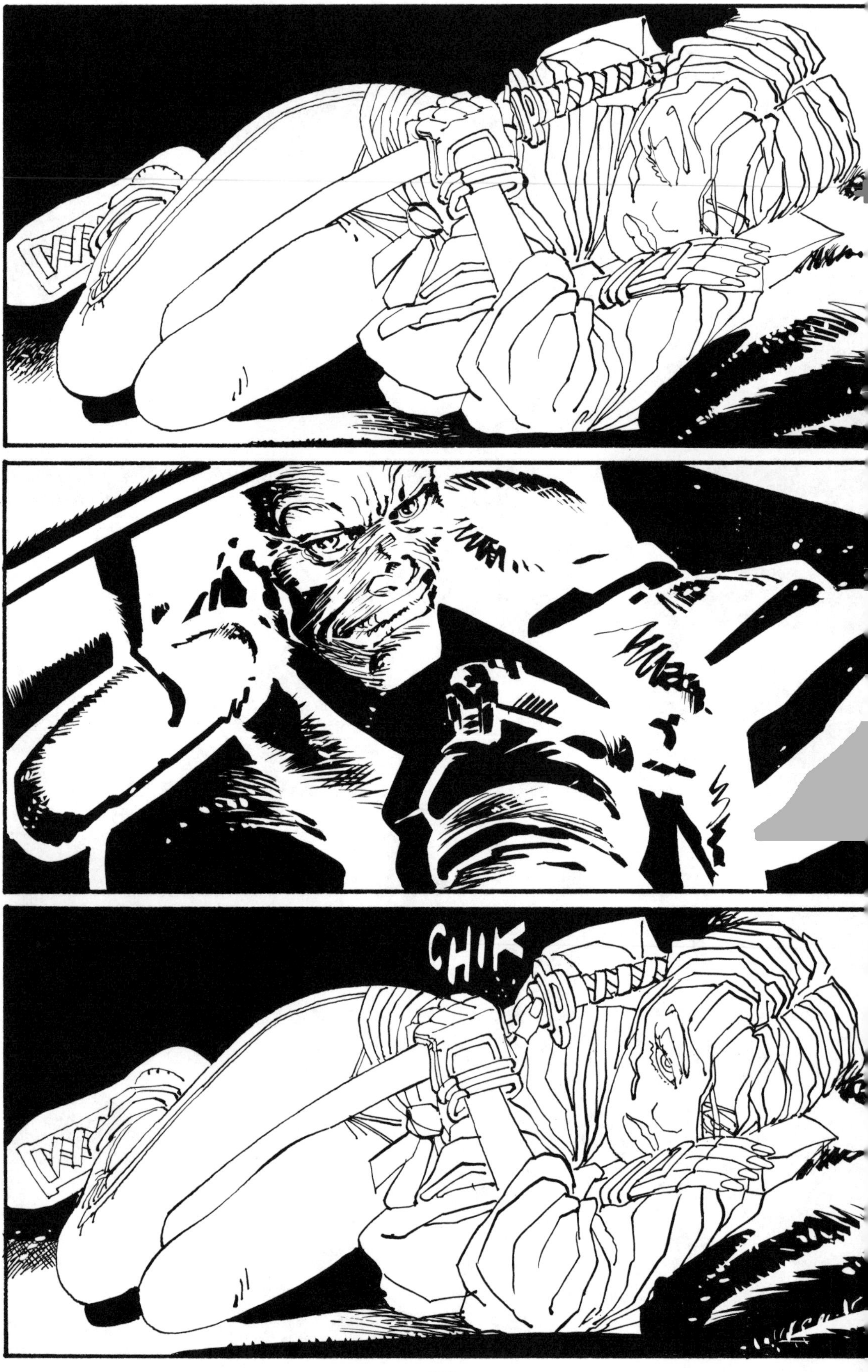
CHIK

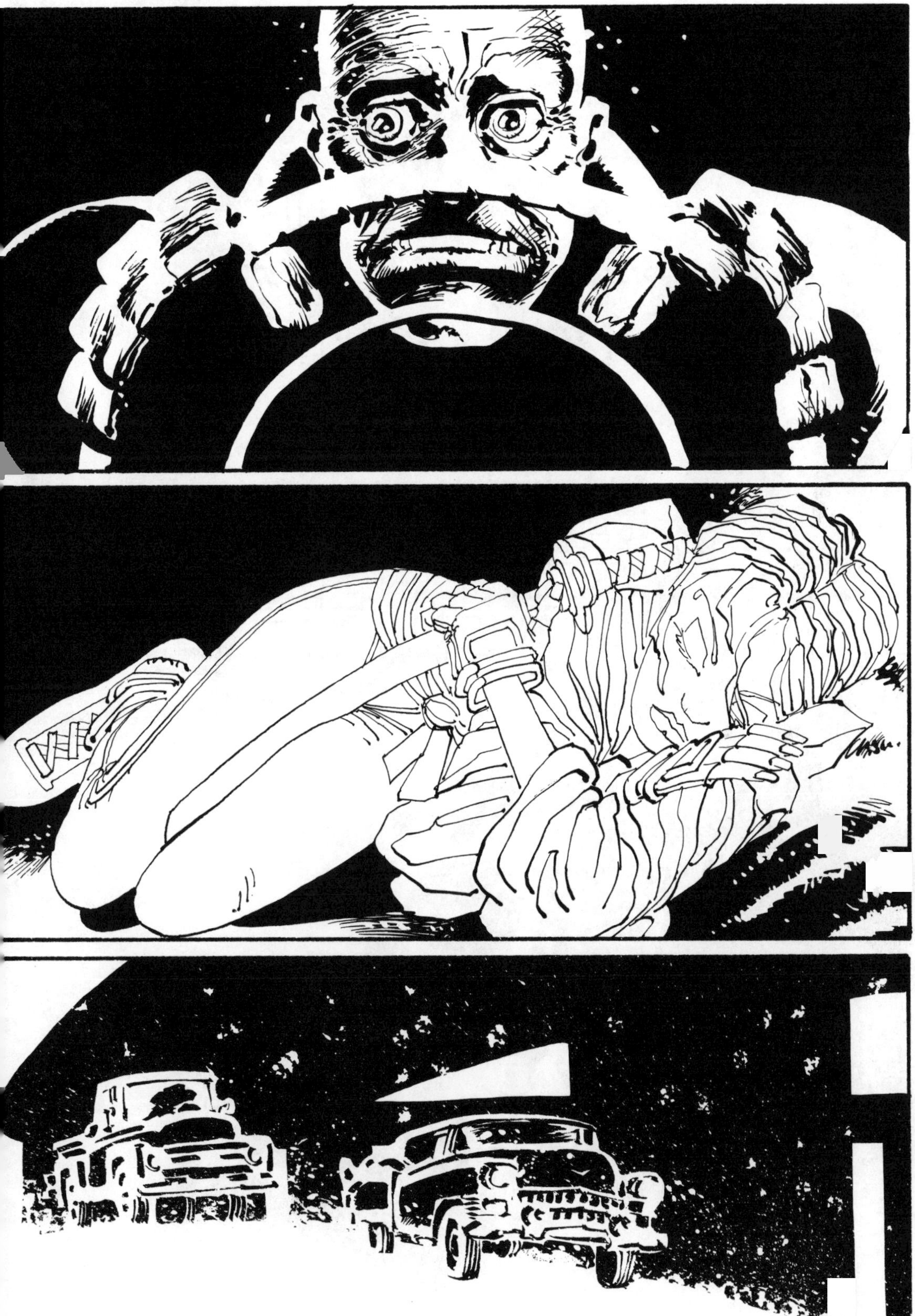

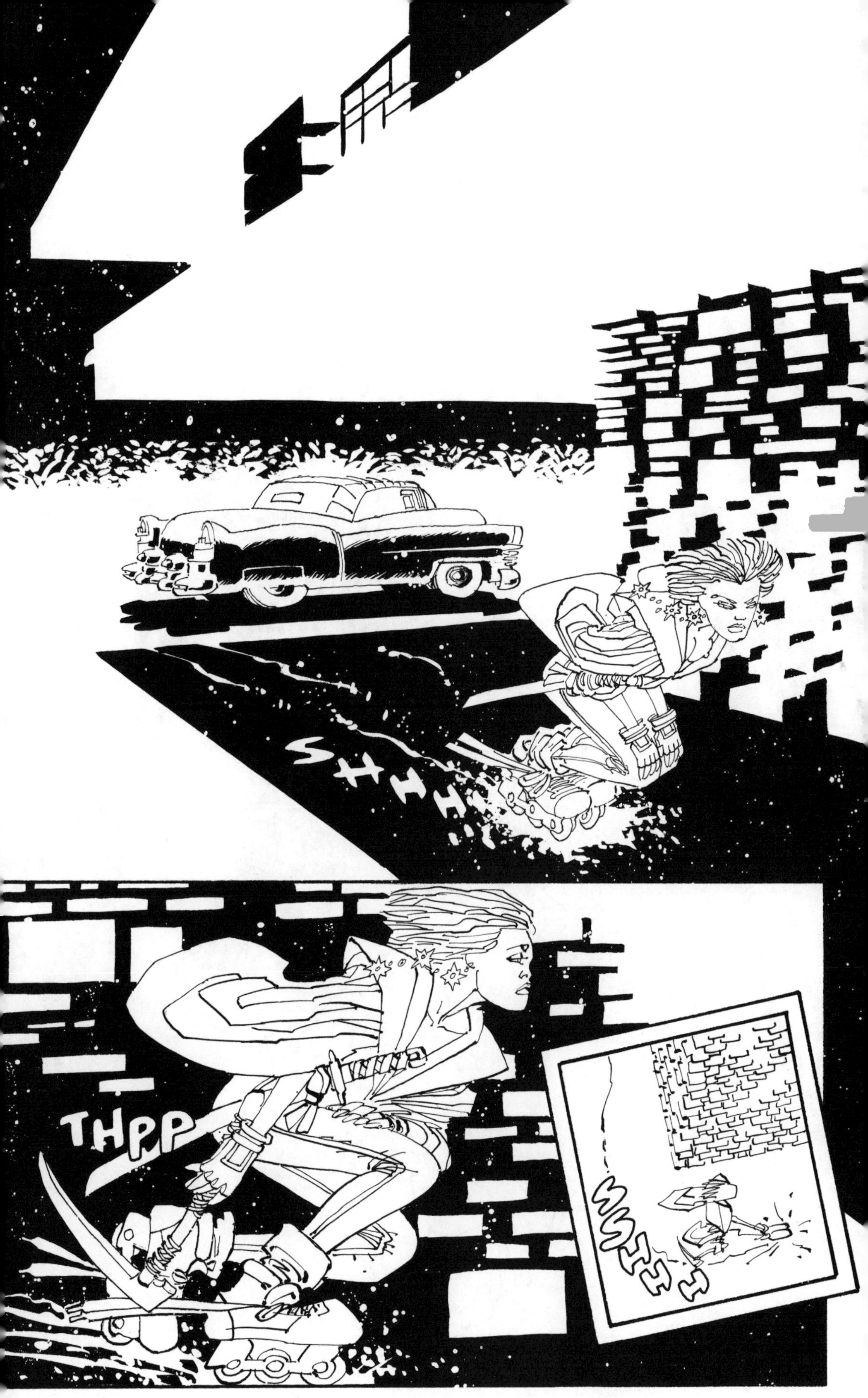
SHHH
THPP

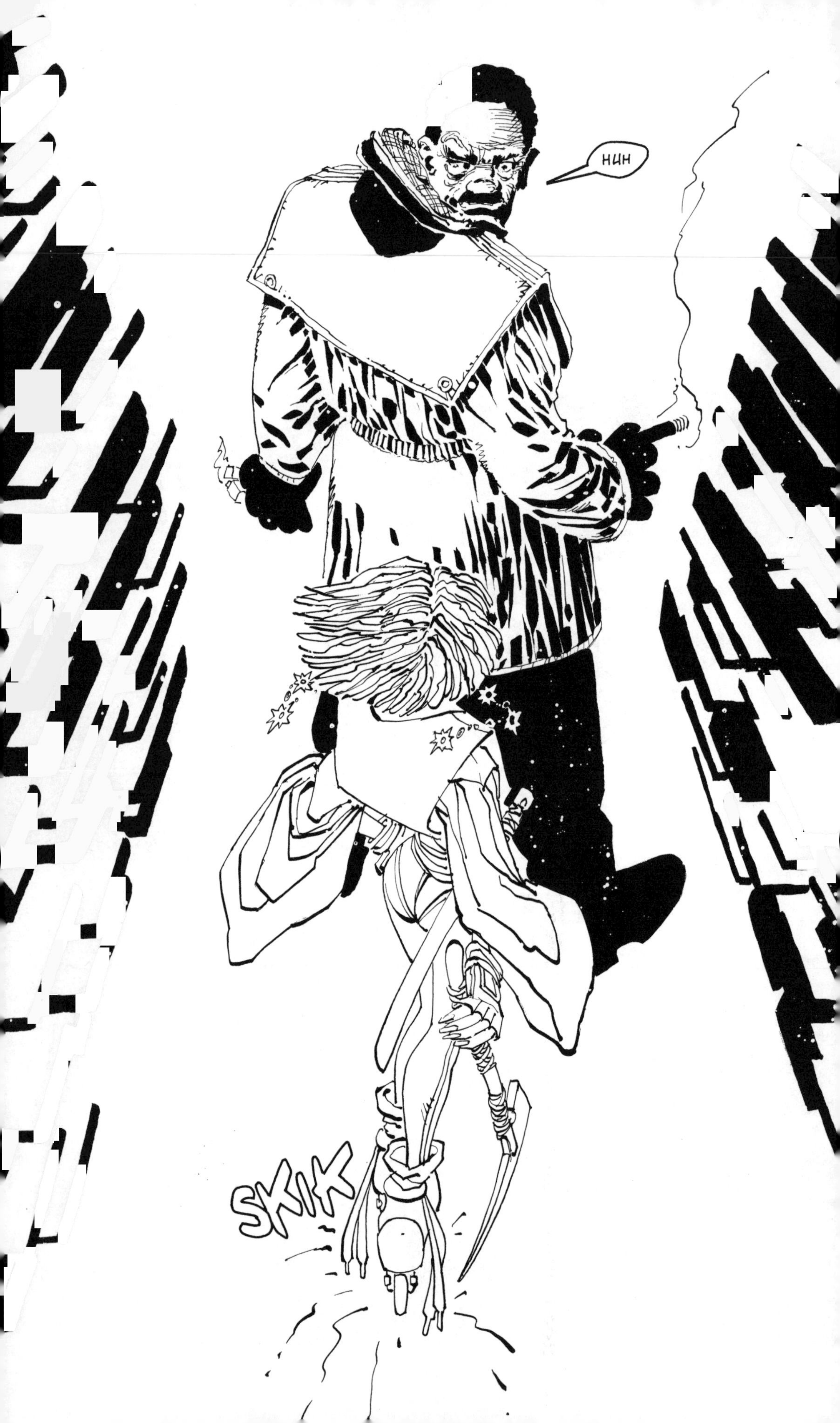
HUH
SKIK

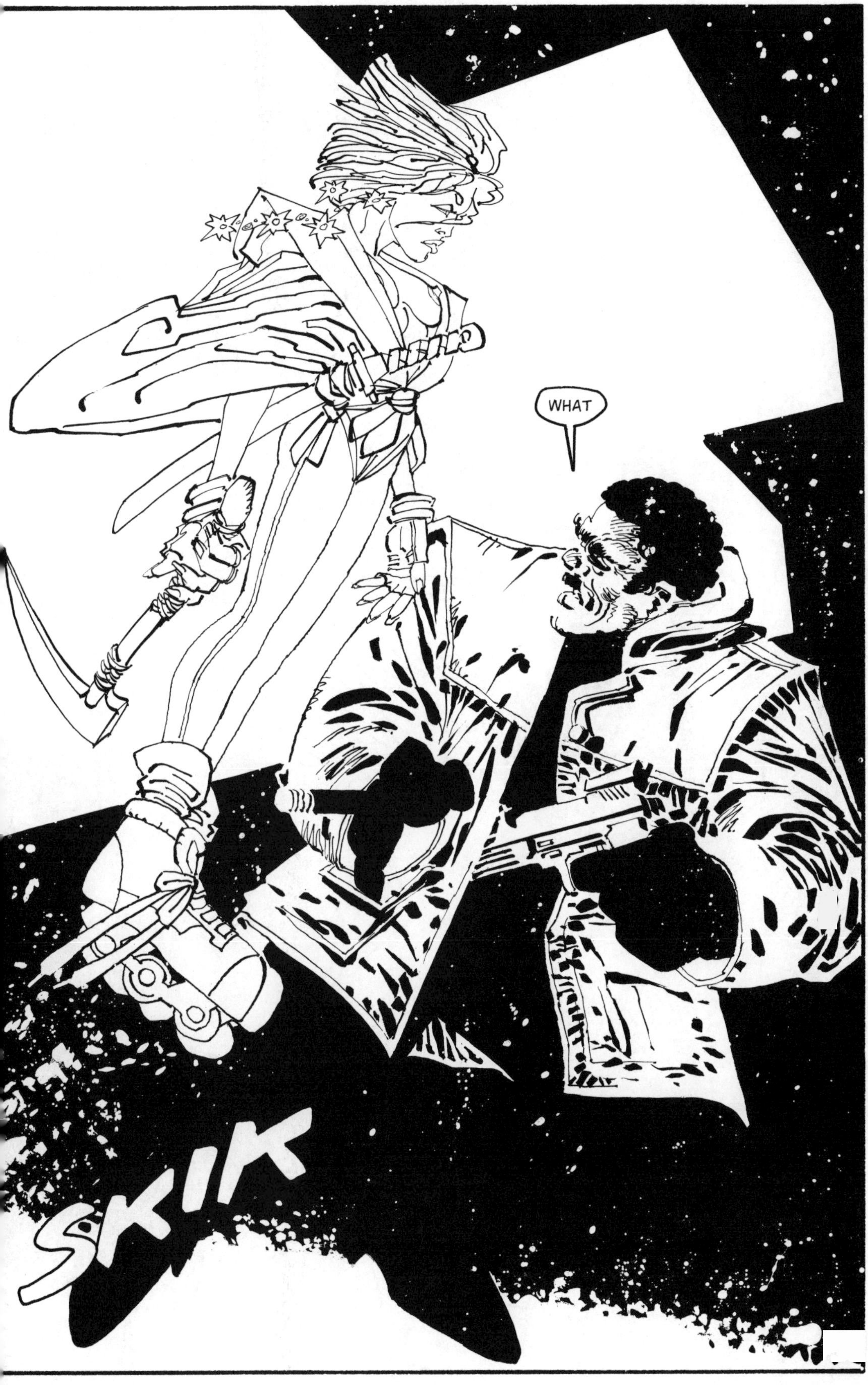
WHAT
SKIK

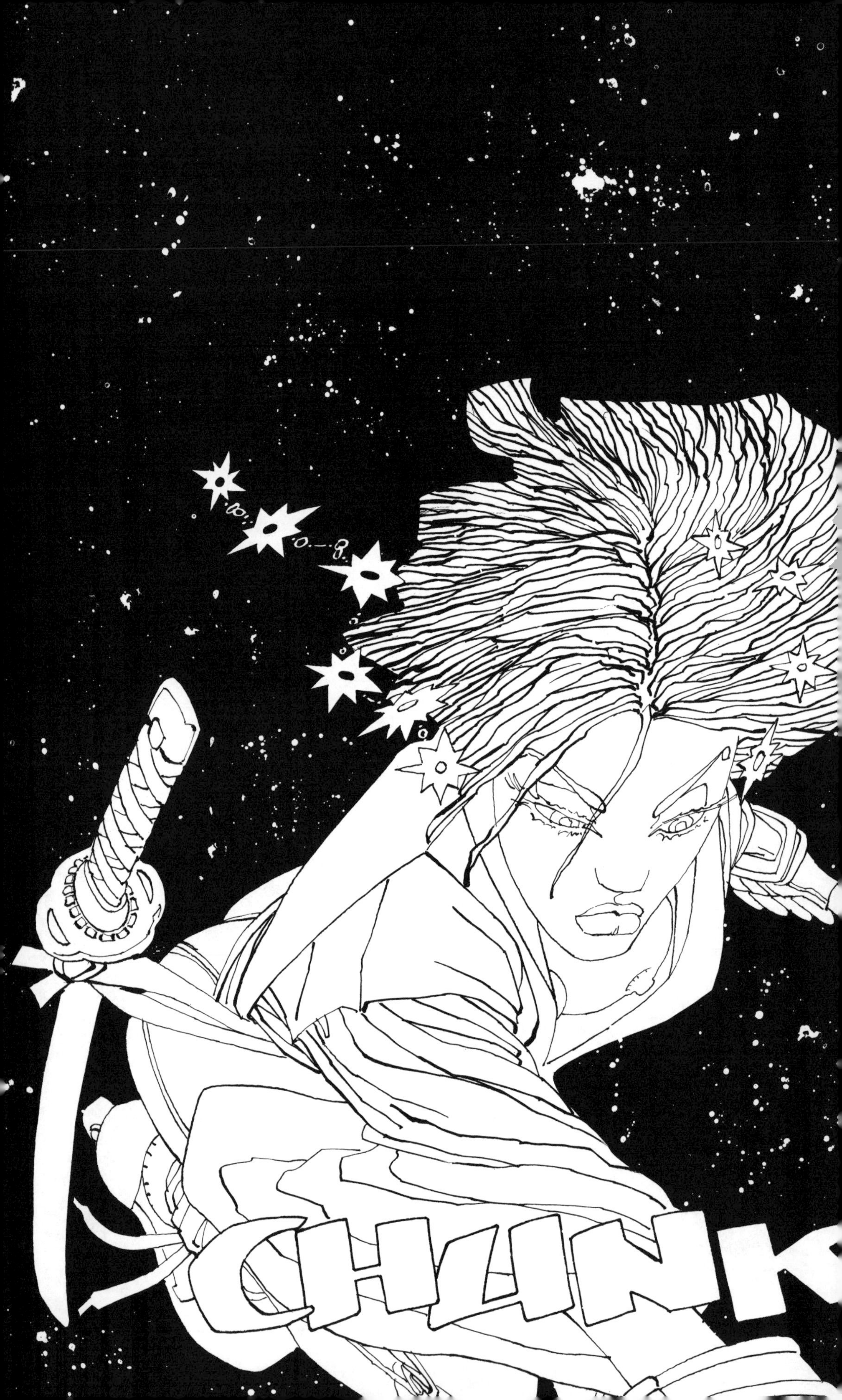
CHUNK

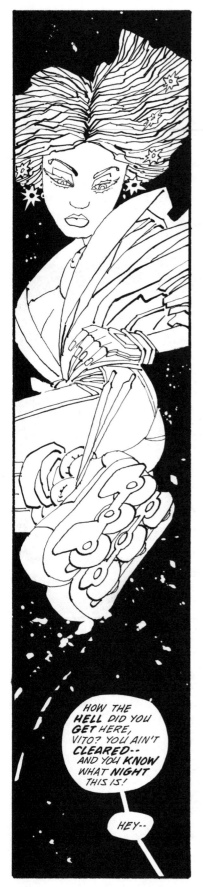

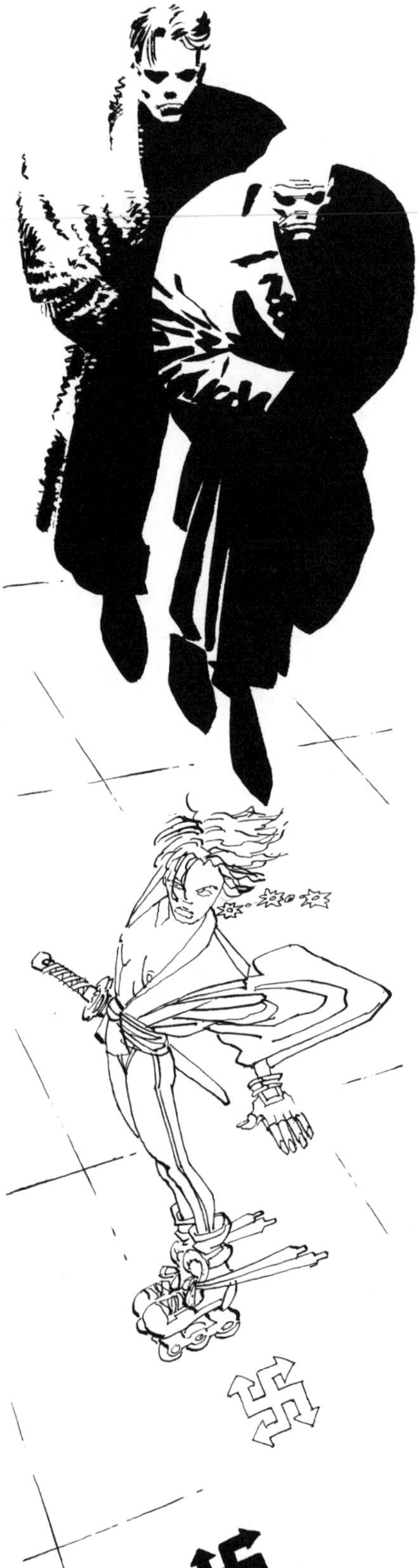

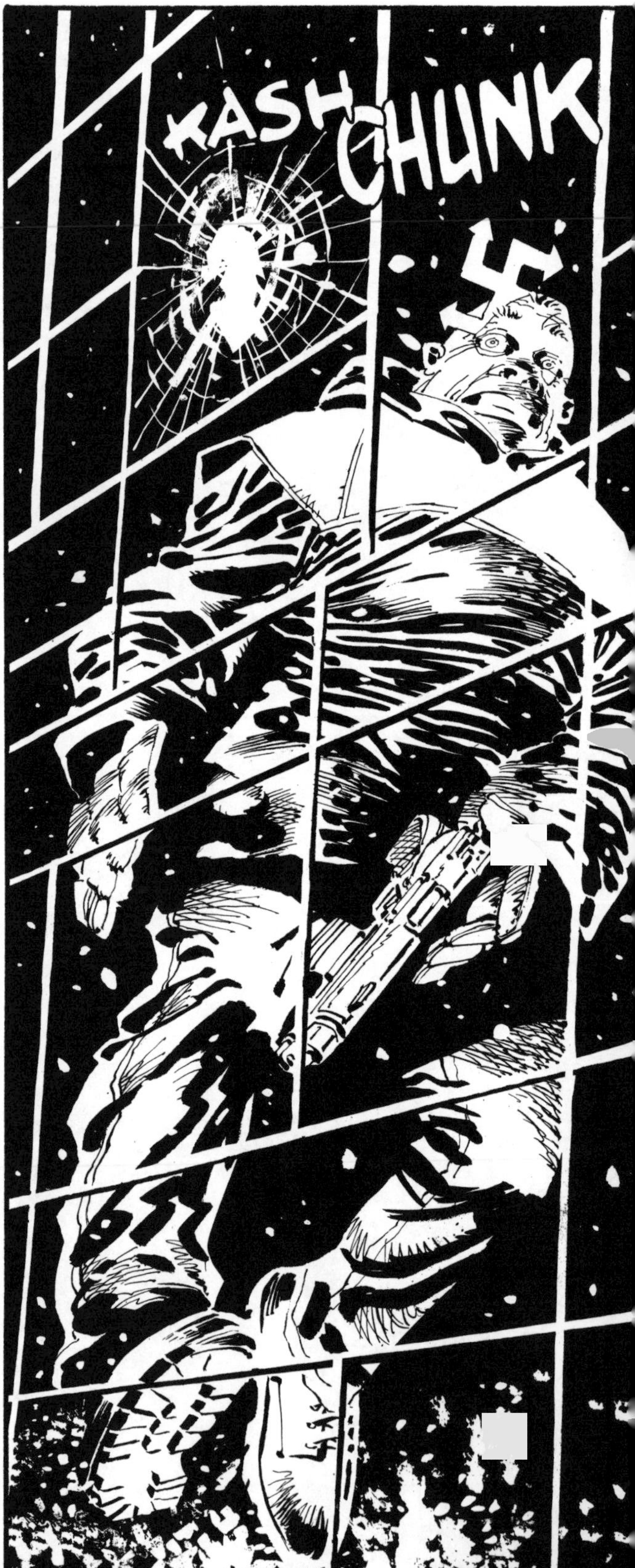
KASH
CHUNK

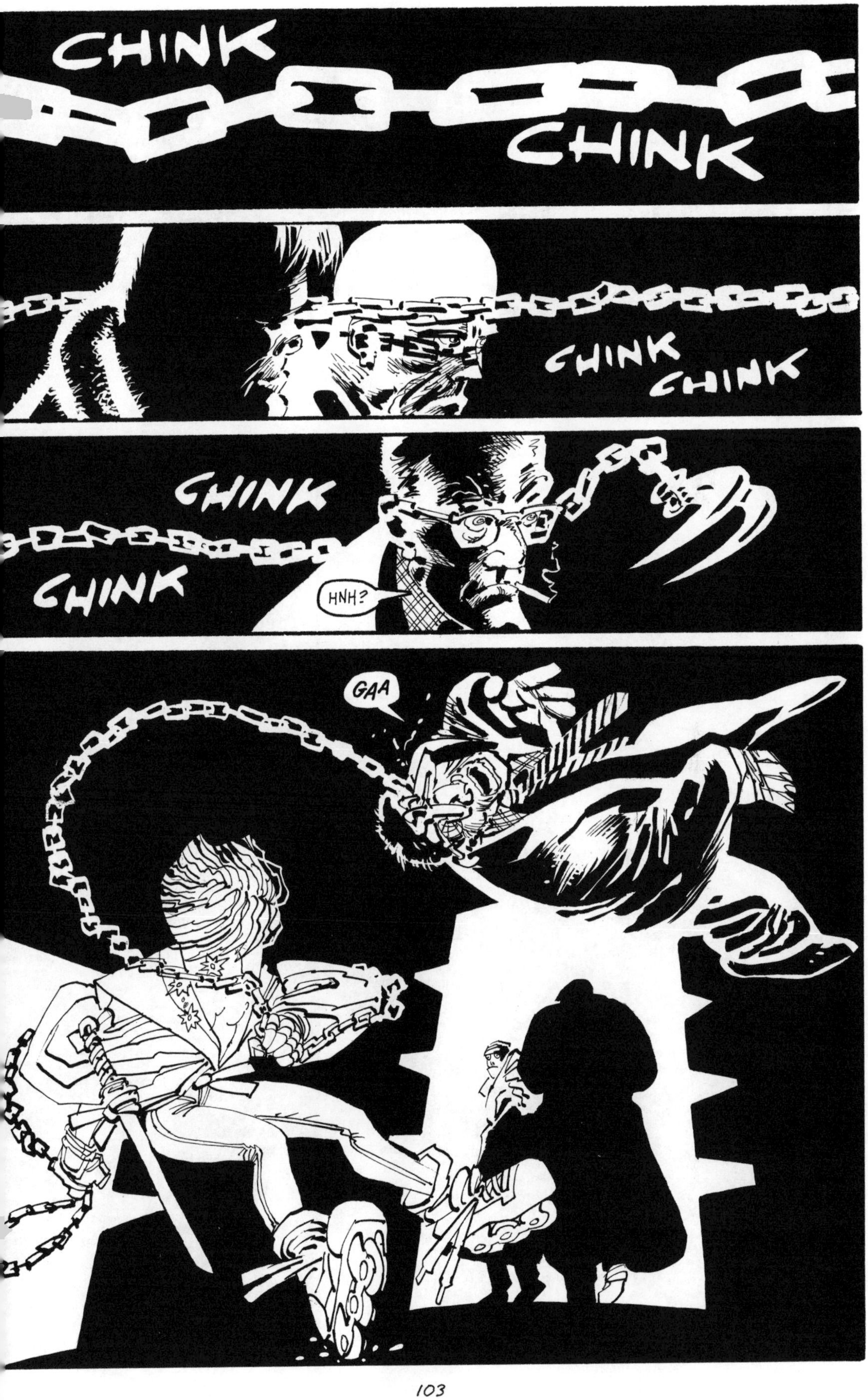

CHINK
CHINK
CHINK
CHINK
CHINK
CHINK
HNH?
GAA

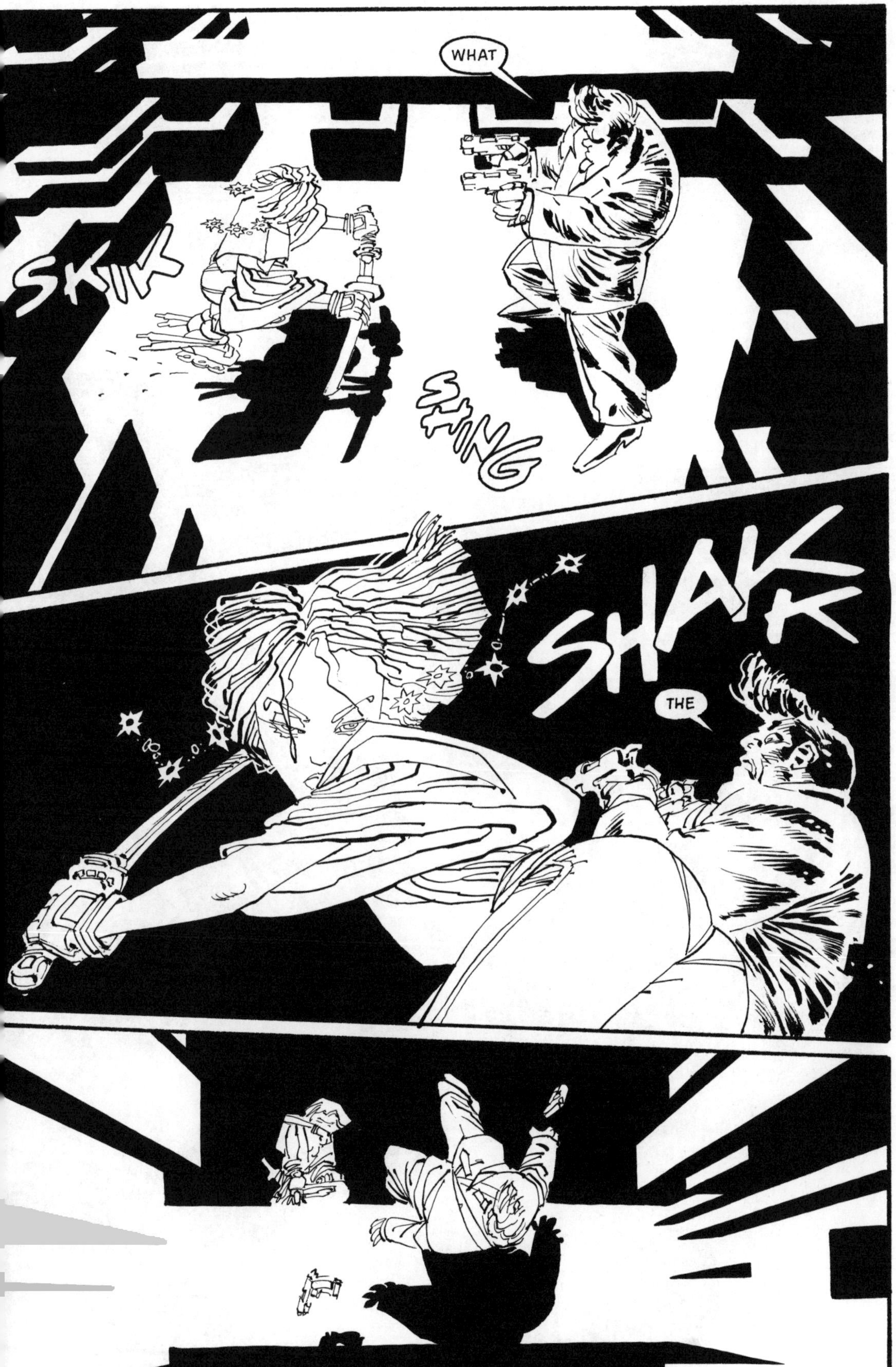
WHAT
SKIK
SHING
SHAK
THE

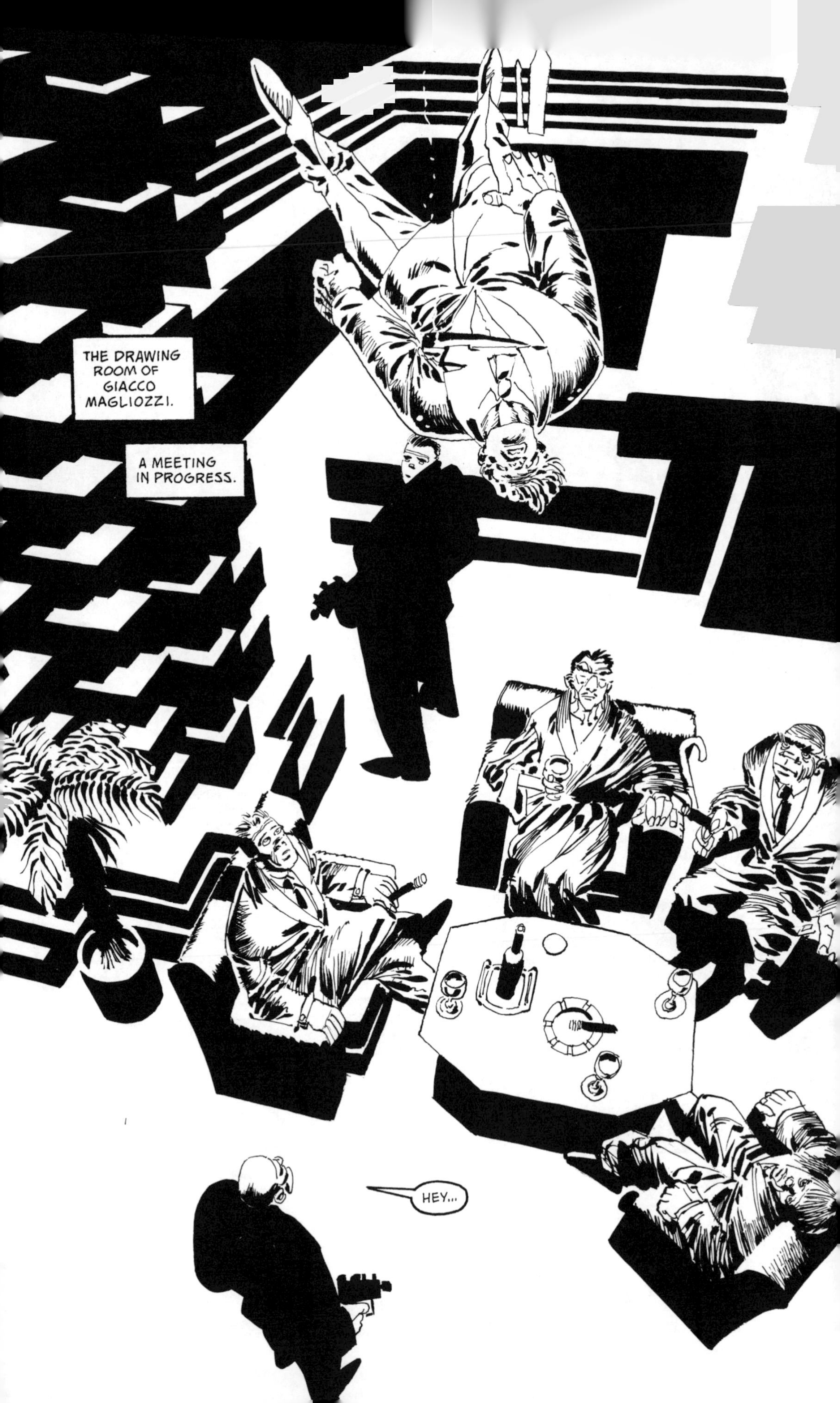
THE DRAWING ROOM OF GIACCO MAGLIOZZI.
A MEETING IN PROGRESS.
HEY...

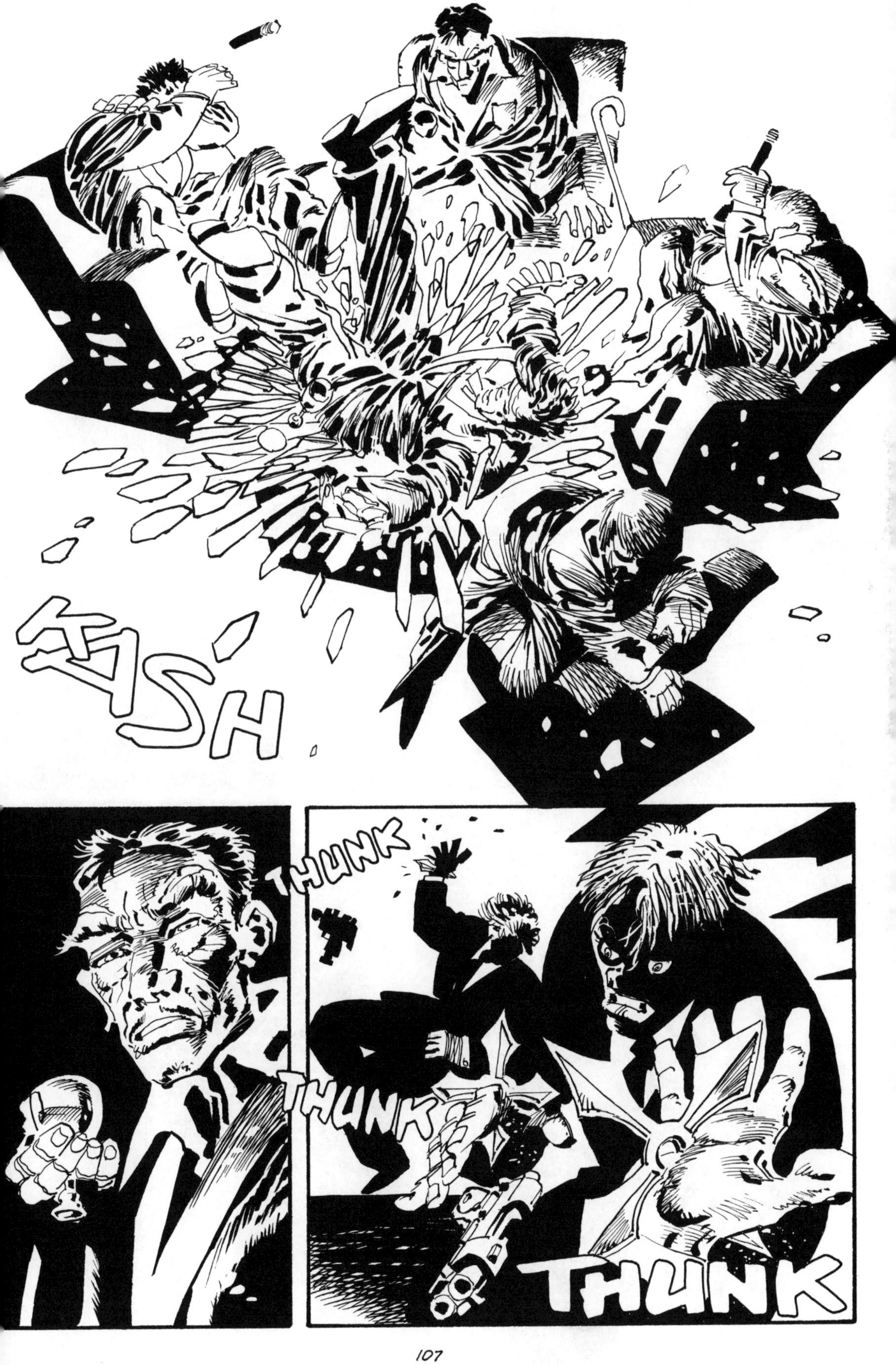
KASH
THUNK
THUNK
THUNK

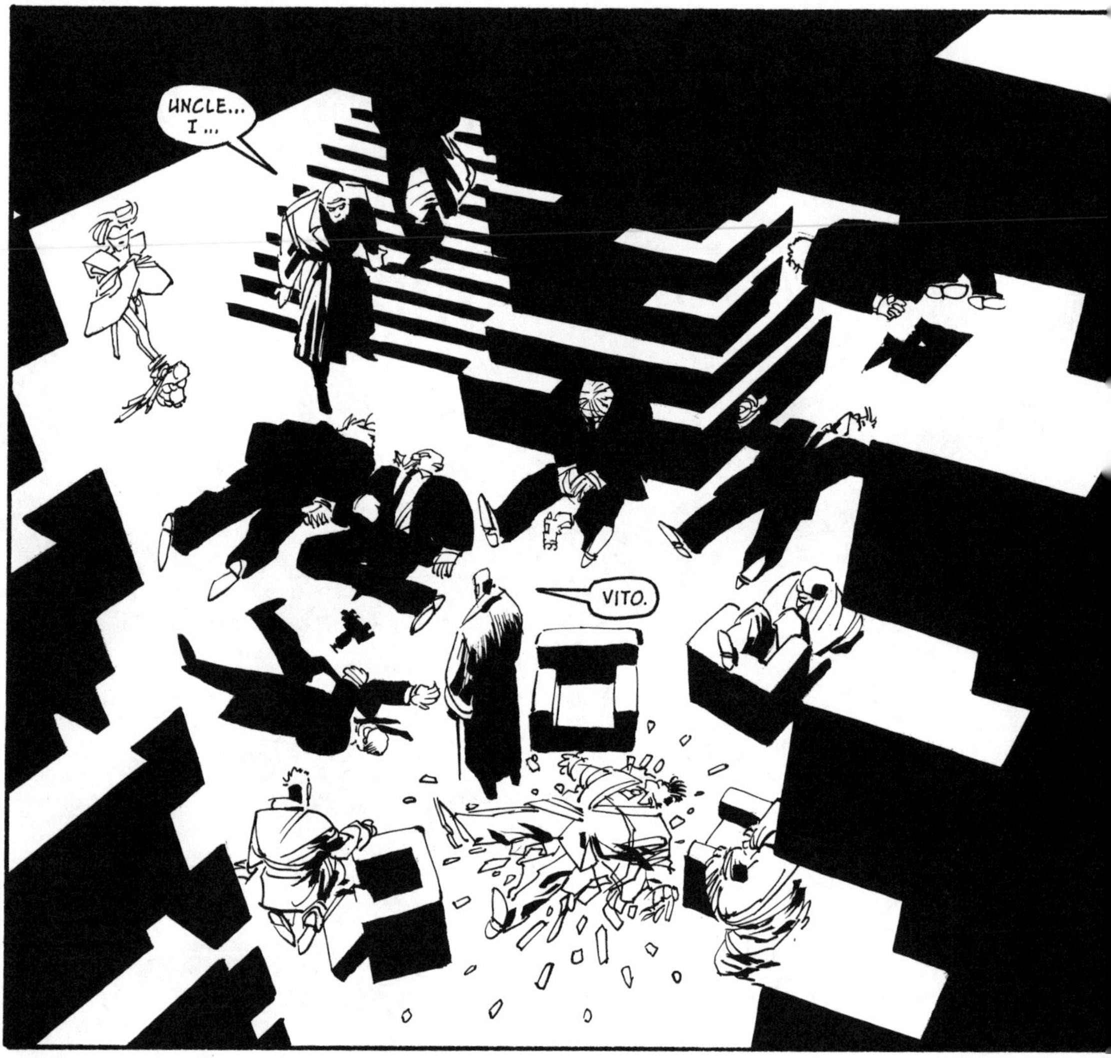
UNCLE... I...
VITO.

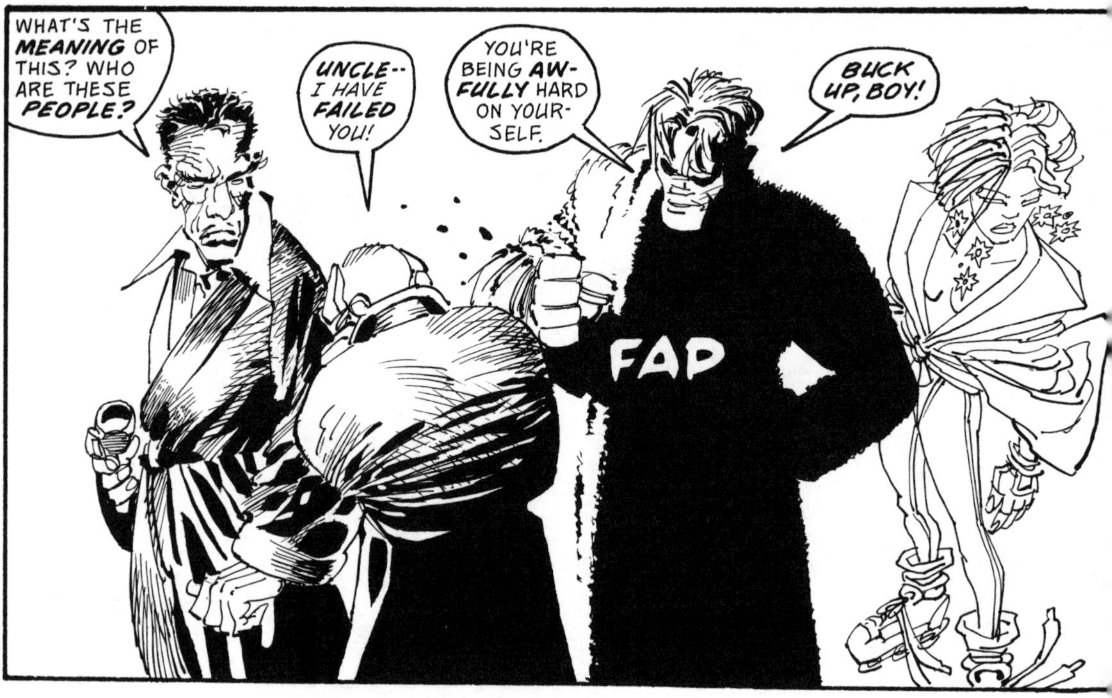
WHAT'S THE **MEANING** OF THIS? WHO ARE THESE **PEOPLE?**
*UNCLE-- I HAVE **FAILED** YOU!*
YOU'RE BEING **AW-FULLY** HARD ON YOUR-SELF.
BUCK UP, BOY!
FAP

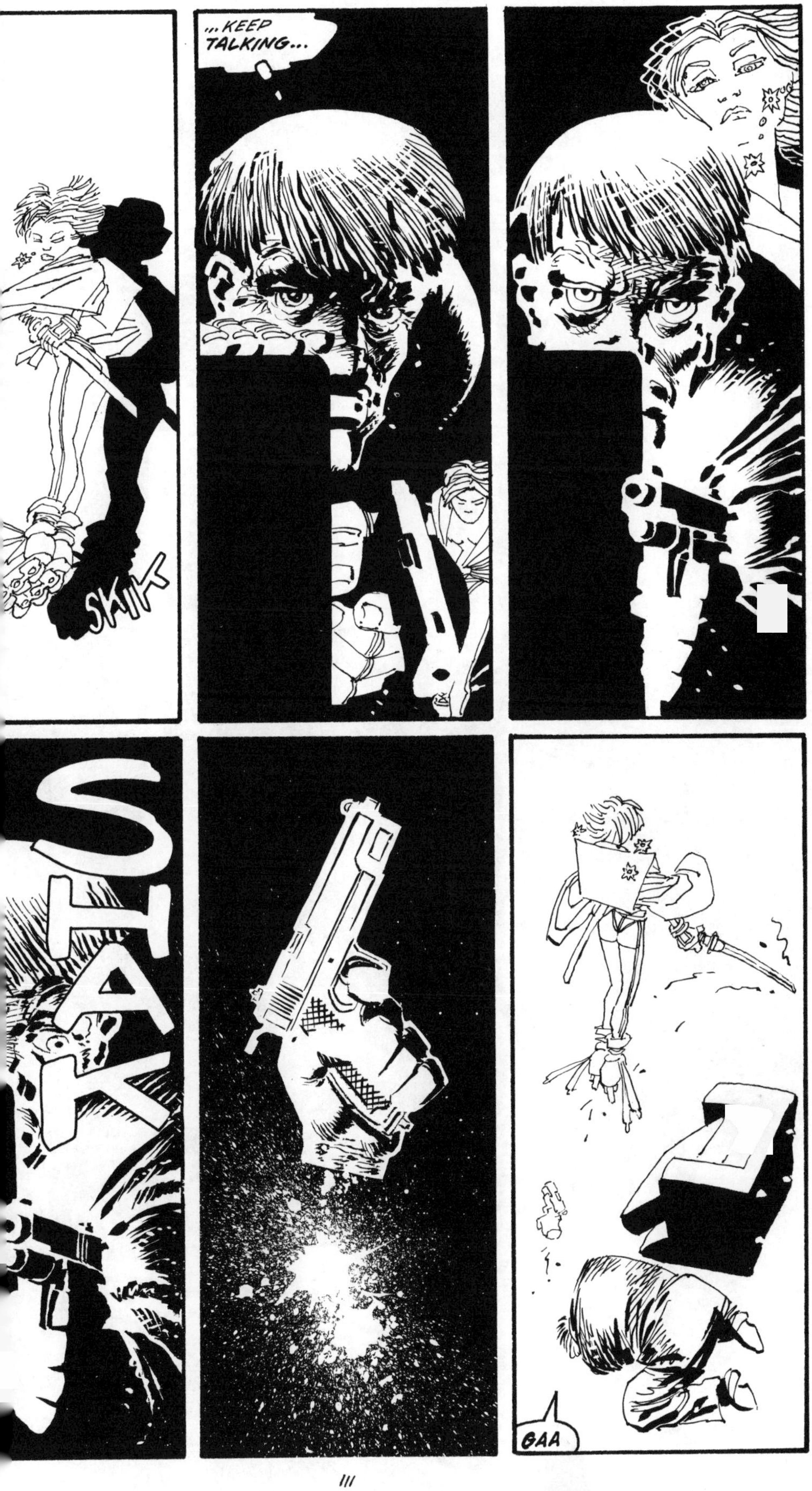
SKITT
...KEEP TALKING...
S
H
A
K
GAA

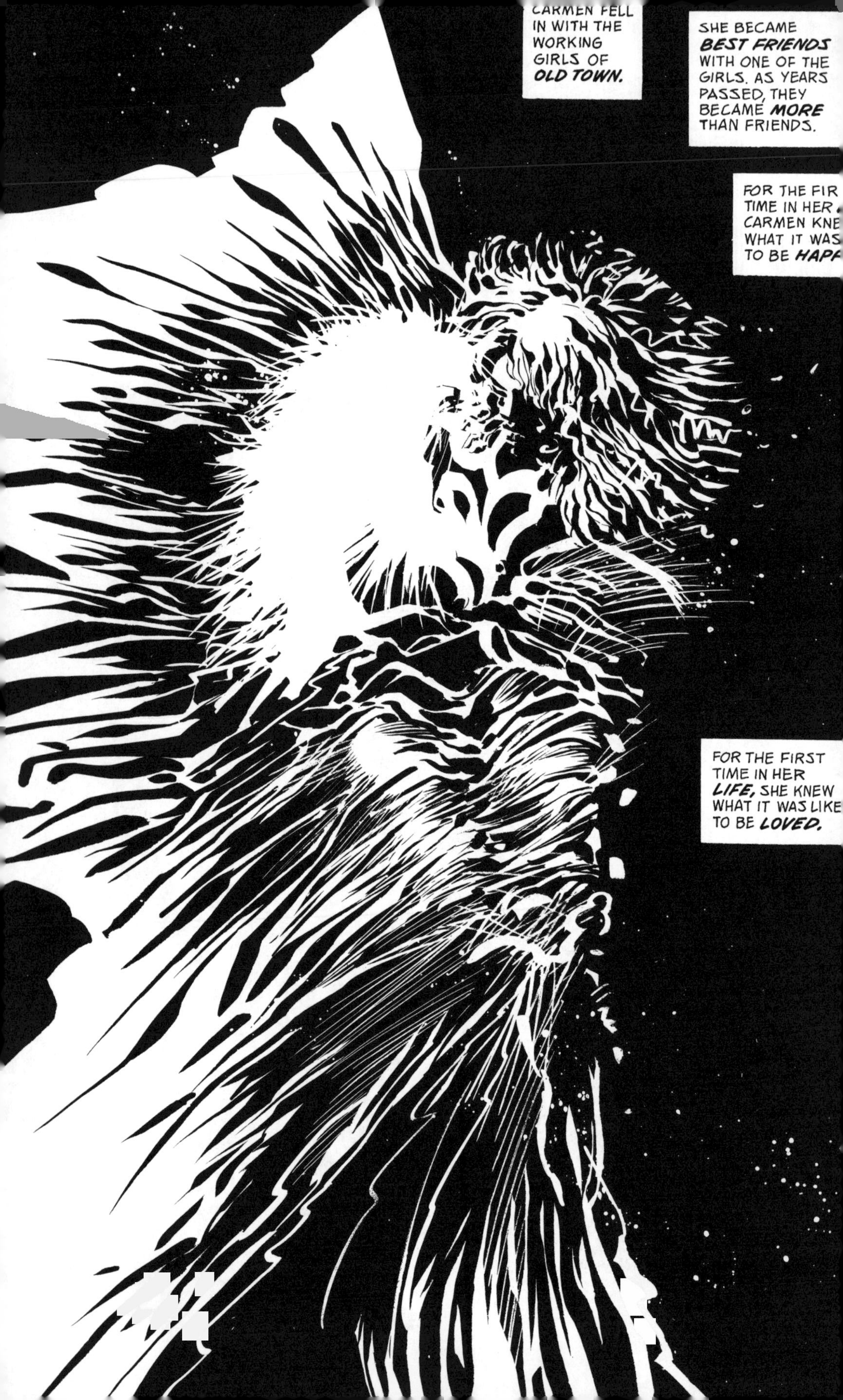
CARMEN FELL IN WITH THE WORKING GIRLS OF OLD TOWN.
SHE BECAME BEST FRIENDS WITH ONE OF THE GIRLS. AS YEARS PASSED, THEY BECAME MORE THAN FRIENDS.
FOR THE FIR TIME IN HER CARMEN KNE WHAT IT WAS TO BE HAPP
FOR THE FIRST TIME IN HER LIFE, SHE KNEW WHAT IT WAS LIKE TO BE LOVED.

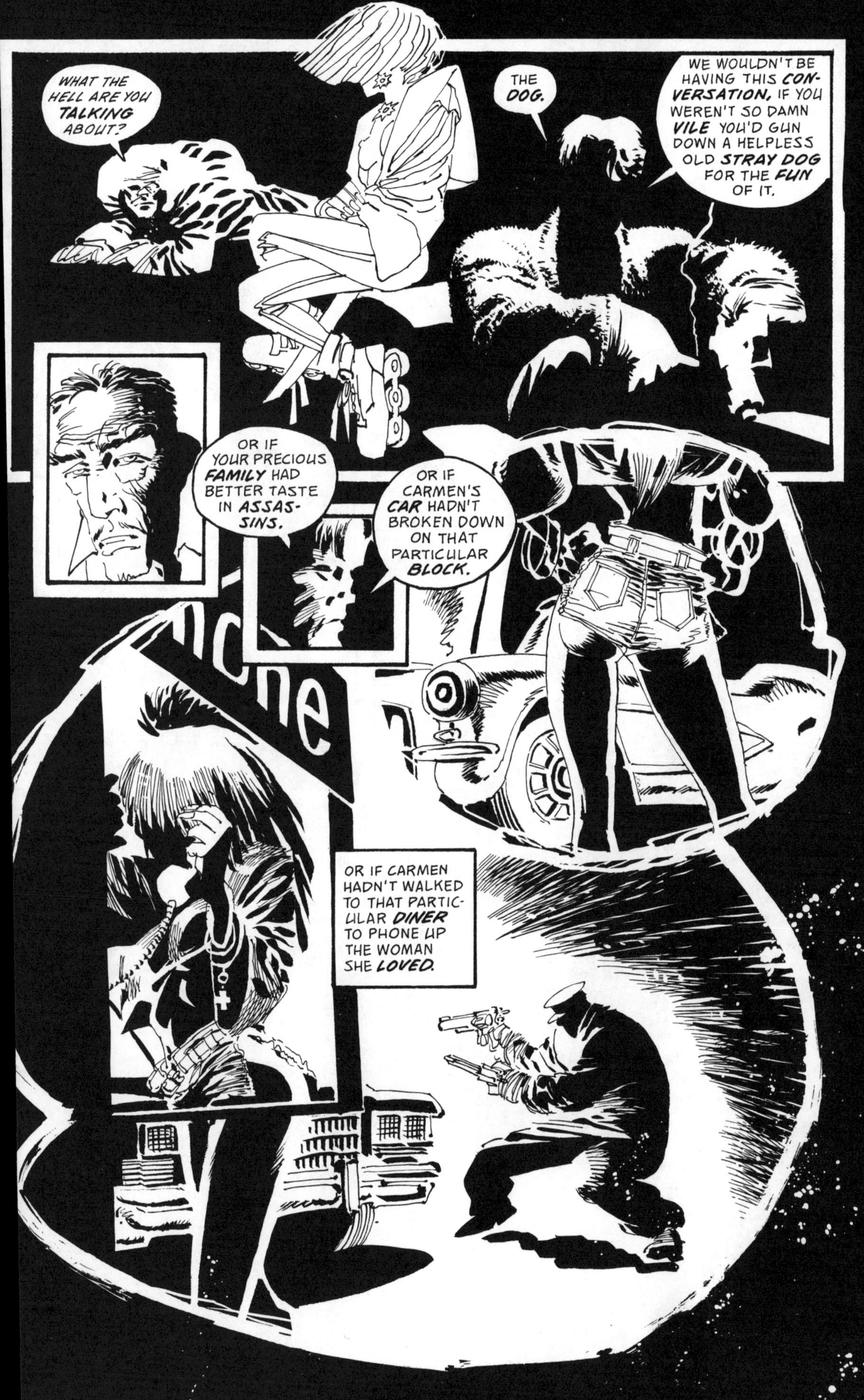

WHAT THE HELL ARE YOU TALKING ABOUT?
THE DOG.
WE WOULDN'T BE HAVING THIS CONVERSATION, IF YOU WEREN'T SO DAMN VILE YOU'D GUN DOWN A HELPLESS OLD STRAY DOG FOR THE FUN OF IT.
OR IF YOUR PRECIOUS FAMILY HAD BETTER TASTE IN ASSAS-SINS.
OR IF CARMEN'S CAR HADN'T BROKEN DOWN ON THAT PARTICULAR BLOCK.
OR IF CARMEN HADN'T WALKED TO THAT PARTIC-ULAR DINER TO PHONE UP THE WOMAN SHE LOVED.

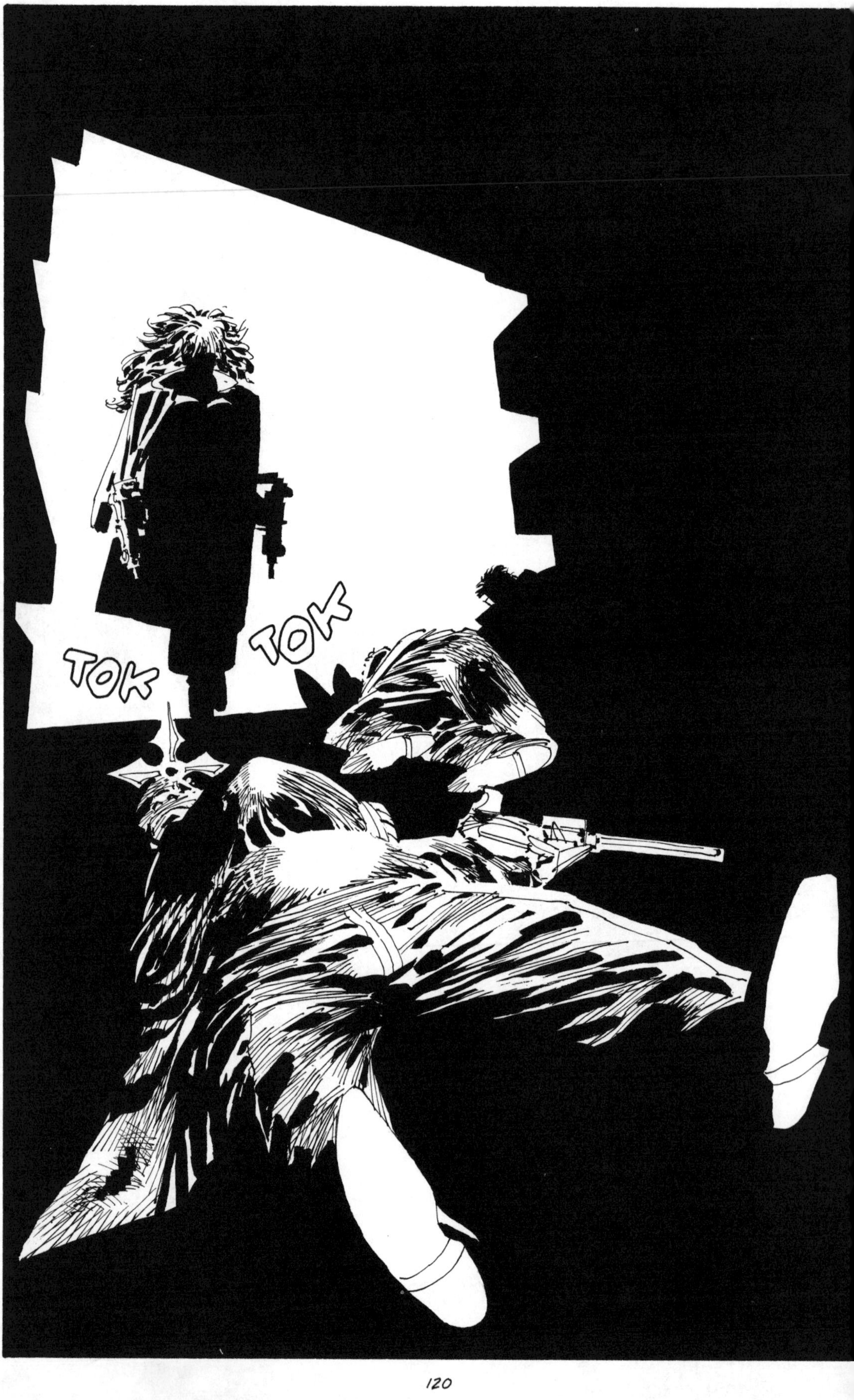
TOK
TOK

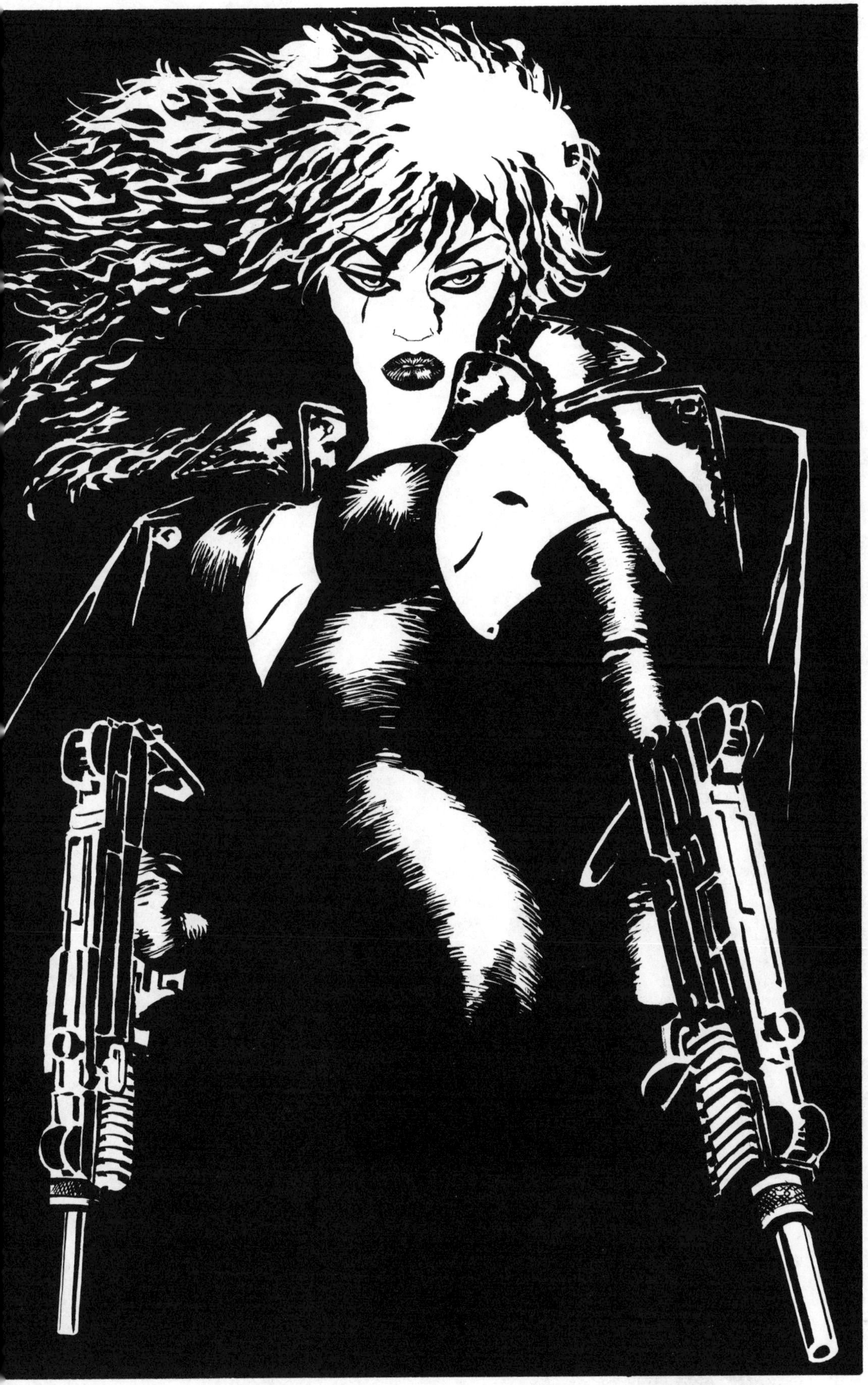

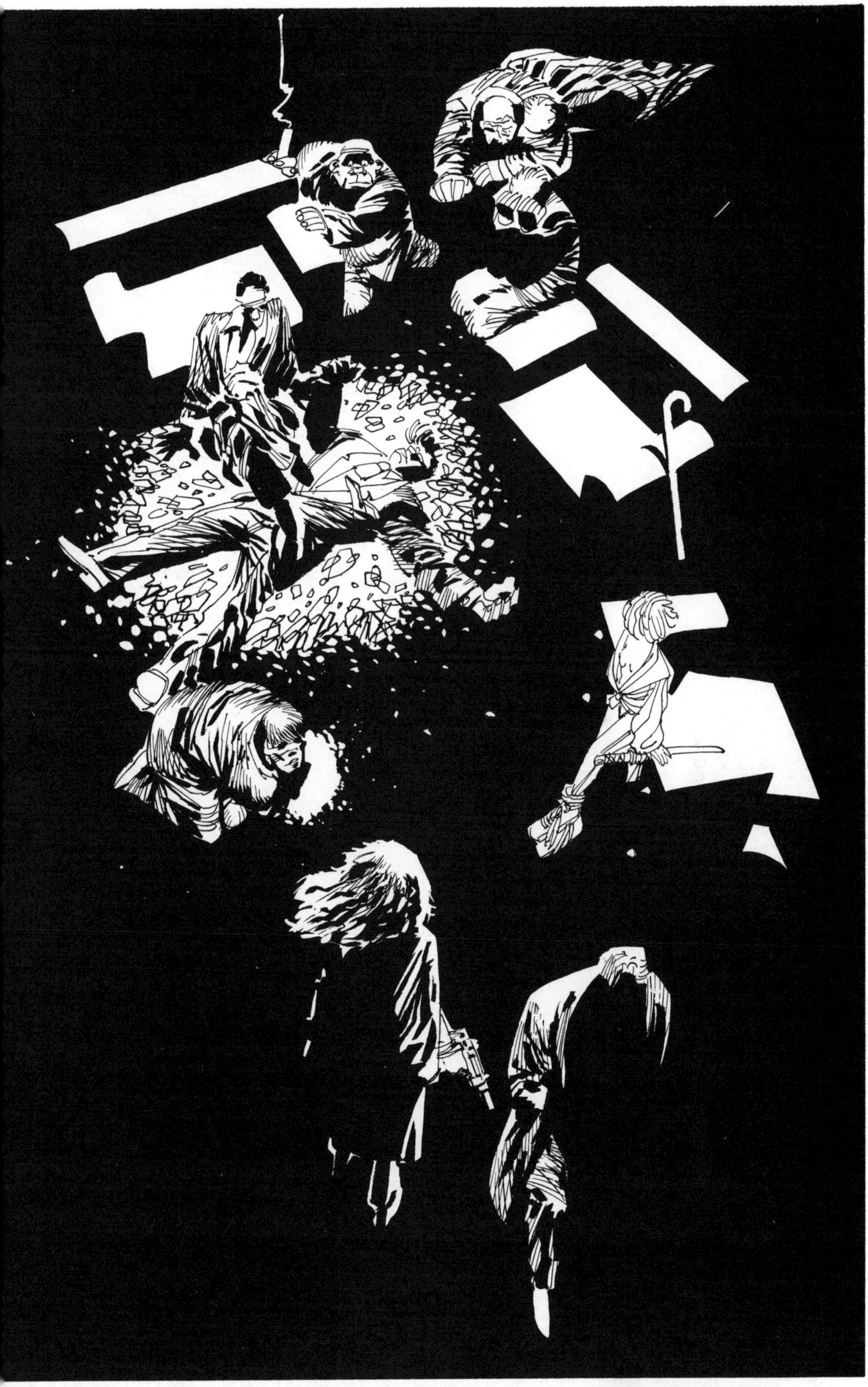

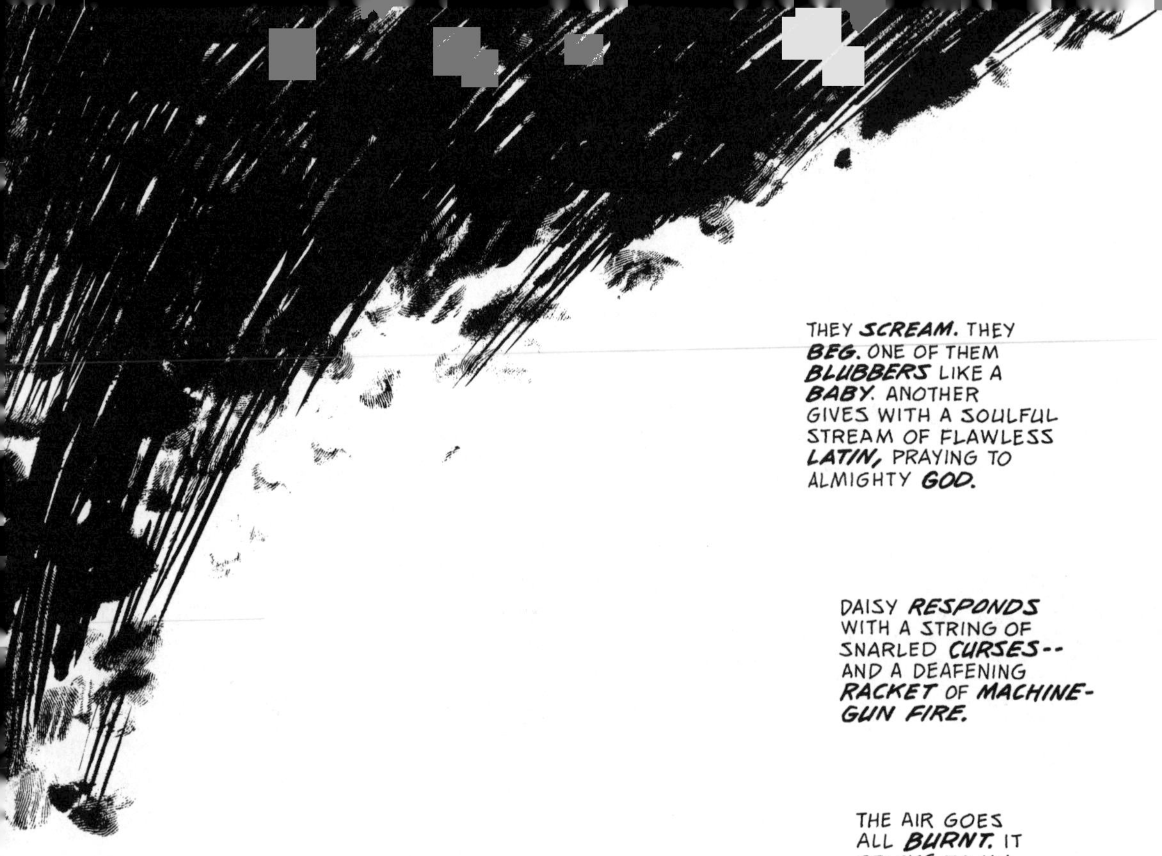
THEY SCREAM. THEY BEG. ONE OF THEM BLUBBERS LIKE A BABY. ANOTHER GIVES WITH A SOULFUL STREAM OF FLAWLESS LATIN, PRAYING TO ALMIGHTY GOD.
DAISY RESPONDS WITH A STRING OF SNARLED CURSES-- AND A DEAFENING RACKET OF MACHINE-GUN FIRE.
THE AIR GOES ALL BURNT. IT STICKS TO MY TONGUE.
AT LEAST I DON'T HAVE TO WATCH.

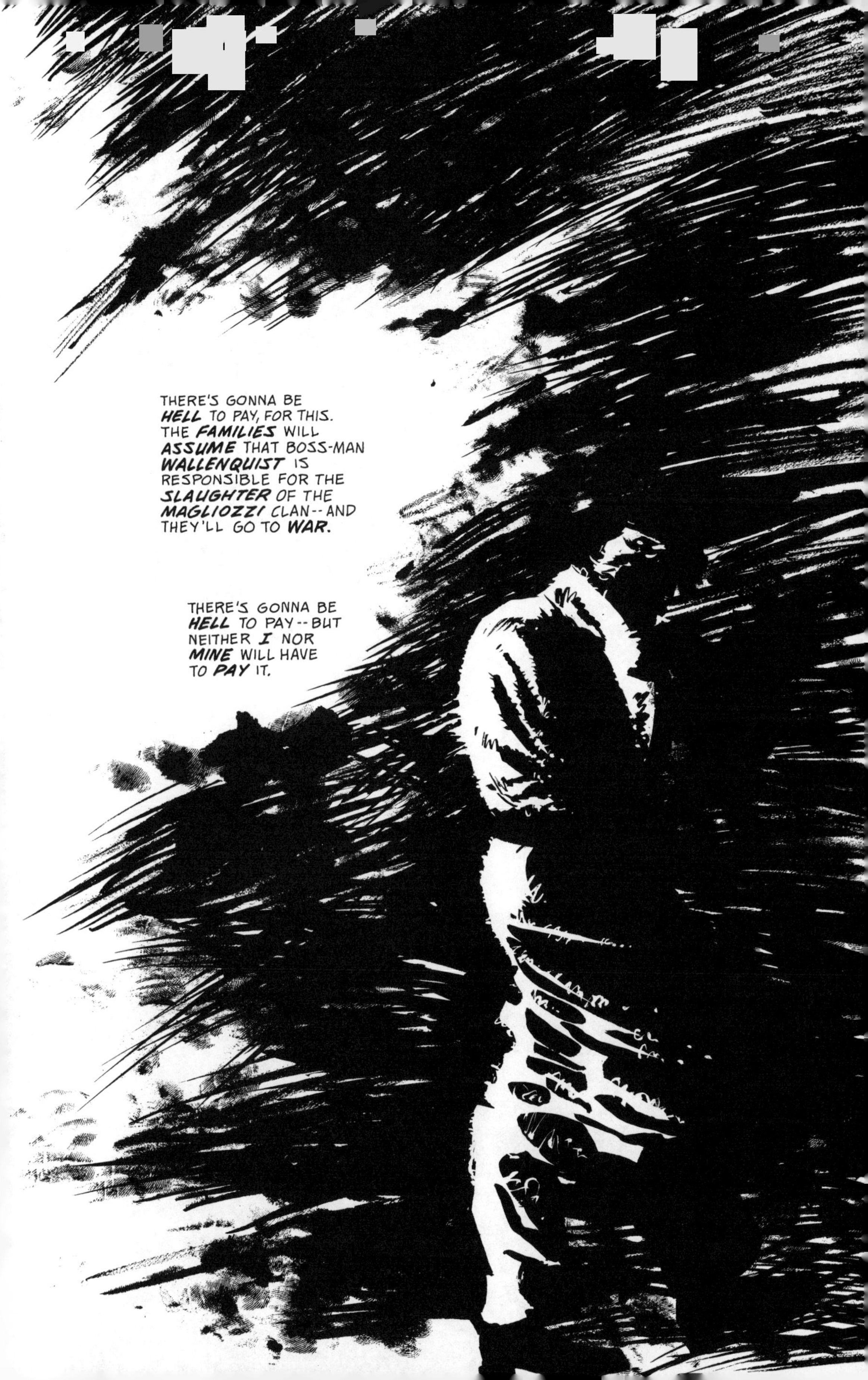
THERE'S GONNA BE HELL TO PAY, FOR THIS. THE FAMILIES WILL ASSUME THAT BOSS-MAN WALLENQUIST IS RESPONSIBLE FOR THE SLAUGHTER OF THE MAGLIOZZI CLAN--AND THEY'LL GO TO WAR.
THERE'S GONNA BE HELL TO PAY--BUT NEITHER I NOR MINE WILL HAVE TO PAY IT.

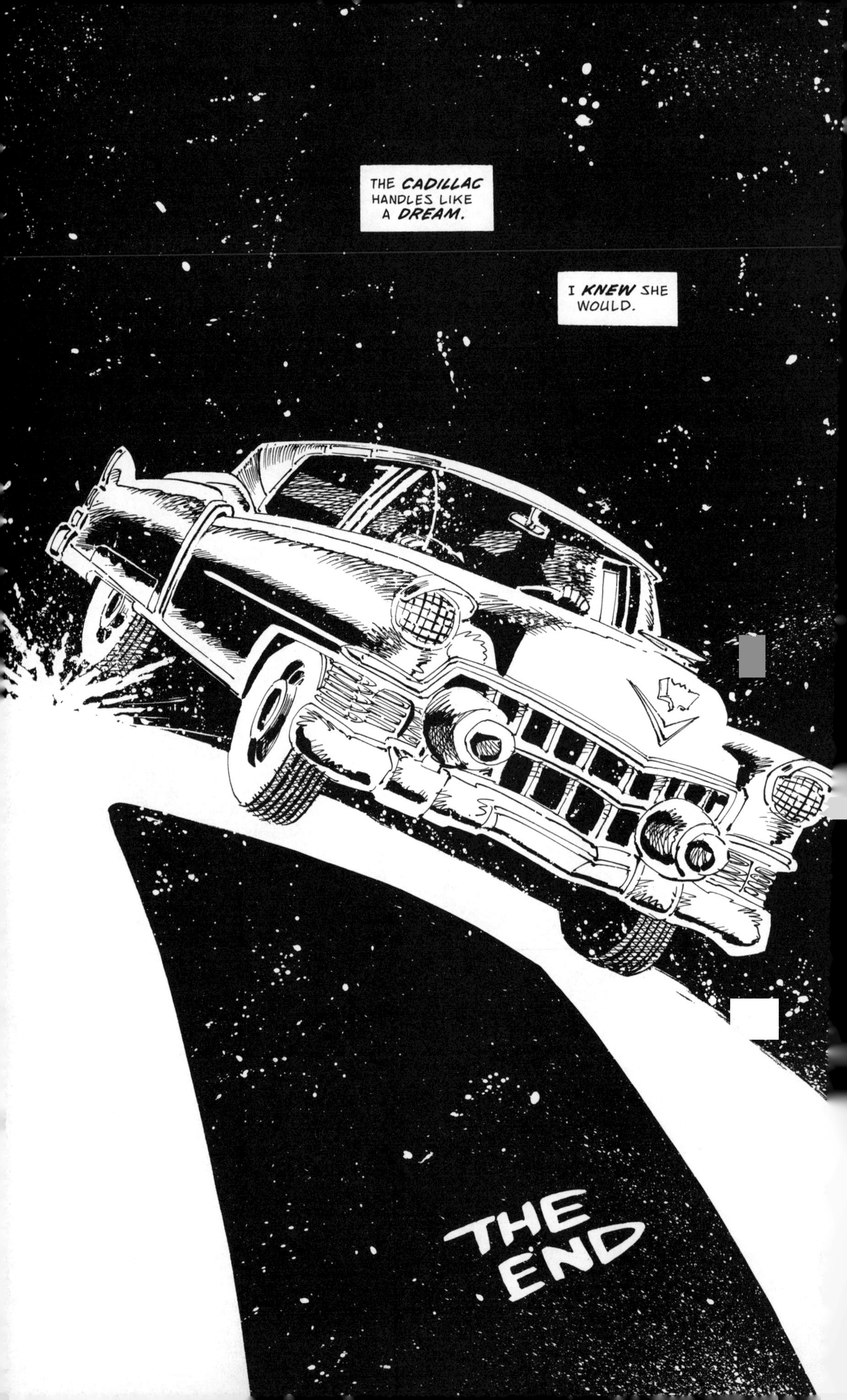
THE CADILLAC HANDLES LIKE A DREAM.
I KNEW SHE WOULD.
THE END

OTHER YARNS FROM SIN CITY

SIN CITY

A DAME TO KILL FOR

THE BIG FAT KILL

THAT YELLOW BASTARD

THE BABE WORE RED

SILENT NIGHT

LOST, LONELY, & LETHAL

SEX & VIOLENCE

MIKE RICHARDSON • publisher

NEIL HANKERSON • executive vice president

DAVID SCROGGY • product development

ANDY KARABATSOS • vice president & controller

MARK ANDERSON • general counsel

RANDY STRADLEY • director of editorial

CINDY MARKS • director of production & design

MARK COX • art director

SEAN TIERNEY • computer graphics director

MICHAEL MARTENS • director of sales & marketing

TOD BORLESKE • director of licensing

DALE LAFOUNTAIN • director of m.i.s.

KIM HAINES • director of human resources

SIN CITY®: Family Values

Published by Dark Horse Comics, Inc.
10956 SE Main Street
Milwaukie, Oregon 97222

First edition: October 1997
ISBN: 1-56971-313-8

3 5 7 9 10 8 6 4 2
Printed in Canada